lonely
SCOTLAND
Laurie Goodlad, Susanne Arbuckle, Colin Baird, Kay Gillespie,
Mike MacEacheran, Joseph Reaney, Neil Robertson, Neil Wilson

Meet Our Writers

Laurie Goodlad

𝕏 ◎ *@shetlandwithlaurie*

Writer and tour guide Laurie is a Shetlander with a passion for her island home and culture. Her favourite experience is witnessing the return of the storm petrels to the 2000-year-old Mousa Broch at midsummer. The culmination of nature and archaeology is breathtaking.

Susanne Arbuckle

𝕏 *@ScotAdventures*

Born in Glasgow, Susanne is the founder of Adventures Around Scotland travel blog and a travel writer based in Orkney. Her favourite experience is the Aberdeenshire Coastal Trail as the route encompasses an enthralling diversity over a relatively short distance.

Colin Baird

𝕏 *@cyclingscot*

Colin lives in Edinburgh, blogging about cycling and travelling in Scotland. His ambition is to see the whole country by bike. Colin's favourite experience is the Far North Line. He loves the changing landscape and hopping off at rural stations to explore on his bike.

Kay Gillespie

𝕏 ◎ *@thechaoticscot*

Edinburgh-local Kay travels Scotland for a living and shares her experiences online as The Chaotic Scot. Her favourite experience is taking a boat trip with Staffa Tours to the turquoise-fringed shores of Lunga to see thousands of puffins up close: a sight you never forget.

Mike MacEacheran

𝕏 *@MikeMacEacheran*

Mike is an award-winning, Edinburgh-based travel journalist. His favourite experience is skiing in Glencoe. On a golden winter's day, with the right snow conditions, nowhere in the world beats it.

Dugald Stewart Monument, Calton Hill (p53), Edinburgh

Joseph Reaney

josephreaney.com

Joseph Reaney is a travel journalist and editor who divides his time between Edinburgh and Prague. His favourite experience is St Kilda. When it comes to off-the-beaten-track adventures in Scotland, it's hard to beat this beautiful, isolated archipelago.

Neil Robertson

@travelswithakilt

Neil has been exploring his home country extensively since 2012 as a travel writer and blogger as Travels with a Kilt. A Glasgow boy at heart, he has recently become a Highlander. His favourite experience is a relaxed wander along the River Kelvin, between Kelvingrove Park and the Botanics, through the heart of the city's West End.

Neil Wilson

@neil3965

Based in Perthshire, Neil has been a full-time writer since 1988, working on more than 80 guidebooks for various publishers. His favourite experience is climbing Schiehallion. The view from the summit never gets old, with the peaks of Glen Coe shimmering beyond Rannoch Moor.

Contents

Best Experiences 6
Calendar 18
Trip Builders 26
7 Things to Know About Scotland 34
Read, Listen, Watch & Follow 36

Edinburgh 38
Festival Fringe 44
History & a Royal Mile 46
The Water of Leith 48
Writers, Witches & Wizards 50
Seven Hills 52
Foodie Leith 54
Listings 56

Glasgow 58
A Night on the Town 64
A Splash of Colour 66
Glasgow's Story 68
Footsteps of Legends 72
Listings 74

Southern Scotland 76
Immersion in the Lowlands 80
Majestic, Stately Homes 82
Lands of Sieges & Raids 84
Ride to the Sea 86
Listings 88

Stirling, Fife & Perthshire 90
Seafood & Sea Views 96
The Road to Rannoch 98
Kings, Queens & Castles 102
Listings 108

Northeast Scotland 110
A Coastal Trail 116
Whisky Tour of Speyside 120
Dundee Design Trail 122
Listings 124

Southern Highlands & Islands 126
Inner Hebrides Hopscotch 132
Whisky Island Discovery 134
From Sea to Plate 138
Secret Coast Road Trip 140
Enter the Ancient Kingdom 142
Listings 146

Central Highlands 148
Monster Hunting 154
Up Ben Nevis 158
Royal Road Trip 160
Listings 162

JUSTINE KIBLER/SHUTTERSTOCK ©

Northern Highlands 164
Wonders of Wester Ross 168
Cape Wrath 172
On the Clearances Trail 174
Gateway to the Highlands 176
Listings 180

Skye & the Outer Hebrides 182
Hiking Trotternish 188
Unwind in Uist 192
Skye's Secret Sister 194

Struan Cottage, Uist (p192)

St Kilda: Edge of the World 196
Hebridean Island Hopper 198
Road Trippin' Lewis & Lewis 200
Listings 202

Orkney **204**

Hop to Papa Westray 208
Neolithic Orkney 210
Creative Orkney Trail....... 212
St Magnus Way Walk 216
Listings 218

Shetland **220**

Exploring Fair Isle............224
Unforgettable Unst 228
Mousa Broch's Petrels....232
Exploring Geology...........234
Listings 236

Practicalities **238**

Arriving 240
Getting Around................242
Safe Travel 244
Money 245
Responsible Travel 246
Accommodation 248
Essentials 250

ESSAYS

What Makes Glasgow So?...............70
The River Tay 100
Meet the Master Distiller......................136
5000 Years of Orkney Creativity 214
Land of the Vikings 226

VISUAL GUIDES

A Castle Glossary.....106
Treasures of Kilmartin Glen 144
On Screen: The Highlands on Film 156
Highland Games 178
Flora & Fauna 230

WHISKY STATS

- There are more than 150 malt and grain distilleries – making Scotland home to the world's greatest concentration of whisky production.
- Opened in 1786, Strathisla is the oldest continuously operating distillery in the Highlands.
- Whisky exports totalled £5.6bn in 2023.

WHISKY **COUNTRY**

Nowhere else in the world is as indebted to a drink as Scotland is to whisky. The country's bounty of ingredients, from soft spring water gushing from the mountains to fields of barley flourishing in the peaty highlands, helps create a landscape that's ripe for exploration. Then there are the scenic distilleries and joyous whisky festivals – they burst with history, flavour and the potential for a long, if life-affirming, night out.

Left Strathisla Distillery (p121)
Right Copper stills at Glenfiddich Distillery (p121)
Below A dram being poured

→ THE MALT WHISKY TRAIL

If the number of distilleries to choose from leaves you feeling dizzy, the world's only Malt Whisky Trail offers the perfect solution. The route introduces you to the guardians of Glenlivet, Glenfiddich, Glen Moray and Glen Grant, among others, as well as Cardhu – the only distillery pioneered by a woman.

▶ Learn more about the Malt Whisky Trail on p120

13THREEPHOTOGRAPHY/SHUTTERSTOCK ©

ISLAY WHISKY

With 10 distilleries – since the reopening of Port Ellen in 2024 – on an island only 25 miles wide, Islay could be described as the 'whiskiest' place in the world. Most distilleries offer tours and tastings, exclusive drams and food pairings.

▶ See our guide to Islay whisky on p136

RIGHT: BARMALINI/SHUTTERSTOCK ©
LEFT: SUE BURTON PHOTOGRAPHY/SHUTTERSTOCK ©

↑ HOW TO DRINK A SINGLE MALT

Whiskies vary as much as wine: so treat both a single origin malt and blended whisky (a mix of different cask spirits) with respect. Drink it straight at room temperature, or mix it with a little still water to bring out its flavours and aromas. Before drinking, inhale deeply and raise your dram with the traditional toast: *slainte mhath!*

Best Whisky Experiences

▶ **Savour a beach tasting on the sand at Machir Bay to learn all about Islay's only farm distillery.** (p135)

▶ **Discover the highest distillery in Scotland with an original smokestack that can be seen for miles.** (p162)

▶ **Explore the Speyside Cooperage to watch Britain's only barrel makers mastering their craft.** (p121)

LAND OF ISLANDS

With 900 islands to choose from, and with most offering silvery sands, craggy mountains, charming crofting communities and bucket-list wildlife, it's not hard to find an offshore paradise. Reassuringly, despite the timely ferry connections to the mainland, many remain secluded spots where you can get away from it all and enjoy the rhythm of island life.

Harris

Photo-worthy beaches

This stunning island does vast beaches, sweeping mountains and trendsetting textiles in spades. For the picture-postcard Scottish beach, beeline to the powdery sands and primrose-dotted machair of Seilebost (pictured left) or wind through the Golden Road.

1hr 40min to Tarbert from Uig on Skye

▶ p200

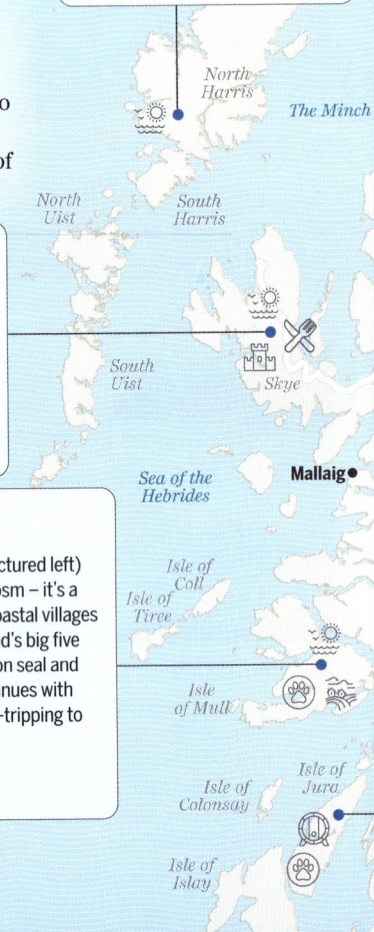

North Harris

The Minch

North Uist

South Harris

Skye

Scotland in miniature

Simply put, the Isle of Skye has it all. Two clan-rich castles, fine-dining restaurants with rooms, Jurassic-era dinosaur fossils, dazzling coral beaches, the lunar landscapes of the Trotternish peninsula, the seismogram-ragged Cuillin mountains and the smoky whisky at Talisker Distillery.

Across the Skye Bridge from Kyle of Lochalsh

▶ p182

South Uist

Skye

Sea of the Hebrides

Mallaig

Mull

Wildlife and island-hopping

Gateway to the Inner Hebrides, Mull (pictured left) offers the best of the islands in microcosm – it's a marriage of beaches, mountains and coastal villages inhabited by friendly locals and Scotland's big five (golden eagles, red deer, otters, common seal and harbour porpoise). The adventure continues with island-hopping to Iona and Ulva, or day-tripping to Staffa and the Treshnish Isles.

50min from Oban

▶ p132

Isle of Coll

Isle of Tiree

Isle of Mull

Isle of Jura

Isle of Colonsay

Isle of Islay

Neolithic Orkney

Archaeology in action

Step back in time for a tour of mysterious stone circles, ghostly burial cairns and ancient dwellings shrouded in secrets. Then there's a range of eras to jump through, from the Neolithic and Iron Age to the time of Vikings and earls. Here the sense of history is tangible.

1½hr from Scrabster to Stromness

▶ p210

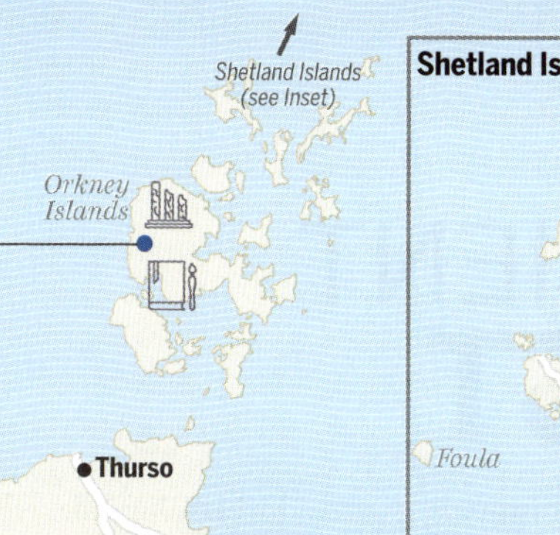

Britain's Most Northerly

Nature at its wildest

At the northernmost point of the northernmost island, this is the Shetland most don't see. Laden with wildlife, from colonies of puffins (pictured left), gannets and skuas to songbirds, whales and more, Unst is an unforgettable experience. This small island in the far north is rich in geology and otters, and also features an offshore lighthouse marking the furthest reaches of Scottish soil: Muckle Flugga Lighthouse.

2hr from Lerwick

▶ p228

Thurso
Wick
Helmsdale
Inverness
Aberdeen
North Sea
Cairn Gorm
Ben Macdui
Cairngorms National Park
Fort William
Ben Nevis
Dundee
Perth
Loch Lomond & the Trossachs National Park
Stirling
Kirkcaldy
EDINBURGH

Jura

Deer Island

Neighbouring Islay draws the crowds because of its whisky distilleries, but Jura rewards travellers with a far wilder experience. You'll find one hotel, one shop, one pub, one end-of-the-road gin distillery, one whisky distillery, one rum distillery, and 6000 roaming red deer.

2½hr to Islay, then 10min ferry from Port Askaig

▶ p146

0 100 km
0 50 miles

ANCIENT PAST

Exploring history is so much more satisfying when you have so many strata to delve into. Here you can follow in the footsteps of time-honoured kings and queens, or tread where Jurassic-era dinosaurs, Neolithic humans and Vikings once roamed, rewarding you with a whole new perspective of a place rich with history through the ages.

LEFT: JULIETPHOTOGRAPHY/SHUTTERSTOCK ©, BOTTOM: TOMASZ WOZNIAK/SHUTTERSTOCK ©

→ SEE CASTLE COUNTRY

Aberdeenshire has more than 260 castles, stately homes and turreted chateaux. Must-sees include Dunnottar Castle (p118) near Stonehaven; Crathes Castle near Banchory; Balmoral Castle (p161) near Braemar; and fairy-tale Craigievar Castle in Ballater.

Best History Experiences

- **Discover the most besieged place in Europe at heavily fortified Edinburgh Castle.** (p47)
- **See where Macbeth, Robert the Bruce and Charles II were crowned at sacred Scone Palace.** (p108)
- **Step into a traditional Hebridean home and see crofting life firsthand at a thatched blackhouse on the Isle of Lewis.** (p200)

← HIKE THROUGH HISTORY

Dozens of pilgrim trails and long-distance routes thread through the country. From the Fife Pilgrim Way to the Rob Roy Way, the routes are studded with standing stones, abbeys, stories and secrets.

Above left St Andrews Castle (p108)
Left Dunnottar Castle (p118)

CELTIC DELICACIES

Don't miss these only-in-Scotland treats:

Tablet A sweeter-than-fudge sugary confection (pictured).

Cranachan Raspberries, oats, cream and whisky in a dessert glass.

Cullen Skink Thick, smoked fish and potato soup.

LOCAL FLAVOURS

Forget the deep-fried Mars bar. This is a country with a larder jam-packed with just-landed langoustine, mussel and lobster, estate-reared venison, hand-dived scallops, wood-smoked salmon, Aberdeen Angus beef, Stornoway black pudding, Ayrshire cheddar, sea-salt fudge, crumbly oatcakes, vegan haggis and stovies, Arbroath smokies, Dundee cake, teeth-melting Irn Bru, and the world's best single malt whisky. Put simply, Scotland is the kind of place where indulging is practically a human right.

Best Food Experiences

- **For crab feasts, curries and whisky, head to Glasgow's trendiest neighbourhood for a big night out.** (p64)

- **Fish and chips, farmers markets, Michelin stars and local lobster – loosen your belt for the foodie hot spot of Fife.** (p96)

- **All gannets flock to Oban, the 'Seafood Capital of Scotland', for sustainable shellfish platters.** (p138)

BY HIKE OR BY BIKE

Breathe in the invigorating sea air from a clifftop, follow a historic pathway into the cradle of a silent mountain, pedal deep into some of Europe's most undiscovered landscapes – or challenge yourself to all three. Scotland's short- and long-distance walking trails and bike routes reward you with a wealth of second-to-none history, culture and wildlife experiences.

Cape Wrath

Britain's final frontier

This remote corner feels untouched: cut off by road and accessible only by ferry, take your bike and cycle the 11-mile dirt road through Scotland's last great wilderness to the lighthouse at Scotland's most northwesterly point.

52 miles/2 days

▶ p172

Trotternish

Showstopping geology

Take your pick from three soul-stirring day hikes: the spectacular Quiraing (pictured right) hike; the short but steep Old Man of Storr; or the easy-going Scorrybreac circuit. All cross geomorphic landslips and escarpments that take you to another world entirely.

1 day

▶ p188

Dalriada Heritage Trail

Hike through history

Plot Kilmartin Glen in Argyll on the map, then walk through 5000 years of brain-scrambling history in one long ramble. Explore standing stones, rock carvings, burial chambers and ancient graves in the quiet surrounds of a storied glen.

7 miles/½ day

▶ p142

Cape Wrath
Port of Ness
The Minch
Lewis
Stornoway
Ben More Assynt
North Outer Hebrides
Harris
Tarbert
Ullapool
St Kilda
ATLANTIC OCEAN
South Harris
An Teallach
Gairloch
Wester Ross
Beinn Dearg
The Little Minch
North Uist
Lochmaddy
Achnasheen
Trotternish
Dunvegan
Skye
Portree
Isle of Mull
Oban
Isle of Jura
Lochgilphead
Cowal Peninsula
Tarbert
Kintyre
Isle of Arran
Firth of Clyde

Rannoch Moor

Scenic bike adventure

Follow the twisty-turn road from Pitlochry to Rannoch Station, past glittering lochs and beautifully contoured mountains, to arrive at the daunting expanse of Rannoch Moor (pictured right).

35 miles/2 days

▶ p98

West Highland Way

Wild walks and wild camping

This rollercoaster route (pictured above) through the Highlands' finest scenery starts north of Glasgow and winds to Fort William. Wild camping is a thrill among the heather, but a permit is needed while in Loch Lomond and the Trossachs National Park.

96 miles/7–10 days

▶ p163

Fife Coastal Path

Seafood-packed shores

The country's most delicious trail, this 25-mile route from Elie to St Andrews is the perfect place to taste Scotland's larder. From humble fish and chip shops to gourmet restaurants, the East Neuk's fishing villages never fail to deliver.

25 miles/3 days

▶ p96

SPEED LIMITS

MOTORWAYS

70mph (112km/h) for cars, 60mph (96km/h) for caravans/camper vans

CITIES

30mph (48km/h)

OUTSIDE BUILT-UP AREAS

60mph (96km/h) for cars, 50mph (80mph) for caravans/ camper vans

ON THE ROAD

Driving across Scotland isn't for the faint-hearted. The single-track roads and moving obstacles (sheep, cattle, deer) offer a crash course in the slower pace of life beyond the cities – but be sure to pull over and let the locals pass! But the country's highways and coastal routes open up a world of adventure that lives up to the hype. Seen through the windscreen or during spontaneous pitstops, it'll blow you away.

Left Sheep on a Scottish road
Right Kylesku Bridge, on the North Coast 500 (p181)
Below Motorist in Dumfries and Galloway

→ THE ROAD TRIP BOOM

Following the success of the North Coast 500, there are plenty of sign-posted touring routes to pack your itinerary with. The K66 around the Kintyre Peninsula; the South West Coastal 300 around Dumfries and Galloway; the Deeside Tourist Route from Perth to Aberdeen; or the Coig, around Ayrshire and the Clyde Islands.

RICHARD P LONG/SHUTTERSTOCK ©

THE ULTIMATE PLAYLIST

When touring, you need a fitting soundtrack. The folky and ambient refrains of Erland Cooper and Kris Drever are ideal for Orkney, while Runrig remains Skye's most popular rock band. The Gaelic lilts of Mànran, Skipinnish and Julie Fowlis help bring the Outer Hebrides to life, while bands such as The Proclaimers, Chvrches and Franz Ferdinand will have you singing down the M8 motorway.

▶ Learn about more Scottish albums on p36

RIGHT: HELEN HOTSON/SHUTTERSTOCK ©
LEFT: OTMARW/SHUTTERSTOCK ©

↑ DON'T DRINK & DRIVE

There is a zero tolerance policy for driving under the influence of alcohol in Scotland. The legal limit is 50mg of alcohol in 100mL of blood – just one drink can put you over the threshold.

Best Road Trips

Stop off at whitewashed lighthouses, soft-sieved sands and cliff-hugging harbours on the Aberdeenshire Coastal Trail. (p116)

Hit the road to discover forest paths, hidden beaches and gastro highlights on the crowd-free Cowal Peninsula. (p140)

Follow the Snow Roads Scenic Route to see a royal palace, ancestral clan homes and distilleries east of the Cairngorms. (p162)

Tour Wester Ross and explore the stunning coastal scenery and mountain views between Ullapool and Applecross. (p168)

ARTS & CULTURE

For all the wild landscapes and scenic excursions, this is a country imbued with a deep-rooted love for Scots, Gaelic and Celtic cultures in all their forms. From Hogmanay and the Highland Games to the world's largest arts festival in Edinburgh, there's plenty of art, song, design, poetry, literature, theatre and film to capture your imagination – and your heart.

LEFT: DOUBLECLIX/SHUTTERSTOCK ©. BOTTOM: JAN KRANENDONK/SHUTTERSTOCK ©

★ FAB FESTIVALS

Not a month goes by without a memory-making festival and there are as many small-scale events as there are zeitgeist-defining epics like the Edinburgh Festival Fringe, Glasgow's Celtic Connections and Belladrum's Tartan Heart Festival. There are more than 200 every year.

▶ Find out more at scotland.org/events

Best Culture Experiences

▶ **Snap up tickets for a premiere at the genre-defying Edinburgh Festival Fringe.** (p44)

▶ **Gawp at Glasgow's larger-than-life murals on an ever-changing street art tour.** (p66)

▶ **Meet the artisans who carve, spin, engrave, paint and weave on the Creative Orkney Trail.** (p212)

← MUST VISIT

Dundee's V&A Museum encapsulates a city that is on the rise. The country's first design museum, its galleries are spectacular: expect identity-unravelling exhibits on fashion, art, furniture and architecture.

▶ Follow the design trail on p122

Above left V&A Dundee (p123)
Left Street performers, Edinburgh Festival Fringe (p44)

↘ GO CROWD FREE

Leave the tourists behind for somewhere new:

Isle of Raasay A wilder alternative to Skye. (p194)

Angus Glens Swap Glencoe for the Grampians.

East Lothian Stay on the coast, rather than in Edinburgh.

WIDE OPEN **SPACES**

There is no more rewarding way to experience Scotland than to really get away from it all. Words such as remote and off-grid are buzz-worthy today and Scotland is, in effect, a gigantic outdoor classroom, delivering a lesson on how to lose yourself in a landscape. Whether you hike in to cut-off Knoydart (Europe's so-called last wilderness) or tour Flow Country (Europe's largest expanse of blanket bog), there's a wide open space waiting for you.

Best Wide Open Spaces

- **Wild camp or stargaze amid the epic beauty and rolling silence of Galloway Forest Park.** (pictured above; p81)
- **Explore the wilderness of Cape Wrath with birdwatching and beach camping.** (p172)
- **Discover Loch Ness away from the crowds and be rewarded with rolling moorlands, mountains and clear waters.** (p154)

Demand for accommodation peaks in summer, particularly during the school holidays in July and August. Book tours and overnight adventures in advance.

▸ lonelyplanet.com/bookings

↙ The World Pipe Band Championships

Ditch the earplugs: pipers and drummers compete to see who's the best in the world.

Glasgow

▸ theworlds.co.uk

Belladrum Tartan Heart Festival

Inverness-shire does Woodstock at this alternative rock festival held every July.

▸ Beauly

▸ tartanheartfestival.co.uk

It's golf season: the home of golf has a course for every day of the year (550, in fact), but 18 holes are best played under sunny skies.

JUNE

Average daytime max: 17°C
Days of rainfall: 10

JULY

Scotland in SUMMER

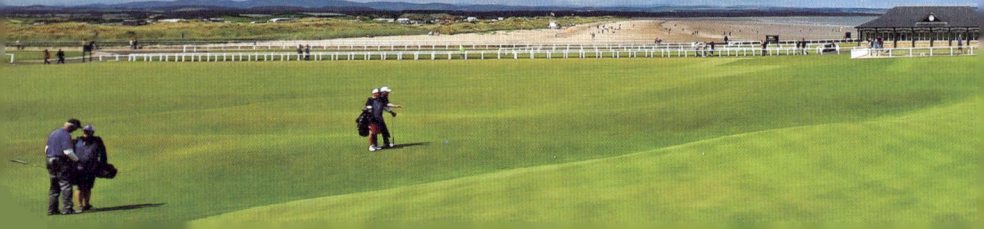

↓ Edinburgh Festival Fringe

The world's largest arts festival brings the capital to a standstill in August.

Edinburgh

▸ edfringe.com

↑ Royal Highland Show

Scotland's largest agricultural get-together – a showcase of rural life, farm produce, arts and crafts.

Edinburgh

▸ royalhighlandshow.org

↑ The Hebridean Whale Trail

Cetacean sightings peak from June to September, when long summer nights make it easier than ever to shore watch along Scotland's west coast.

Average daytime max: 19°C
Days of rainfall: 10

AUGUST

Average daytime max: 19°C
Days of rainfall: 10

Packing notes

Beach clothes and sun cream, but also a raincoat or umbrella. Maybe golf clubs too. Midge repellent essential.

Check out the full calendar of events

Go stargazing: autumnal skies and shooting stars light up Galloway Forest Park, the UK's first Dark Sky Park.

↘ Halloween

The Celtic roots of this scare-fest are celebrated nationwide on 31 October. Take a ghost tour in Edinburgh, or follow Scotland's Ghost Trail.

▸ visitscotland.com/blog/attractions/ghost-trail

↘ Braemar Gathering

Skirling, whirling, caber tossing, tug of war and highland dancing – the world-famous Highland Games is a one-day bash (literally) in September. Always a sell-out.

▸ p160

As part of the breeding season, stag ruts are shows of strength from the largest population of red deer in Europe. Best seen before dusk or dawn in the Highlands.

SEPTEMBER

Average daytime max: 16°C
Days of rainfall: 10

OCTOBER

Scotland in AUTUMN

↘ St Andrews Day

A celebration of Scotland's patron saint and the country's national day. Expect haggis, whisky and tipsy singalongs of 'Auld Lang Syne'.

Shetland Wool Week

Travel north for a week-long celebration of all things textiles; learn traditional skills and meet the makers at this festival held each October.

Royal National Mòd

The biggest celebration of Gaelic literature, song, arts and culture. Held in October in a different city each year.

▶ ancomunn.co.uk

Largs Viking Festival

More than an excuse to dress up in a horned helmet: a commemoration of the last great battle between the Scots and the Vikings.

📍 Largs

▶ largsvikingfestival.org

Average daytime max: 12°C
Days of rainfall: 12

NOVEMBER

Average daytime max: 9°C
Days of rainfall: 11

Packing notes

A backpack and hiking boots for forest rambles, plus a fleece or puffy jacket for cooler nights.

↘ Winter sports

Scotland's six ski resorts are a great way to see the country's most spine-tingling scenery. Choose Glenshee or Cairngorm for beginners, or Glencoe for gnarlier terrain.

📍 Glencoe

▸ p163

↘ Burns Night

A celebration of the life and poetry of the national bard – or poet – Robert Burns on 25 January.

Christmas Day, Boxing Day, New Year's Day and 2 January are all public holidays. Restaurants and pubs are busy with revelry and especially welcoming.

DECEMBER

Average daytime max: 3°C
Days of rainfall: 12

JANUARY

Scotland in WINTER

Celtic Connections

The UK's largest Celtic music festival, with folk, roots and jazz. Late-night sessions and stadium stars.

Glasgow

▸ celticconnections.com

Edinburgh's Hogmanay

A carnival of Hogmanay – the Scottish celebration of New Year – with *ceilidhs*, a torchlit procession and a city-stopping street party.

Edinburgh

▸ edinburghshogmanay.com

↑ Up Helly Aa

Viking-themed fire festival held at the end of January – a no-holds-barred celebration, culminating in 1000 torch-bearers burning a replica Viking longship.

Shetland

▸ uphellyaa.org

FEBRUARY

Average daytime max: 4°C
Days of rainfall: 12

Average daytime max: 5°C
Days of rainfall: 9

Northern Lights

Get lucky, and on a clear night Scotland's night sky turns into a disco. Sutherland, Caithness and Shetland are prime areas for the Northern Lights.

Snow Roads Scenic Route

Drive the 90-mile road through the Cairngorms National Park – it's the highest mountain road in the UK.

Packing notes

Cosy hat, gloves, a puffy jacket and a warming dram to ward off the cold and often snowy conditions.

Spirit of Speyside Whisky Festival

Tastings, tours and morning-after sore heads at this single malt extravaganza. In a word: slainte!

Speyside

▸ spiritofspeyside.com

→ Beltane Fire Festival

Celtic festival in April which heralds the beginning of summer. Don't miss the Calton Hill bonfire.

Edinburgh

▸ beltane.org

→ Six Nations

Pan-European rugby tussle that brings the UK together every spring. Hard to get a ticket, but the pubs around Murrayfield Stadium are just as packed.

Edinburgh

▸ scottishrugby.org

↓ West Highland Way

Demand for accommodation on the West Highland Way peaks in summer – tackle it in late April or May and avoid the crowds and midges!

▸ westhighlandway.org

MARCH

Average daytime max: 9°C
Days of rainfall: 10

APRIL

Scotland in SPRING

Mountain biking

All eyes are on Fort William in May for the annual World Cup event, which attracts thousands from around the globe.

Fort William

▶ fortwilliamworldcup.co.uk

The beginning of the salmon-fishing season starts in February, but the most reliable time for landing a whopper is April and May. The Spey, Tay and Tweed have the best spring runs.

Average daytime max: 12°C
Days of rainfall: 9

MAY

Average daytime max: 15°C
Days of rainfall: 10

The long Easter holiday from school (and work) lasts for two to three weeks every spring.

World Whisky Day

The centrepiece of Scotland's Whisky Month held every May (yet another excuse for a dram).

▶ worldwhiskyday.com

Packing notes

Woolly sweater and waterproof jacket, plus scarf and warm hat. Feeling brave? Pack shorts for Easter.

CITIES & THE SOUTH
Trip Builder

TAKE YOUR PICK OF MUST-SEES AND HIDDEN GEMS

Experience Scotland's two extremes: the here-and-now arts, music, dining and drinking scenes of its two greatest cities, then take the road less travelled to the serene landscapes and scenic coastlines of Arran, Ayrshire, the Borders, and Dumfries and Galloway.

Trip Notes

Hub towns Edinburgh, Glasgow

How long Allow for 10–12 days

Getting around Take the bus or train to see the cities, then pick up a hire car to go at your own pace. Otherwise, public transport will take you to all but the most remote destinations.

Tips Plan for more time than you think you will need: many roads hide a castle, cove or creaky historic attraction that you'll want to stop and linger at. The roads here are designed to be driven slowly.

Islay
Said to be the 'whiskiest place in the world' – breathe in the peaty aromas of Islay's 10 distilleries, then sample the single malts on a trail around the Southern Hebrides.
4hr from Arran

Arran
Hike, bike, wildlife watch, distillery tour or beachcomb – maybe all five. This west coast isle's 'best-in-Scotland' billing lives up to expectation.
2½hr from Glasgow

Glasgow

There's no time to catch your breath in Scotland's buzziest city: discover mind-boggling art, music, museums and Mackintosh, before staying up late for the ultimate night out.

1hr from Edinburgh

Edinburgh

Time travel down the Royal Mile to medieval Scotland with atmospheric visits to Edinburgh Castle, Holyrood Palace and Greyfriars Kirkyard before settling in for a dram in a cosy pub.

Rosslyn Chapel

Take a day trip to Scotland's 'celebrity church', made famous by its role in *The Da Vinci Code*, to discover the mysterious Knights Templar legend that lives on in Midlothian.

45min from Edinburgh

Robert Burns Country

The epicentre of Burns-mania, the bard was born and raised in Ayrshire, steeping the region in literature. Alloway holds the keys to unlock the story of Robert Burns, Scotland's national bard.

1½hr from Glasgow

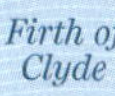

Tweed Valley

Lose yourself in the Walter Scott–era romance of historic estates and stately homes along the River Tweed, then fish for salmon, or mountain bike the south's greatest downhill trails.

1hr from Edinburgh

Galloway Forest Park

Take the slower route through the deer-filled wild hills and lochs of this natural wonderland. It's the UK's first Dark Sky Park and the most memorable stargazing spot.

1hr from Glasgow

Loch Lomond & the Trossachs National Park
Cowal Peninsula
Isle of Bute
Falkirk
Firth of Forth
Edinburgh
Glasgow
Peebles
Firth of Clyde
Ayr
Girvan
Merrick
Galloway Forest Park
Dumfries
Newton Stewart
Castle Douglas
Solway Firth

0 40 km
0 20 miles

WESTERN HIGHLANDS & ISLANDS
Trip Builder

TAKE YOUR PICK OF MUST-SEES AND HIDDEN GEMS

Year-round adventures, soul-stirring landscapes and unforgettable food and drink. This four-season wonderland is the Scotland of your imagination, where epic mountains tickle the shores of wild sea lochs and wild Atlantic breakers collide with glistening sands and towering cliffs to create one life-affirming trip.

Trip Notes

Hub towns Fort William, Oban, Portree, Ullapool

How long Aim for two weeks

Getting around Hire a car to explore at your own speed. Bus and train travel are limited, but the ferry network makes up for it. A bike is a great option for touring the islands.

Tips Summer is peak season on the west coast. To discover it in solitude, avoid July and August and instead come in May, June or September.

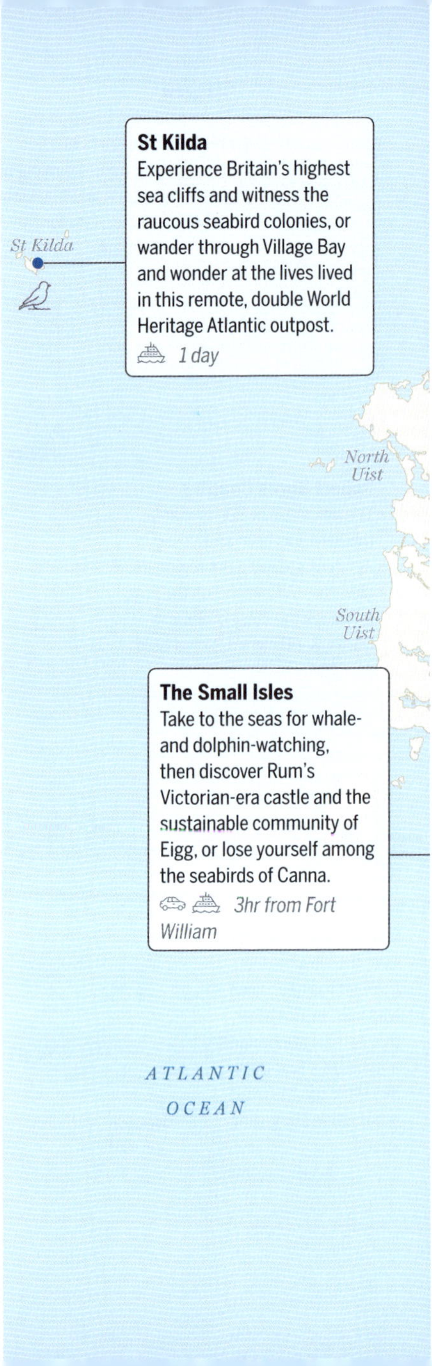
St Kilda
St Kilda
Experience Britain's highest sea cliffs and witness the raucous seabird colonies, or wander through Village Bay and wonder at the lives lived in this remote, double World Heritage Atlantic outpost.
1 day
North Uist
South Uist
The Small Isles
Take to the seas for whale- and dolphin-watching, then discover Rum's Victorian-era castle and the sustainable community of Eigg, or lose yourself among the seabirds of Canna.
3hr from Fort William
ATLANTIC OCEAN

Lewis

The Minch

0 40 km
0 20 miles

North Harris

Harris

Pick up some hand-woven Harris Tweed or kelp-infused gin in Tarbert. Feel the wind in your hair and sand on your toes at the mesmerising beaches of Luskentyre and Seilebost.

6hr from Fort William

Tarbert

Harris

Loch Ness

Whether you believe in monsters or not, go monster hunting where pine-skirted mountains plunge into the clear waters of Scotland's deepest loch and the ruins of Urquhart Castle stand sentry.

2½hr from Oban

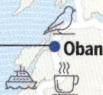

Skye

Hike to the Quiraing through one of Scotland's most remarkable landscapes, then hunt for Jurassic-era fossils in Staffin and explore storied clan history in Dunvegan Castle.

3½hr from Oban

Portree

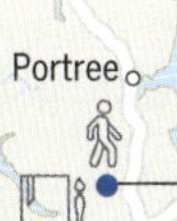

Skye

Loch Ness

Glen Nevis

Scale the heights of Ben Nevis, Britain's highest mountain, then tackle the UK's gnarliest mountain-biking routes at the Nevis Range.

1hr from Oban

Cuillin Sound

Rum

Mallaig

Eigg

Muck

Glencoe

This is the feel-good drive of your life: discover some of the Highlands' most iconic landscapes from Rannoch Moor to Glen Etive to Glencoe.

1–2hr from Oban

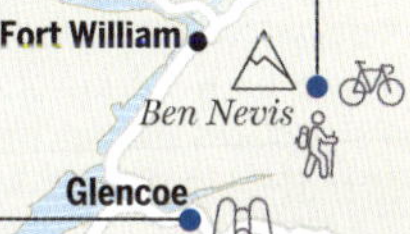

Fort William

Ben Nevis

Glencoe

Sea of the Hebrides

Isle of Coll

Oban

The Gateway to the Islands: enjoy fresh shellfish at the harbour and an island-hopping adventure from Mull to Iona and Ulva, with a Staffa boat tour for puffins and Fingal's Cave.

5–7 days

Isle of Mull

Oban

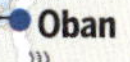

THE NORTH
Trip Builder

TAKE YOUR PICK OF MUST-SEES AND HIDDEN GEMS

One of the wildest swathes of Europe, Scotland's north is a mysterious riddle of snow-capped summits, forgotten-by-time sea lochs and windswept island archipelagos. There are abundant hillsides and coastlines to explore and open roads to follow – and a winter that bites harder than the midges!

Trip Notes

Hub towns Inverness, Kirkwall, Lerwick

How long Go for two weeks

Getting around Hire a car in Inverness to run to your own schedule. Alternatively, if touring Orkney and Shetland, take the ferry and hire a car locally.

Tips Driving here can feel like being on roads at the edge of the world. Explore slowly, use passing places and watch out for deer, sheep and Highland cows.

Assynt
Experience mind-boggling geology, where three billion years of history collide with dramatic beauty and white-knuckle outdoor thrills.
30min from Ullapool

Ullapool
Stop off in this mini Highland capital, and buzzing ferry port, for seafood, seal-spotting, cruising the Summer Isles or climbing Stac Pollaidh.
3hr from Fort William

Westray

Explore the sea cliffs and sandy beaches of the Queen o' the Isles. Afterwards, island-hop to Papa Westray on the world's shortest scheduled flight.

3hr from Orkney

Fair Isle

Knit, hike, birdwatch or revel in the isolation and incredible community spirit of the UK's most geographically remotely inhabited island.

2 days

Neolithic Orkney

Once upon a time, Skara Brae and the Ring of Brodgar were Orkney's lifeblood – today they are archaeological treasure troves older than the pyramids of Egypt.

5hr from Iverness

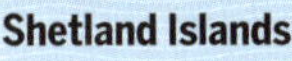

Shetland Islands (see Inset)
Fair Isle
Westray
Orkney Islands
Mainland
Kirkwall
Stromness
Hoy
John O'Groats
Thurso
Tongue
Wick
Helmsdale
Lairg
Golspie
North Sea
Banff
Fraserburgh

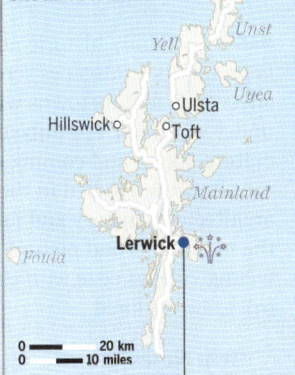

Shetland Islands

Yell
Unst
Uyea
Ulsta
Hillswick
Toft
Mainland
Lerwick
Foula
0 20 km
0 10 miles

North Coast 500

This road trip is to Scotland what Route 66 is to the USA. Mountains, marvellous beaches, malty distilleries and more.

7–10 days

Lerwick

January's dark days see Shetland's madcap Up Helly Aa fire festival transform a town with Viking-style hijinks. For those chasing the light, visit in June for 19 hours of daylight.

14hr from Aberdeen

Torridon

Hike the ragged spurs of Beinn Eighe, then plan a canoe or kayak adventure on Loch Maree or Loch Torridon, below the magnificent ridge of the Liathach massif.

3hr from Fort William

0 50 km
0 25 miles

CENTRAL SCOTLAND & THE EAST
Trip Builder

TAKE YOUR PICK OF MUST-SEES AND HIDDEN GEMS

Scotland's historic northeast is proud; its landscapes scream adventure, and its towns will get under your skin. For unbeatable culture, its up-and-coming cities are almost unrivalled in the arts, architecture, history and food, while the mountains and picture-perfect fishing villages ooze with charm and call to be explored.

Trip Notes

Hub towns Aberdeen, Dundee, Perth, St Andrews

How long Allow for 10–12 days

Getting around Public transport is a great way to explore, with all major cities and towns connected by train and bus. If adventuring to the Cairngorms or exploring Speyside, hire a car.

Tips Festivals are part of life – time a visit to coincide with St Andrews Golf Week (April and October), Spirit of Speyside (May), East Neuk Festival (July) or the Braemar Gathering (September).

Cairngorms National Park
Discover the UK's largest national park, offering thrillseekers biking, paddling and winter sports, or solitude for those who wish to slow down in nature with a hike and outstanding wildlife.
1 day

Loch Lomond & the Trossachs National Park

Stirling
Enjoy sweeping castle views, the knee-busting climb of Wallace's Braveheart Monument, storied battlefields and gothic landmarks.
1 day

0 40 km
0 20 miles

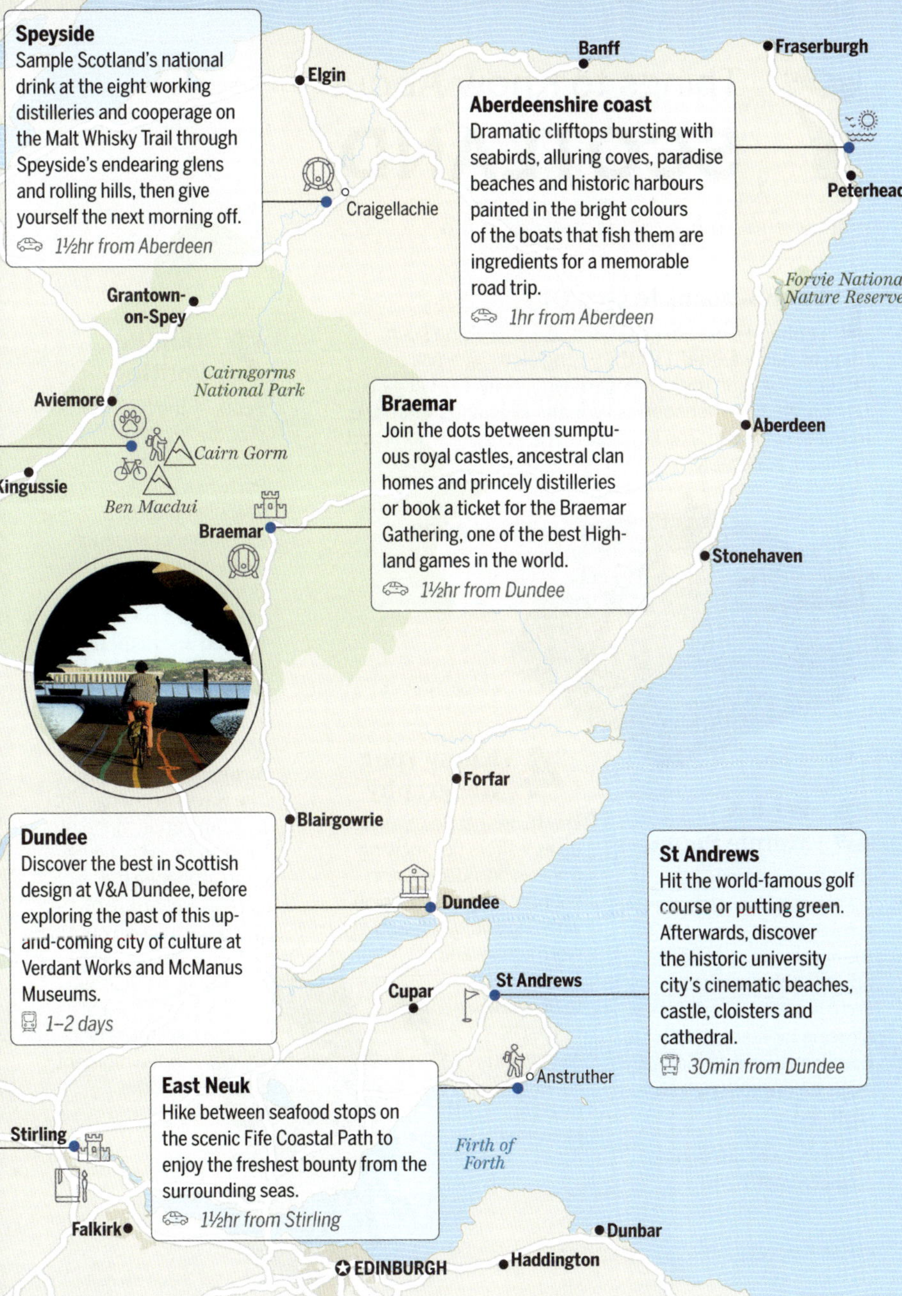
Speyside
Sample Scotland's national drink at the eight working distilleries and cooperage on the Malt Whisky Trail through Speyside's endearing glens and rolling hills, then give yourself the next morning off.
1½hr from Aberdeen
Elgin
Banff
Fraserburgh
Aberdeenshire coast
Dramatic clifftops bursting with seabirds, alluring coves, paradise beaches and historic harbours painted in the bright colours of the boats that fish them are ingredients for a memorable road trip.
1hr from Aberdeen
Craigellachie
Peterhead
Forvie National Nature Reserve
Grantown-on-Spey
Cairngorms National Park
Aviemore
Cairn Gorm
Kingussie
Ben Macdui
Braemar
Braemar
Join the dots between sumptuous royal castles, ancestral clan homes and princely distilleries or book a ticket for the Braemar Gathering, one of the best Highland games in the world.
1½hr from Dundee
Aberdeen
Stonehaven
Forfar
Blairgowrie
Dundee
Discover the best in Scottish design at V&A Dundee, before exploring the past of this up-and-coming city of culture at Verdant Works and McManus Museums.
1–2 days
Dundee
St Andrews
Hit the world-famous golf course or putting green. Afterwards, discover the historic university city's cinematic beaches, castle, cloisters and cathedral.
30min from Dundee
Cupar
St Andrews
Anstruther
East Neuk
Hike between seafood stops on the scenic Fife Coastal Path to enjoy the freshest bounty from the surrounding seas.
1½hr from Stirling
Stirling
Firth of Forth
Falkirk
Dunbar
EDINBURGH
Haddington

7 Things to Know About SCOTLAND

INSIDER TIPS TO HIT THE GROUND RUNNING

1 Four Seasons in One Day

Scotland's old adage rings true – there's no such thing as bad weather, just the wrong clothing. Pack a raincoat, even on the sunniest Glasgow day. Expect gales in Edinburgh. And monsoon rains in the Highlands when the forecast is for sun. The key is to manage expectations and dress appropriately.

▶ See more about the weather on p18

2 Talking Politics

Scots fly the flag proudly, and the Scottish National Party has spent years fighting for a second independence referendum. Fuelled by Brexit, this has been an era-defining period for a proud and patriotic nation split between those desperate for an independent Scotland and those who want to maintain the status quo. The waves of change are alive, and understanding the history will not only deepen the pleasure of travelling but also act as a reminder that you are not just visiting a place but a moment in time.

3 Wi-fi & Mobile Signal

Broadband, 4G and 5G coverage is improving across rural Scotland, particularly the Highlands and Islands, but don't be surprised if there is none. While this is a blessing for many, it's best to download any essentials or maps before your plans are scotched.

▶ See more about getting connected on p240

4 Know Your Geography

Few things get Scots as riled up as visitors not knowing that it is an independent country. It's part of a union with England, Wales and Northern Ireland, and referring to Scotland or the UK as England will only result in glowering.

5 Passing Places

On meeting a car, pull over in a passing place. If it's on your left, pull into it. If it's on your right, stop on the road – allowing the other vehicle to weave in-and-out of it. If there's a car – or queue – behind you, let them pass. Locals know the roads and won't appreciate driving 25mph behind you. Be prepared to reverse to allow someone to pass!

▶ See more transport tips on p242

6 Local Lingo

Learning some Scots vernacular will help you get by and make local friends along the way.

Munro bagging – hiking Scotland's highest mountains

fizzy juice, ginger – a soft drink or soda

gutties – shoes

banter – chat

scran – food

dreich – cold, wet and miserable

gie it laldy – give it your best

roaster, rocket, walloper – an idiot

blootered, bladdered, hammered, steamin', smashed, wrecked – drunk

If you're visiting the west coast Highlands and Islands, particularly the Outer Hebrides, a few token words of Gaelic will go a long way with locals. Many road signs are in both English and Gaelic.

Madainn mhath – *(matin va)* Good morning.

Ciamar a tha sibh? – *(kimmer a ha shiv)* How are you?

slainte mhath – *(slanj-a-va)* cheers

Alba – Scotland

uisge beatha – *(ishke behe)* literally 'water of life', but also the name of whisky

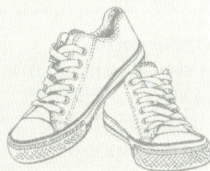

7 Midges

Scotland's most ferocious foe can single-handedly ruin a summer's evening. From May to September, the hard-to-see biting insects swarm riverbanks, lochsides, campsites and anywhere without a breeze. Pack midge repellent and cover up to avoid itchy red spots. If they're bad, put a stocking over your head and run for cover. Seriously.

▶ See more about midges on p244

Read, Listen, Watch & Follow

READ

Trainspotting (Irvine Welsh; 1993) A literary assault on the senses, hinged on the dark exploits of heroin users in 1980s Edinburgh.

Lanark (Alasdair Gray; 1981) A dystopian, surrealist distillation of Glasgow in four colossal parts.

The Life & Death of St Kilda (Tom Steel; 1988) A moving portrayal of St Kilda's evacuation in 1930 and challenges faced by island communities.

Sunset Song (Lewis Grassic Gibbon; 1932) Rural life in the Northeast, as seen through the lens of postwar Scotland.

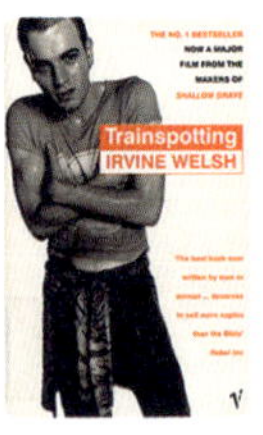

LISTEN

This is The Life (Amy Macdonald; 2007) With its heartfelt lyrics, and topping eight European singles charts, this was Amy's most successful release.

Screamadelica (Primal Scream; 1991) Rave-meets-rock-meets-gospel-meets-psychedelic-acid-house, spanning 11 tracks that changed British music forever.

Sunshine on Leith (The Proclaimers; 1988) Scotland's favourite sons, thanks to the country's unofficial singalong national anthem, 'I'm Gonna Be (500 Miles)'.

The Boy with the Arab Strap (Belle and Sebastian; 1998) Breakthrough third album from Glasgow's unlikely pop-folk troubadours.

TOM ROSE/SHUTTERSTOCK ©

Divinely Uninspired to a Hellish Extent (Lewis Capaldi; 2019) Broody, blue-eyed soul and torch ballads from busking singer-songwriter turned down-to-earth Billboard superstar.

WATCH

Harry Potter saga (2001–11) Wizards, witches and whomping willows – JK Rowling's epic inspired by and shot in her homeland.

Braveheart (1995) Mel Gibson channels his inner warrior for this Oscar-winning classic about claymore-wielding hero William Wallace.

Shetland series (2013–present) Popular TV crime drama based in Shetland.

Brave (2012) Disney does Scotland, with kilts, curses and a fiery cartoon princess.

Whisky Galore! (1949) Ealing Studio classic about a shipwrecked cargo and the Hebridean community out to hijack it.

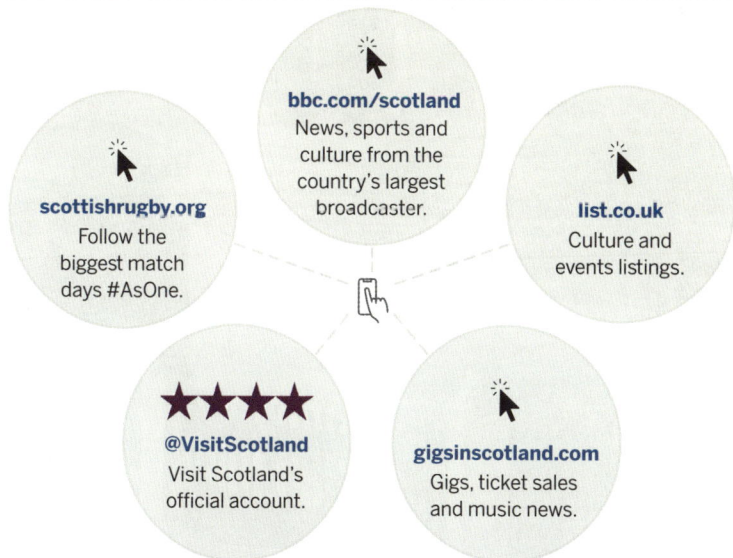

FOLLOW

bbc.com/scotland
News, sports and culture from the country's largest broadcaster.

scottishrugby.org
Follow the biggest match days #AsOne.

list.co.uk
Culture and events listings.

@VisitScotland
Visit Scotland's official account.

gigsinscotland.com
Gigs, ticket sales and music news.

EDINBURGH
CULTURE | HISTORY | FESTIVALS
DUGALD STEWART

▸ **Trip Builder** (p40)
▸ **Practicalities** (p42)
▸ **Festival Fringe** (p44)
▸ **History & a Royal Mile** (p46)
▸ **The Water of Leith** (p48)
▸ **Writers, Witches & Wizards** (p50)
▸ **Seven Hills** (p52)
▸ **Foodie Leith** (p54)
▸ **Listings** (p56)

EDINBURGH

Trip Builder

Where history, hospitality and higgledy-piggledy hills collide, discover a captivating city steeped in legend and lore. Edinburgh is a dynamic city, filled with castles, cathedrals and storybook alleys that inspired the greatest minds in science, philosophy and literature, but it's also where visitors can experience new waves of art, design and culture.

Stroll the **Water of Leith** to **Stockbridge** for a window on local Edinburgh life (p48)
1 day

Get smart and land tickets for the best shows at the world's largest **arts festival** (p44)
2–3 days

Discover life as it was during the Middle Ages at **Edinburgh Castle** (p47)
½ day

Take a scenic trip to **Rosslyn Chapel** for divine masonry and mystery (p47)
½ day

Firth of Forth
TRINITY
WARRISTON
INVERLEITH
Inverleith Park
CANONMILLS
DRYLAW
BLACKHALL
NEW TOWN
DEAN VILLAGE
WEST END
LAURISTON
MARCHMONT
Murrayfield (SRU Ground)

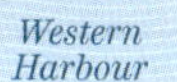

Western Harbour

0 — 1 km
0 — 0.5 miles

CLOCKWISE FROM LEFT: GREIG GALLAGHER/SHUTTERSTOCK ©, ALBERT PEGO/SHUTTERSTOCK ©, KOLLAWAT SOMSRI/SHUTTERSTOCK ©

NEWHAVEN

Feast on Scotland's larder on a foodie walking tour of **Leith** (p54)

1 day

LEITH

ABBEYHILL

Leith Links

Craigentinny Golf Course

Sample the clichés – fudge, whisky and shortbread – on the **Royal Mile** (p46)

½ day

Explore Edinburgh's seven hills, finishing with sunset on top of **Calton Hill** (p53)

1 day

PIERSHILL

Drop in on the late 17th century at **Palace of Holyroodhouse** (p47)

½ day

OLD TOWN

Holyrood Park

Begin 335 million years ago with a scramble to the top of volcanic **Arthur's Seat** (p52)

½ day

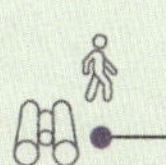

Step into the world of Harry Potter in **Greyfriars Kirkyard** and on bewitching **Victoria Street** (p50)

½ day

Practicalities

NITSAWAN KATERATTANAKUL/SHUTTERSTOCK ©

ARRIVING

Edinburgh Airport Located 8 miles from the city. The Airlink 100 service runs from the terminal to Haymarket, Princes St and St Andrew Sq (for Waverley). The journey is around 25 minutes and costs £4.50 one way. Taxis cost around £25 to £30.

Trains Trains arrive from other parts of Scotland at Waverley Station in the middle of the city centre. The taxi rank is on Market St and various car-hire options are available within the station.

HOW MUCH FOR A

Pint of local beer £5

Edinburgh Castle ticket £19.50

Haggis meal £14

GETTING AROUND

Walking Edinburgh is compact, easily navigable and best explored in a pair of comfy shoes. The city has seven hills – offering a different perspective from almost every angle.

Tram Edinburgh's modern tram network includes 23 stops throughout the city, including the airport, Haymarket, Princes St and St Andrew Sq (for Waverley).

Bus Lothian Buses operates an extensive 24/7 network around the city. All maps and timetables can be found on the website. City Sightseeing hop-on, hop-off buses have stops at all the major attractions in the city centre.

WHEN TO GO

JAN–MAR

Chilly weather, snow-globe scenery and dark nights.

APR–JUN

Comfortably warm, relatively rain free and with blossoming flowers.

JUL–SEP

Festival season, with the sunniest weather and the most visitors.

OCT–DEC

Thinner crowds, but busy around the city's raucous winter festivals.

EATING & DRINKING

Michelin menus Blow your budget on a tasting menu with paired wines at Martin Wisharts, The Little Chartroom, Fhior or Aizle (p57).

Coffee and cake The Pastry Section (p56) serves the best city bakes and Semifreddo Ice-cream Sandwiches.

Must try divine cocktails
Bramble (p56)

Best whisky alternative
Edinburgh Gin Distillery (p57)

CONNECT & FIND YOUR WAY

Wi-fi All hotels, bars, cafes and restaurants have guest wi-fi, while the city has its own free wi-fi service (edinburghfreewifi.com) with no restrictions on time.

Navigation The city centre is one of the smallest in Europe and a joy to explore on foot. Use Google Maps or grab a free local map from any tourist information point in the city.

FESTIVALS

The Scottish capital is turned upside down in August, December and at Hogmanay with more than three million visitors. Arrange your trip for midweek, when the crowds are more manageable.

WHERE TO STAY

Area	Pro/Con
Old Town	Buzzing hub of restaurants, shops, pubs and hotels, with excellent transport links and views. Pricey accommodation.
West End	Upmarket streets with terrace houses and hotels, boutiques and cocktail bars. Perfectly quiet in the evening.
Stockbridge	Affluent suburb wedged between the Royal Botanic Gardens and the Water of Leith. Wonderful restaurants, cafes, pubs and markets with a family-friendly feel.
Leith	Hipster central with hostels and the city's most happening restaurants and nightlife. A little rough around the edges.
Bruntsfield	Colourful southern suburb overlooking the green spaces of the Meadows with a village-like vibe.
Newington	Up-and-coming neighbourhood in the shadow of Arthur's Seat. Popular with students and right in the thick of things come Festival Fringe time in August.

MONEY

Plenty of Edinburgh's most popular attractions are free, including the National Museum of Scotland, the Scottish National Gallery and Scottish National Gallery of Modern Art. All are certainly worthy of a donation.

01 Festival FRINGE

ARTS | CULTURE | LATE NIGHT

From performances in pubs and playhouses to genre-defying shows in caravans and even toilets, the Edinburgh Festival Fringe turns the capital into Scotland's cultural heartbeat every August. Nothing beats it for drama or spectacle (weirdness, too). But with so much to make sense of, knowing where to start can leave you spinning.

KENNY TELFER/SHUTTERSTOCK ©

How to

When to go August. Stay longer than you think you'll need. Three days is ideal.

How much Ticket prices vary from free to upwards of £40 for a marquee act. 2-for-1 previews over the first weekend are the norm. Consider the Half Price Hut (The Mound) for last-minute bargains.

Don't forget An umbrella or raincoat. August is notoriously fickle weather-wise and queueing outside a venue in torrential rain is no one's idea of a great day out.

Get smart With 3500 shows, 1900-odd premieres and around 55,000 performances spread across 300 city-wide venues, deciding on what to see is a minefield. For the most memorable shows, read up on the critics' picks beforehand in *The Scotsman*, trust word of mouth, and remember that spontaneity is key. For the quintessential day, settle on one of the big four venues, turn up by lunchtime with at least one show pre-booked, then see where the mood takes you.

The venues The four main Fringe hubs all offer something different. Try the

Above left Edinburgh Festival Fringe on the Royal Mile
Above right A Festival Fringe street perfomer
Right A street musician plays for a Festival Fringe crowd

YATZEK PHOTOGRAPHY/SHUTTERSTOCK ©

Other Festivals

Edinburgh's Hogmanay The world's biggest Hogmanay bash sees a tartan army crammed beneath Edinburgh Castle to *ceilidh* and drain a dram of whisky every 31 December.

Edinburgh International Film Festival This carnival in late June sees red carpet galas, world premieres and talks with both local and A-list stars and directors.

Edinburgh International Book Festival Held from mid to late August, with 1000 writers, conversations and Q&As.

Pleasance for celeb-spotting and comedy; take a picnic blanket to Assembly at George Sq for street food and the big top Spiegeltent; consider Underbelly for cabaret; and catch topical comedy and theatre at the Gilded Balloon. Elsewhere, Summerhall is a stellar multi-arts venue, while The Stand is a don't-miss basement comedy club.

Need to know By the second and third weeks, the critics' picks are often sold out. Conversely, newcomers and on-the-up performers hand out free or next-to-nothing tickets outside venues. You might see a flop, but before they were famous the likes of Stephen Fry, Mike Myers and Flight of the Conchords performed for less than £5.

POWEROFFLOWERS/SHUTTERSTOCK ©

02 History & a ROYAL MILE

HISTORY | CULTURE | WALK

With a storied skyline of Gothic tolbooths, Georgian turrets and dizzying spires, Edinburgh is Britain's most full-blooded city. There are dozens of world-class sights to discover, with each offering time travel of a sort through the centuries from the medieval to the present day.

ESSEVU/SHUTTERSTOCK ©

How to

Getting around Most sights are easily navigable through Edinburgh's most romantic cobbled passageways. To get to Rosslyn Chapel, take Service 37 with Lothian Buses, or hire a bike for the 10-mile round-trip along Route 61 (The Rosslyn Chapel Way).

When to go Summer sees the city's high-profile attractions at their busiest; spring and September are quieter times to visit.

Best photo op From rugged Salisbury Crags, next to Holyrood Palace at last light.

FOTOKON/SHUTTERSTOCK ©

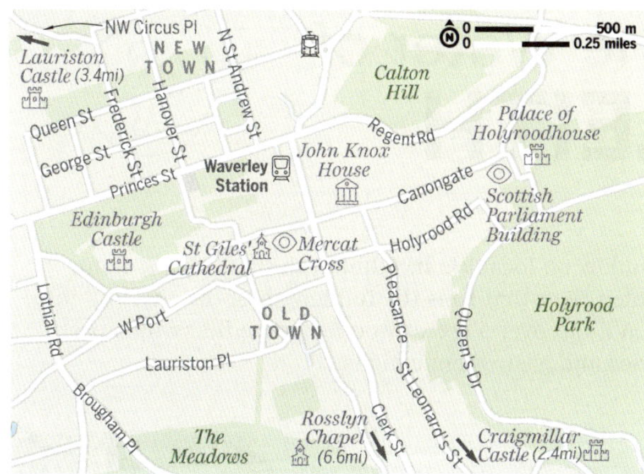

Skyline views Edinburgh Castle is the Scotland of fantasies. Stride past the Braveheart face-painters and bagpipe-players to the top of Castle Rock to discover 10 centuries of nation-defining wars. To bypass the crowds, go straight to the Honours of Scotland, Britain's oldest surviving set of crown jewels, and take a quiet moment in St Margaret's Chapel, Edinburgh's oldest building.

Living history The **Royal Mile** is the city's larger-than-life high street, where the past and present come face to face. Start in front of the Castle Gate House before strolling east, past the Tolbooth Kirk, St Giles' Cathedral and Mercat Cross. Between glimpses of 73 time-stopped closes (medieval alleyways), highlights include the Canongate Tolbooth, John Knox House and the Scottish Parliament.

Of kings and queens The Royal Mile abruptly ends at the gates to **Palace of Holyroodhouse**, the official residence of His Majesty the King in Scotland. Join a morning private tour to learn the secrets of the Throne Room and State Apartments before the palace opens for the day.

All saints A sanctuary for the faithful since 1446, mysterious **Rosslyn Chapel** took on a second life as a 'celebrity' church following its role in Dan Brown's *The Da Vinci Code*. Try to find connections to the Knights Templar in the crypt, then admire 200-plus keystone carvings that cover the nave, apse and altar.

Left Edinburgh's Royal Mile
Below left Canongate Tolbooth

Fortress Edinburgh

With more time to explore further afield, here are three other medieval keeps to help inspire your imagination.

Craigmillar Castle The capital's 'other' imposing castle, located 2.5 miles southeast of the Royal Mile. Once a safe haven for Mary Queen of Scots and brimming with nooks and crannies.

Lauriston Castle A supposedly haunted 16th-century tower house with lovely Japanese garden, museum and family-run bakery.

Blackness Castle A seafront garrison and prison stronghold with second-to-none Firth of Forth views. Located 15 miles west near Linlinthgow.

03 The Water of LEITH

WALK | ART | FOOD

There's no better window on local life in Edinburgh than a walk along the Water of Leith, the hidden river that runs the full length of the city. Slip into your comfiest shoes and you'll discover a secret wooded gorge that winds past impeccable gardens, galleries and gastronomic highs.

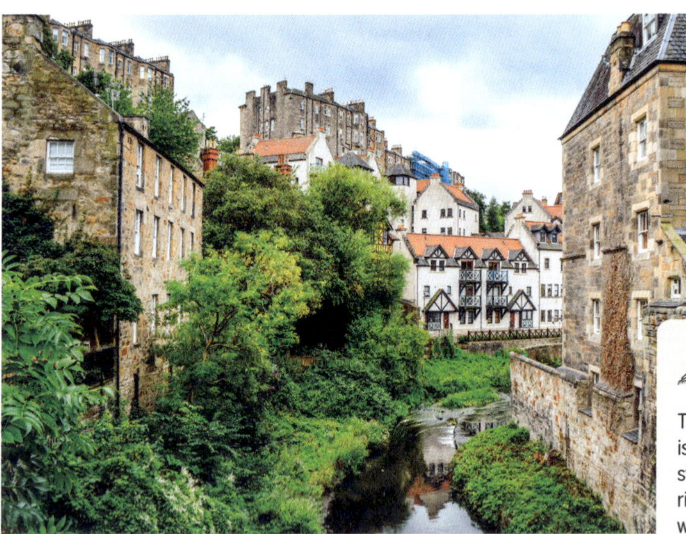

KORNELIJA CAKARUN/SHUTTERSTOCK ©

Trip Notes

Getting around At 12 miles long, this walk is best broken into chunks. Our featured section can be reached on a bus or tram from Princes St to Murrayfield Stadium. Alternatively, hire a bike from Cycle Scotland (29 Blackfriars St) to tackle it in one go.

When to go Year-round, but especially on Sunday when the Stockbridge Market is in full swing.

Top tip The Scottish National Gallery of Modern Art is split into Modern One and Modern Two: fuel up at Modern One's garden cafe.

Wildlife-Watching

The Water of Leith isn't only home to strolling couples, harried dog walkers and weekend joggers. It's an urban sanctuary for a staggering 250 species of wildlife and there's almost as much diversity as at nearby Edinburgh Zoo. Look for heron, kingfisher, mink and otter, as well as swan, fox, squirrel and bat.

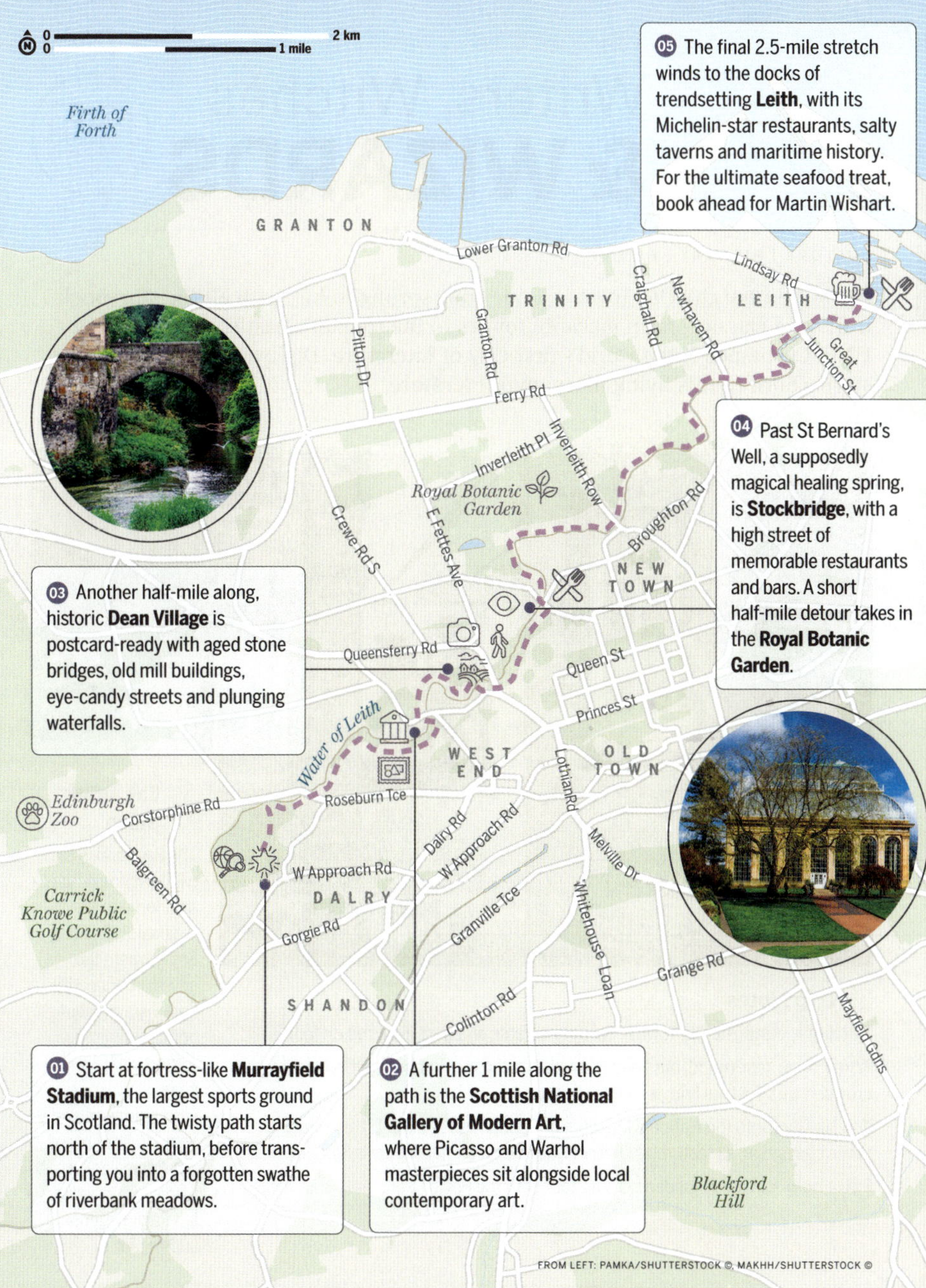

0 2 km
0 1 mile
Firth of Forth
GRANTON
Lower Granton Rd
TRINITY
LEITH
Lindsay Rd
Craighall Rd
Newhaven Rd
Granton Rd
Pilton Dr
Great Junction St
Ferry Rd
Inverleith Pl
Inverleith Row
Royal Botanic Garden
Broughton Rd
Crewe Rd S
E Fettes Ave
NEW TOWN
Queensferry Rd
Queen St
Princes St
Water of Leith
WEST END
OLD TOWN
Lothian Rd
Edinburgh Zoo
Corstorphine Rd
Roseburn Tce
Dalry Rd
W Approach Rd
Balgreen Rd
Melville Dr
W Approach Rd
DALRY
Carrick Knowe Public Golf Course
Gorgie Rd
Granville Tce
Whitehouse Loan
Grange Rd
SHANDON
Colinton Rd
Mayfield Gdns
Blackford Hill
05 The final 2.5-mile stretch winds to the docks of trendsetting **Leith**, with its Michelin-star restaurants, salty taverns and maritime history. For the ultimate seafood treat, book ahead for Martin Wishart.
04 Past St Bernard's Well, a supposedly magical healing spring, is **Stockbridge**, with a high street of memorable restaurants and bars. A short half-mile detour takes in the **Royal Botanic Garden**.
03 Another half-mile along, historic **Dean Village** is postcard-ready with aged stone bridges, old mill buildings, eye-candy streets and plunging waterfalls.
01 Start at fortress-like **Murrayfield Stadium**, the largest sports ground in Scotland. The twisty path starts north of the stadium, before transporting you into a forgotten swathe of riverbank meadows.
02 A further 1 mile along the path is the **Scottish National Gallery of Modern Art**, where Picasso and Warhol masterpieces sit alongside local contemporary art.

FROM LEFT: PAMKA/SHUTTERSTOCK ©, MAKHH/SHUTTERSTOCK ©

04 Writers, Witches & WIZARDS

CULTURE | HISTORY | FAMILY

Edinburgh's Old Town is a fairy tale sprung to life, with all the storybook traits of a classic – from macabre towers to the romantic castle, it's no wonder UNESCO named it the world's first City of Literature. Discover the best-selling stories born in this living museum of literature.

FOTOKON/SHUTTERSTOCK ©

Trip Notes

Getting around The Old Town is easily navigable and best explored on foot.

When to go Year-round, but keep in mind that the most popular sites can get crowded with Festival Fringe goers in August.

Top tip Duck into the National Museum of Scotland to see the 12th-century Lewis chessmen, as featured in *Harry Potter and the Philosopher's Stone*.

Extra help Join a free guided walking tour with the Potter Trail.

Eat, Drink, Sleep

The Balmoral is the city's grandest hotel and home to the magical JK Rowling Suite, where the novelist penned the final instalment of her wizarding saga. A short walk away, some of the most vivid stories can be heard in The Oxford Bar (Young St), a pub where crime writer Ian Rankin regularly sups a pint.

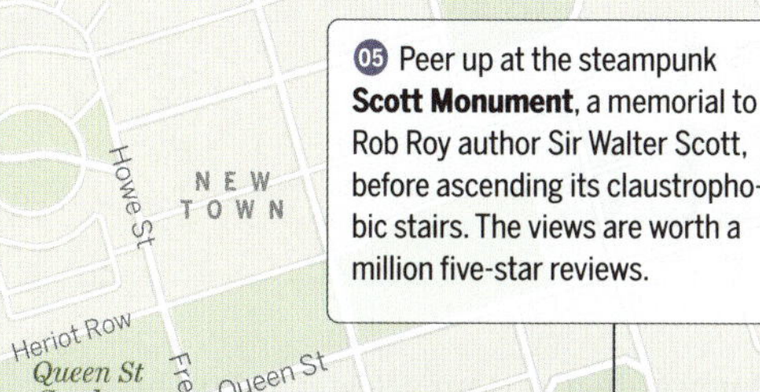

05 Peer up at the steampunk **Scott Monument**, a memorial to Rob Roy author Sir Walter Scott, before ascending its claustrophobic stairs. The views are worth a million five-star reviews.

Regent Gardens

Calton Rd

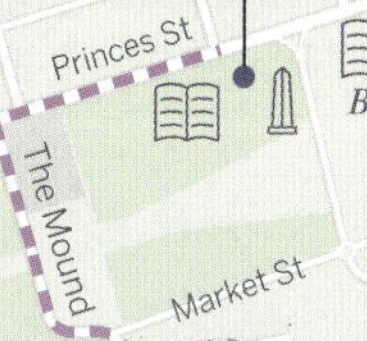

04 Head down the steps to the **Writers' Museum** (pictured left) to learn about the city's famous novelists, including Arthur Conan Doyle, JM Barrie and Robert Louis Stevenson.

High St (Royal Mile)

Edinburgh Castle

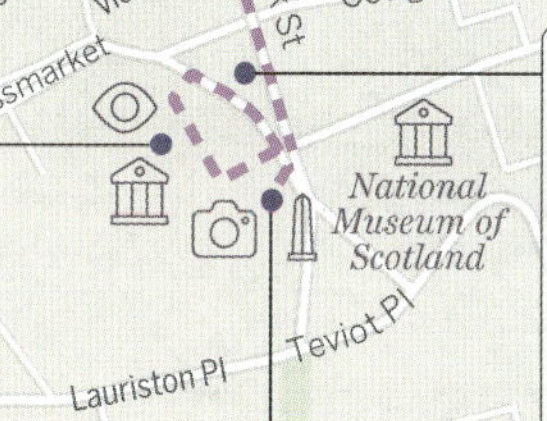

02 Grave-spotting is serious business at **Greyfriars Kirkyard** – JK Rowling found inspiration for some of her most beloved characters here. Look for the headstones of the Potter family.

03 JK Rowling first put Harry Potter onto page at the **Elephant House** (George IV Bridge); she was also inspired by nearby **Victoria Street** (Diagon Alley) and **George Watson's College** (Hogwarts).

Lauriston Pl

George Sq

01 Pick up the trail at the **statue of Greyfriars Bobby** (Candlemaker Row), the Skye Terrier whose story has been turned into novels, picture books and a Disney film.

0 500 m
0 0.25 miles

05 Seven HILLS

WALK | HISTORY | ADVENTURE

Every visitor to Edinburgh knows about Arthur's Seat and Edinburgh Castle, sitting atop the volcanic plug of Castle Rock. But few know the city is built on five other handsome hilltops and combining an exploration of all seven offers the most rewarding way to explore this topographically challenged capital. Here's what to see for a unique perspective of Edinburgh's cinematic plateau.

MAKHH/SHUTTERSTOCK ©

How to

Getting around To reach all of the seven hills, you'll need a Lothian Buses Day Ticket (£5), which allows unlimited journeys on day services (lothian buses.com).

When to go It might be an allusion to the Seven Hills of Rome, but it remains a joy all year round. June sees a hotly contested competition between runners of all ages (seven-hills.org.uk).

Fast fact It's an Edinburgh badge of honour to run or walk the 14 miles between all seven hills, marrying pavement pounding with hill climbing and urban orienteering.

MIGUEL ALMEIDA/SHUTTERSTOCK ©

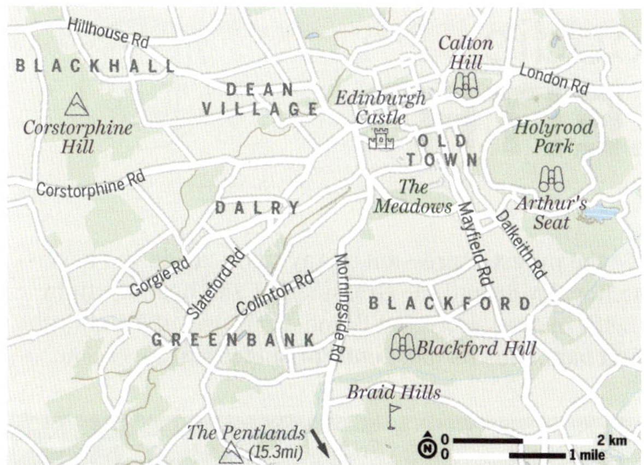

Pick Your Perfect Hill

The panoramic one About 2 miles south of the city centre, **Blackford Hill** is the locals' preferred option on a summer's day. It begins with a ramble through a wooded glen past Hermitage House, a stunning example of 18th-century architecture, before rising steeply through gorse onto a bald summit. From here, you'll discover a picture-perfect view of the trinity of Edinburgh Castle, the Old Town and Arthur's Seat.

The family-friendly one Easy to reach in the city centre, and even easier to climb, UNESCO-worthy **Calton Hill** is the gateway to the city's most photographed sunset view, as well as a series of memorials and crenellated buildings that are a delight to explore. A memorable lunch is an option at The Lookout by Gardener's Cottage restaurant, while late spring sees the hill at its busiest. On 30 April, the Beltane Fire Festival takes place on the hilltop – cue bonfires, masked dancers and pagan traditions.

The golf escape Knowing Scotland is the home of golf helps explain why **Braid Hills**, the southernmost of the seven hills, is blanketed with fairways, putting greens and bunkers – it's home to two golf courses, 27 holes and a driving range. For something other than golf, there's a circular walk that's open to hikers, bikers and horse riders – expect muddy boots.

The wild hill Above Edinburgh Zoo, **Corstorphine Hill** is a forest-topped ridge and nature reserve with a smattering of wooded walks and Corstorphine Hill Tower, a memorial to Sir Walter Scott. As well as a walled garden and gorgeous swathes of oak and birch woods, it's home to a disused stone quarry and a nuclear bunker that's now being converted into a visitor attraction.

Left Royal Observatory (p56), Blackford Hill
Below left National Monument of Scotland, Calton Hill

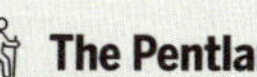

The Pentlands

To the southwest of Edinburgh is the Pentland Hills, which offer a cornucopia of outdoor thrills.

Threipmuir Reservoir Wild swim, canoe or stand-up paddle on this hill-cradled reservoir.

Allermuir Hill The hike to the summit is a 5-mile round-trip, but the reward is views of the entire city.

Scald Law The highest point of the Pentlands at 579m and a 7.5-mile walk from Flotterstone. Plan a whole day to savour all of Edinburgh's heather-topped Himalaya.

06 Foodie LEITH

WALK | FOOD | DRINK

For food and drink – the purest expression of any city – avoid the haggis-touting tourist traps on the Royal Mile and the Grassmarket and head north by northeast to trendsetting Leith instead. Here you'll find a carousel of Edinburgh's most vibrant restaurants and bars, plus its most enterprising grassroots scene.

STEFANO EMBER/SHUTTERSTOCK ©

Trip Notes

Getting around Leith Walk leads from the New Town to the waterfront in Leith. Walk the 2 miles or jump on one of the regular bus or tram services. For an organised tour, Eat Walk Edinburgh is highly recommended (eatwalkedinburgh.co.uk).

When to go Year-round, but especially on a Friday or Saturday, when the tasting rooms, bars and ad hoc summer markets are at their liveliest.

Top tip Take a piece of Leith home with you from Valvona & Crolla, Scotland's oldest delicatessen and wine merchant.

By the Sea

Plenty of seafood in Edinburgh is landed at Newhaven Harbour, a 10-minute walk north from Leith. It's home to a boardwalk promenade, a lighthouse and two memorable fish restaurants. Try the sustainably sourced fish and chips from the **Fishmarket**.

0 500 m
0 0.25 miles

Firth of Forth
Fishmarket
Commercial St
Ocean Dr
Bernard St
Roseleaf
Ferry Rd
King's Wark
LEITH
Salamander St
Links Pl
Leith Links
Great Junction St
Constitution St
Bonnington Rd
Jane St
Duke St
Pilrig Park
Best Kebab House
Leith Walk
Lorne St
Pilrig St
Iona St
Easter Rd
Albert St
The Walnut
Valvona & Crolla
London Rd
Leith St
Holyrood Park

01 Start with a hunger-busting brunch at the **Remedy**, for great coffee, top-notch Turkish eggs, or a sriracha eggs benny. Even better if you manage to grab the window couch. From here, you're in the heart of buzzing Leith Walk.

02 Lunchtime calls for **Eleanore**, by the city's most successful female chef, Roberta Hall-McCarron, or across the street to the **Walnut** for an excellent-value set lunch in a small, intimate setting. The Walnut Whip for dessert is a must.

03 Loosen your belt and stroll down Leith Walk to the Shore, the city's beautiful waterfront, home to several microbreweries. Drop into **Campervan Brewery's** taproom and beer garden for a cold beer.

04 Still got room for dinner? Keep it casual with some final belly-brimming gastropub delights: a mug of kedgeree or mac 'n' cheese at **Teuchter's Landing**, a McLeith Burger and teapot cocktail at **Roseleaf** or a seafood spread at the **King's Wark** (pictured below).

05 If late-night munchies hit, join a queue of merry locals at **Storries** bakery for a post-pub pie or head to the **Best Kebab House** for the legendary roast tatties.

Listings

BEST OF THE REST

Green Spaces & Views

Princes Street Gardens
Slow down and absorb Edinburgh's most accessible park, nestled between the Old and New Town. This park comes to life in December as Christmas markets make the winter city sparkle.

Arthur's Seat
Once an amped-up volcano, now a knuckle of dormant rock, this 251m piton is to Edinburgh what the Sugarloaf is to Rio de Janeiro. Hike through the heather, then gawp at the ludicrous summit panorama.

Royal Observatory
Sweeping Blackford Hill beside the Hermitage of Braid park is home to Edinburgh's premier stargazing spot. Take a bus to Morningside for the round-trip hike.

A Quick Bite

Minami Sushi £
Hidden in plain sight (behind the Apple store), this tiny eatery is run by a Ukrainian family fleeing the war. They have introduced Ukrainian-style sushi to the city, including their unique hot, grilled sushi rolls.

Shrimpwreck £
From award-winning fish-finger sandwiches to their favoured crispy squid, no visit to the beach is complete without a stop at Portobello's favourite seafood shack.

Scran and Scallie ££
All the best bits of Scottish pub culture crammed into the one neighbourhood spot in Comely Bank. It's run by tousle-haired chef Tom Kitchin, who raids the seasonal Scots larder with glee.

Oink £
For the perfect pulled-pork sandwich, visit Victoria St or the Canongate's Oink for an incredible hog roast bun. Get there early, as when it's gone, it's gone!

Pastry Section £
For the most impressively delicious selection of cakes and bakes in the city – strong claim, but true! – head to Leith or Stockbridge.

Whisky, Gin & Cocktails

Scotch Whisky Experience ££
Enter a world of whisky and learn about the regions, flavours and history of the nation's *uisge beatha*, or 'water of life' on a tour and tasting.

Voyage of Buck ££
Taking a cue from *Around the World in 80 Days*, this William St favourite is a showstopper. Food and cocktails come courtesy of Delhi, Kyoto and Casablanca, but the decor is Scottish chic.

Bramble £
Tiny if hard-to-find basement bar on Queen St, but worth it for acclaimed cocktails, beats and resident DJs. The bartenders are as creative as they come.

Edinburgh cityscape, seen from Arthur's Seat

Edinburgh Gin Distillery £

A banner couple of years for Scottish gin has seen this subterranean small-batch distillery thrive. Try raspberry-, rhubarb- or bramble-infused recipes on a behind-the-scenes tour off Lothian Rd.

 Memorable Meals

Prestonfield House ££

Highland-style lodge south of the centre with its own strutting peacocks and herd of Highland cows. Come for afternoon tea, served amid a riot of stag-antler armchairs and gilded mirrors.

Little Chartroom ££

Chef Roberta Hall-McCarron is at the vanguard of new Scots cuisine. Her poky Leith bistro, packed with an ever-changing menu of risky, remarkable food, shows why.

Fhior ££

Chef Scott Smith's vaunted Broughton St restaurant looks modest from the outside but is rewriting Scotland's cultural cookbook. Seasonal cooking at its best.

Aizle ££

Tucked deep inside the Kimpton Charlotte Square Hotel and serving locally inspired, seasonal tasting menus in a lush oasis-style dining room – expect playful plates, experimental flavours and pure food science.

Tattu ££

For a sleek and modern twist on the traditional Chinese restaurant, trendsetting Tattu serves up style, sumptuous sizzling plates and quirky cocktails in their elegant, floral restaurant.

 Arts & Culture

National Museum of Scotland

The only place to time travel through Scotland's history and modern culture. Standout exhibits include Bonnie Prince Charlie's picnic set and Dolly, the first cloned mammal and the most famous sheep in the world.

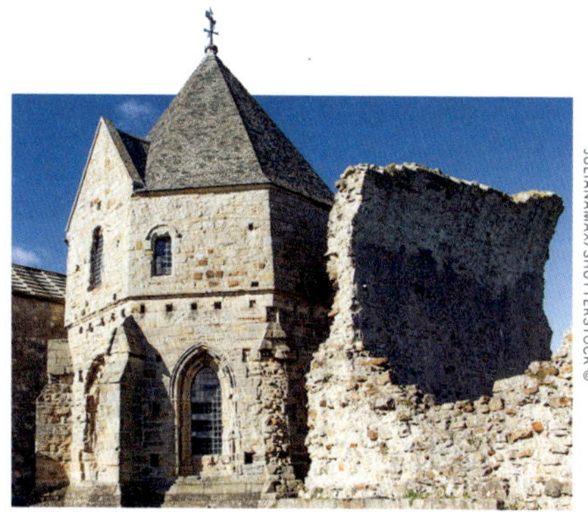

Inchcolm Abbey

Edinburgh Music Tours

Like The Bay City Rollers, The Proclaimers and David Bowie? Every city corner has an echo and it comes to life on a trivia-loaded tour of the city's pop, punk and folk temples.

 Day Trips

Inchcolm Abbey

Set sail from the city's Forth Bridges to eerily empty Inchcolm island to see the best-preserved group of monastic buildings in Scotland.

Dalkeith Country Park

Take a tour of Dalkeith Palace or mooch around the Restoration Yard's store, restaurant and wellness studio. Join one of the walking trails of this 1000-acre park just a 45-minute bus ride from the city centre.

Jupiter Artland

Thirty minutes west of the city, they say, the Guggenheim has competition. This sprawling sculpture park and art gallery in the grounds of Bonnington House is ideal for eye-rubbing art encounters. Open May to September.

GLASGOW

FRIENDLY | GRITTY | DYNAMIC

- **Trip Builder** (p60)
- **Practicalities** (p62)
- **A Night on the Town** (p64)
- **A Splash of Colour** (p66)
- **Glasgow's Story** (p68)
- **What Makes Glasgow So?** (p70)
- **Footsteps of Legends** (p72)
- **Listings** (p74)

GLASGOW
Trip Builder

Glasgow is a place of excitement and round-the-clock energy, offering one of the best nightlife and dining scenes in Europe, backed by superb cultural attractions and eye-catching architecture. Prepare for new friendships and plenty of surprises.

Explore the vast treasure trove of **Kelvingrove Art Gallery & Museum** (pictured right; p69)
½ day

Kelvingrove Park

KELVINGROVE

Taste a dram straight from the source at the **Clydeside Distillery** (p75)
½ day

GOVAN

River Clyde

IBROX

Applaud Charles Rennie Mackintosh's **House for an Art Lover** (p74)
1–2 hr

Gorge on seafood, curries, whisky and more in the food and drink hub of **Finnieston** (p75)
½ day

Bellahouston Park

SOUTH CARDONALD

Admire one of the world's finest personal art collections at the **Burrell Collection** (p69)
½ day

Pollok Country Park

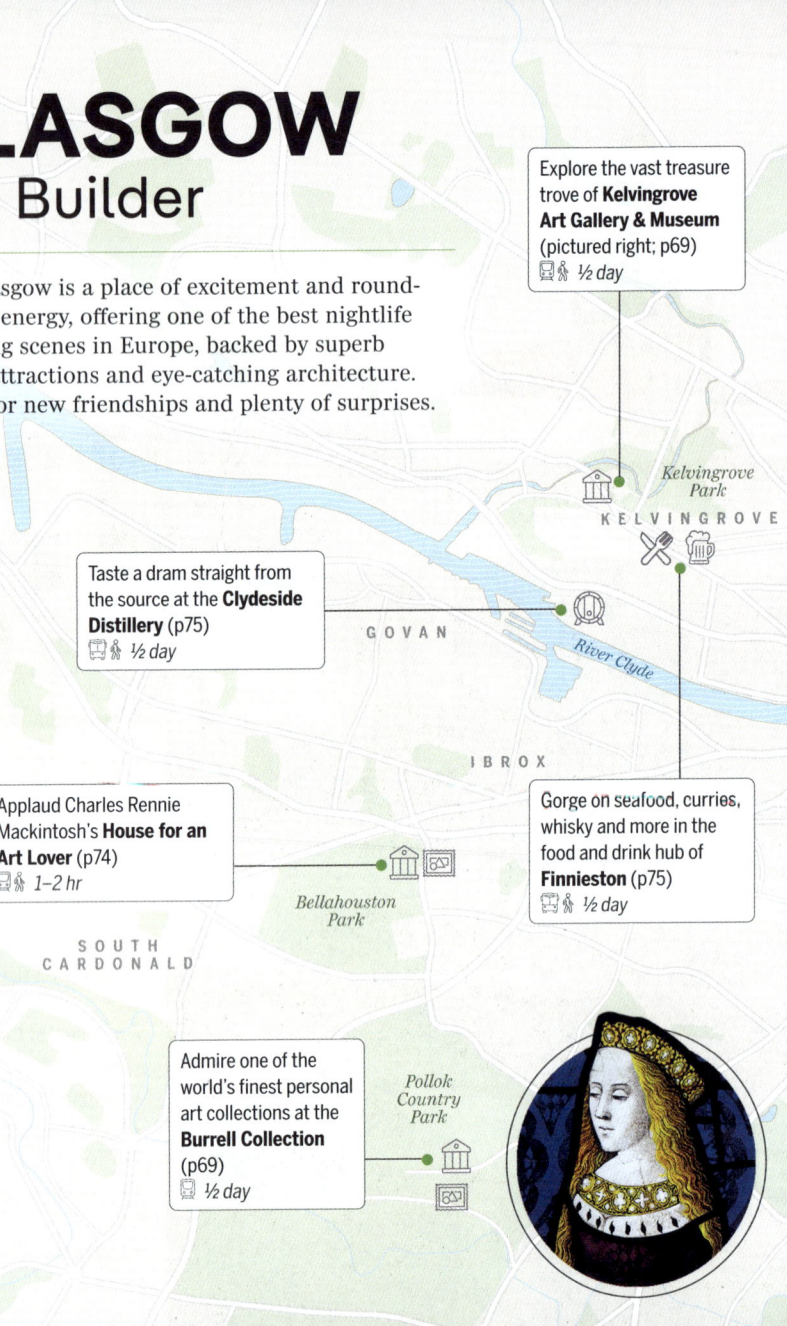

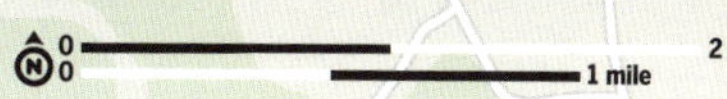

Whisk yourself around town on the wonderfully retro **Glasgow Subway** (p62)
1hr

Marvel at marble in the Victorian masterpiece that is the **City Chambers** (p74)
1–2hr

Step back in time at medieval **Glasgow Cathedral** (p69)
1–2hr

Dance the night away at locally iconic music venue the **Barrowland Ballroom** (p74)
½ day

Lose yourself in shopping along the city centre's **Style Mile** (p63)
½ day

COWCADDENS
GARNETHILL
TOWNHEAD
RIDDRIE
DENNISTOUN
CARNTYNE
Glasgow Green
BRIDGETON
HUTCHESONTOWN
HAMPDEN PARK
RUTHERGLEN
BANKHEAD

CLOCKWISE FROM BOTTOM LEFT: SKULLY/SHUTTERSTOCK ©, JEFF WHYTE/SHUTTERSTOCK ©, WESTWOODST/SHUTTERSTOCK ©

Practicalities

EQROY/SHUTTERSTOCK ©

ARRIVING

Glasgow Airport A shuttle bus service (500) operates from Glasgow Airport's main terminal exit, going to Buchannan St Station in the city centre. Single/return tickets cost £10.50/17. Taxis are also available outside the terminal. The journey time for both to the city is 20 to 30 minutes.

Train In the city centre, trains coming from the south (including direct from London) arrive at Glasgow Central Station while arrivals from the north and Edinburgh pull in at Queen St Station.

HOW MUCH FOR A

Dram of whisky £4

Haggis pakora £6

Gig ticket £7–9

WHEN TO GO

DEC–MAR

Cold and rainy in the quiet season, with short days that call for cosy drams.

APR–JUN

Very mixed weather but a good number of beautiful days.

JUL & AUG

Peak season with stretching days, mild temperatures and moderate rainfall.

SEP–NOV

Autumn weather with crisp days and photogenic light.

GETTING AROUND

Subway The delightfully retro Subway has only 15 stops and travels in a constant loop, making it the most convenient means of getting between the centre and West End.

Bike Hiring bikes is increasingly popular – look for the pink People Make Glasgow branding – there are over 1000 standard bikes and 189 e-bikes at 66 locations across the city. Cyclists can register as a member or casually use the scheme via the Nextbike app.

Bus There are City Sightseeing hop-on, hop-off buses with stops at all the major attractions in the city centre and West End, including audio guides in multiple languages.

EATING & DRINKING

Where to go The West End – and Finnieston in particular – offers the best concentration and range of dining options. Late-night bars and clubs are more prevalent in the city centre.

Regional produce The west coast Highlands and Islands have played a big role in the evolution of the city's social culture, and sampling produce (seafood, venison, lamb, whisky, gin) from these parts is well advised.

Must-try local beer
WEST Brewery's St Mungo lager

Best for seafood
Crabshakk (p65)

CONNECT & FIND YOUR WAY

Wi-fi Available throughout the city in restaurants, bars, cafes and attractions. Glasgow City Free Wi-fi is also available in central locations.

Navigation The city centre is built up with a grid system that can be hard to navigate for first-time visitors. Use navigation apps on your phone (or ask the friendly locals) to keep you right.

WHERE TO STAY

Scotland is rarely cheap but highly competitive Glasgow offers some of the best value. Book ahead wherever possible, certainly in summer peak season, at weekends or if there are big gigs or football matches on.

Area	Pro/Con
Merchant City	Trendy, boisterous and best for nightlife seekers, within walking distance of the central bars and clubs.
City centre	On and around Sauchiehall St you'll find loads of choice from the familiar chain hotels.
Kelvinbridge and Kelvingrove	A relatively quiet happy medium with close proximity to the West End's attractions and restaurants.
Hillhead	Pricey but with immediate access to the West End's main thoroughfare of Byres Rd and its energetic, youthful buzz.
South Side	Less choice but best for mingling with the locals in the calmer residential neighbourhoods south of the Clyde.

SHOPPING

Most city-centre shops and centres are open 9am to 7pm daily. Late-night shopping is on Thursday, when this extends to 8pm for many shops.

MONEY

Most of Glasgow's museums and galleries are free to enter. There are shopping bargains to be had both on the competitive Style Mile and in the West End's vintage shops. All-day tickets on the Subway give unlimited travel.

07 A Night on THE TOWN

NIGHTLIFE | DINING | LIVE MUSIC

From time immemorial, Glaswegians have loved to be entertained. They love having a good laugh at themselves, and each other. They love a good feast, a suitable bevvy, a night of dancing and a singalong. You'd be well advised to join in.

MARION CARNIEL/SHUTTERSTOCK ©

Trip Notes

Getting around While the weather may have other plans, the West End of the city is very navigable by foot. By evening, getting back into the city centre is best done by hailing a taxi.

When to go Friday and Saturday nights are relentlessly boisterous and energetic.

Top tip Keep moving. There are dozens of terrific nightspots in the city so don't settle down too comfortably and keep seeking out the next best thing.

Memories Are There for the Making

Perhaps it was Will Fyffe who captured it best in the 1920s with his timeless song 'I Belong to Glasgow'. Engrossed in conversation with a merry local, Fyffe enquired knowingly if the man belonged to Glasgow. He was slyly reassured that, after a drink or two, on the contrary, it was Glasgow that belonged to him.

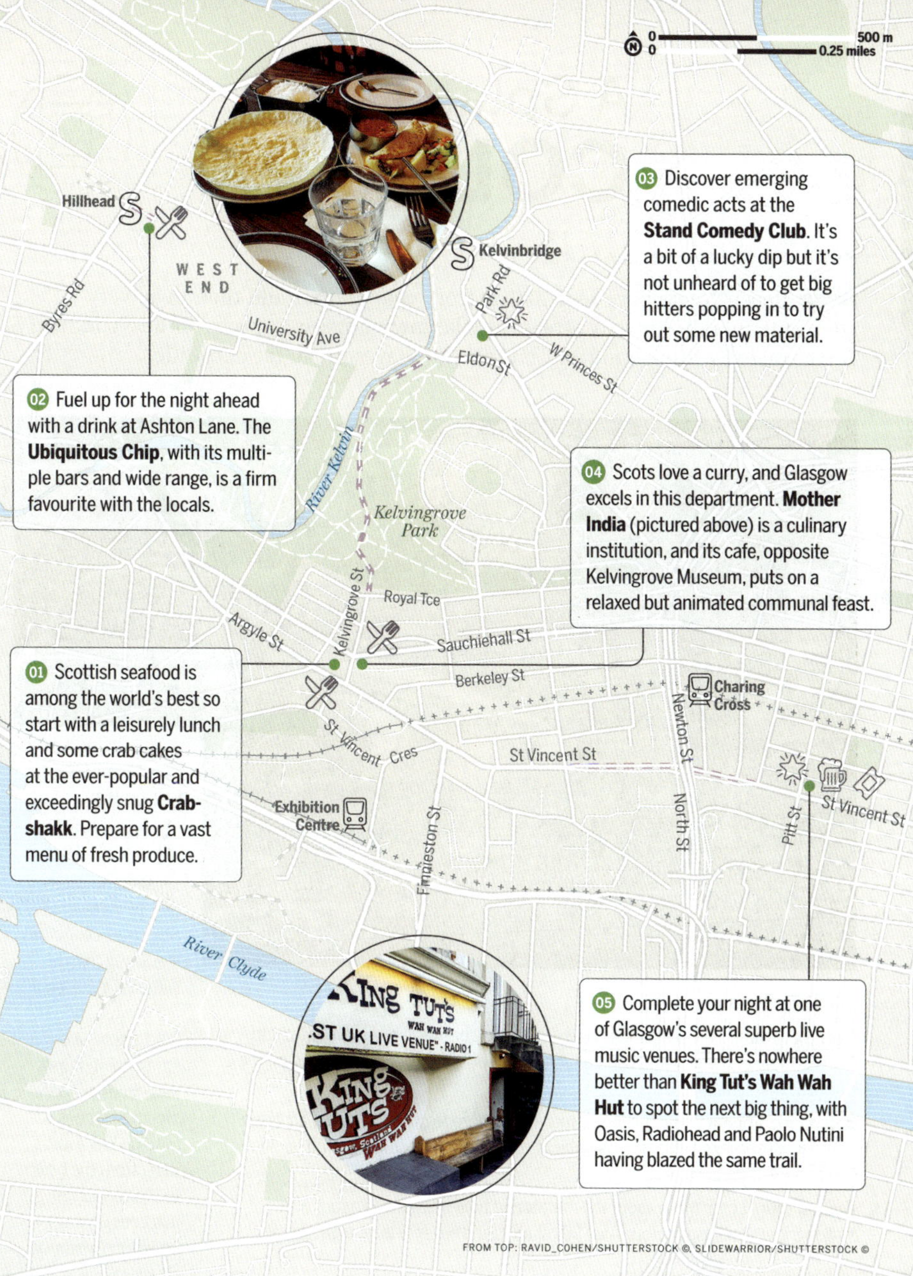

01 Scottish seafood is among the world's best so start with a leisurely lunch and some crab cakes at the ever-popular and exceedingly snug **Crabshakk**. Prepare for a vast menu of fresh produce.

02 Fuel up for the night ahead with a drink at Ashton Lane. The **Ubiquitous Chip**, with its multiple bars and wide range, is a firm favourite with the locals.

03 Discover emerging comedic acts at the **Stand Comedy Club**. It's a bit of a lucky dip but it's not unheard of to get big hitters popping in to try out some new material.

04 Scots love a curry, and Glasgow excels in this department. **Mother India** (pictured above) is a culinary institution, and its cafe, opposite Kelvingrove Museum, puts on a relaxed but animated communal feast.

05 Complete your night at one of Glasgow's several superb live music venues. There's nowhere better than **King Tut's Wah Wah Hut** to spot the next big thing, with Oasis, Radiohead and Paolo Nutini having blazed the same trail.

08 A Splash of COLOUR

MURALS | STREET ART | WALKING TOURS

Recent years have seen artists from near and far add their own, very colourful, mark to the city streets as Glasgow's lingering spectre of heavy industry is contrasted with magnificent murals that have spread far and wide.

ARTIST ROGUE-ONE (@ROGUEONER). IMAGE BY TIM BIEBER/GETTY IMAGES ©

Trip Notes

Getting around The murals selected are located between the city centre and the west end of the city and can be tackled on foot or by hopping on and off the Subway.

A dynamic appeal While the larger murals are here to stay, the street art to be found in all corners of Glasgow is subject to change, with comings and goings keeping fans on their toes.

Guided tours Learn more about the murals and their creators on a tour with Walking Tours in Glasgow. Tours last 90 minutes and cover at least eight murals.

Diversity Is Key

The vibrancy of the murals across Glasgow is matched only by its diversity. Street-art celebrities like Smug mingle with first-time local unknowns, and bold, photo-like spray-paint murals neighbour intricate stencil sketches. Since 2008, everything from the bizarre to the conservative has been raising eyebrows and inspiring chuckles.

01 These two complementary murals – **St Mungo** and **St Enoch with Child** – by international artist Smug are found just off the High St and pay a tribute to Glasgow's patron saint and his mother, with nods to the city's founding story within.

02 In the heart of the Merchant City, you'll find another mural by Smug, **Fellow Glasgow Residents**, a seemingly out-of-place depiction of a resplendent wildlife scene on a forest floor.

03 The back-alley feel of Mitchell St is brought to life by the artist Rogue-One with a Glasgow taxi floating towards a hailing customer: **The World's Most Economical Taxi**. Check out @rogueoner for more information.

04 A tribute to maybe Glasgow's all-time favourite son, comedian and actor Billy Connolly, brightens everyone's day with multiple murals by Rogue-One. His reproduction of Jack Vettriano's painting, **Dr Connolly, I Presume?**, is particularly memorable.

05 The Clutha Bar, the site of a helicopter crash in 2013, is now colourfully marked by the faces of local favourites. None stand out more than the forever-suave **Charles Rennie Mackintosh**, also by Rogue-One.

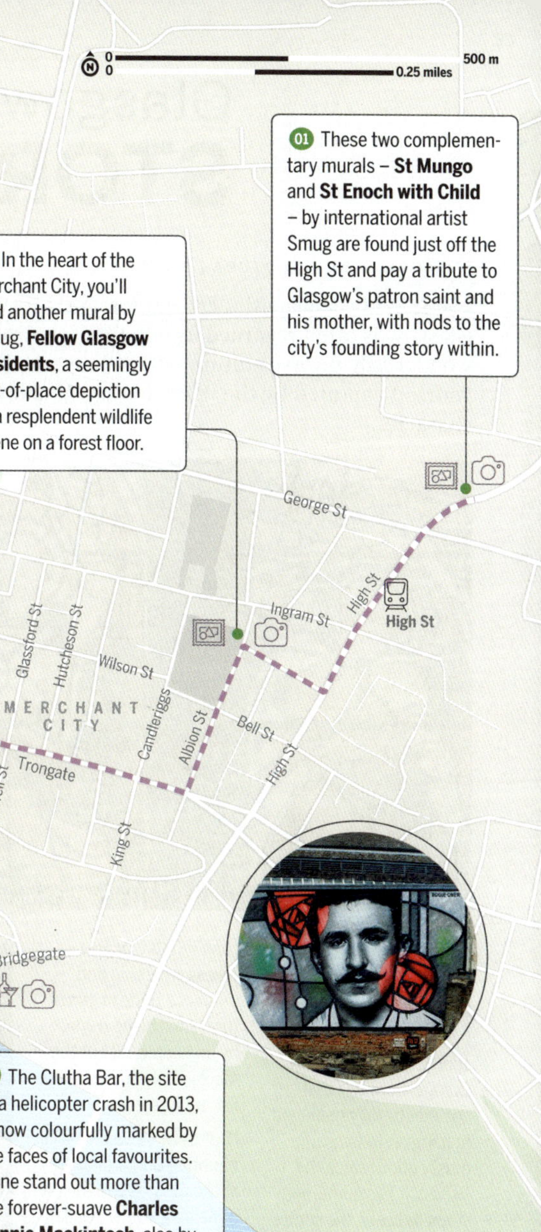

ARTIST ROGUE-ONE (@ROGUEONER), IMAGE BY ROGUE-ONE ©

09 Glasgow's STORY

CULTURE | ARCHITECTURE | MUSEUMS

While some cities cry out for, and often receive, love at first sight, Glasgow is often regarded as one that requires a little more patience. The city's wonderfully diverse cultural attractions are the place to start, where you'll find yourself captured by the many historical chapters that have shaped Glasgow's character.

MEUNIERD/SHUTTERSTOCK ©

How to

Getting around Get between the attractions on foot or via the characterful 'Clockwork Orange' Subway (that has masterfully managed to hang on to the same musty odour since the 1970s). It has numerous stops between the centre and West End.

How much Glasgow takes ownership and immense pride in its cultural sites being owned by its people. All but the Mackintosh House on this list are free to enter.

Highlight Salvador Dalí's haunting *Christ of St John of the Cross* is a highlight at Kelvingrove Art Gallery & Museum.

LOIS GOBE/SHUTTERSTOCK ©

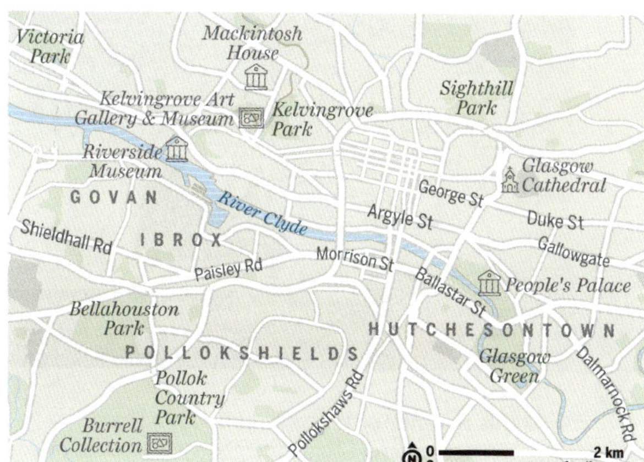

Left Stained glass, Glasgow Cathedral
Below left Art-nouveau brass plate at Glasgow's School of Art

Where it all began Precious little remains of old-world Glasgow, yet 12th-century **Glasgow Cathedral** stands proud as one of the most impressive historic sites in the country. Best viewed from the eerie neighbouring Necropolis graveyard, look down upon what was once the very heart of a fledgling city of trade and gossip.

Glasgow's museums With over five million items, Glasgow Museum's collection is the most visited museum service in the UK outside London. Buckle up for a journey through the ages of transport at **Riverside Museum**. Set within a stunning modern building, vehicles of all shapes and sizes are on display, covering those built for navigating local streets and for taking on the world's high seas. Lose yourself in **Kelvingrove Art Gallery & Museum's** gigantic Victorian palace. Be sure to check ahead for the latest exhibits. Glasgow continually invests in their collections, and following extensive refurbishments in 2022, the **Burrell Collection**, housing an art collection of Sir William Burrell and Constance, Lady Burrell, is open to the public once more – meanwhile, the ever-popular **People's Palace** remains closed for refurbishment.

The iconic Charles Rennie Mackintosh The much-loved art-nouveau style of Glasgow's most famous artist and architect litters the city in timeless tribute. While his masterpiece, the School of Art, was recently and tragically destroyed by fire, there are plentiful alternatives, including the stylishly immaculate **Mackintosh House**, a reconstruction of his own home in the city.

Behind the Scenes

Our museums – the most visited attractions in the city – stimulate imagination, thought and escapism. The city's collection, which belongs to its people, is an important part of who Glaswegians are as individuals, and a key part of their identity. Visitors delight in discovering what made Glasgow the industrial giant of the past and the creative and cultural force it is today.

Our cultural offering enriches the lives of residents and is a powerful draw for new and returning visitors. We put people at the heart of preserving Glasgow's past and I love watching our visitors being surprised and wowed by what they discover.

Recommended by Stewart Thompson, *Manager at Riverside Museum @riversidemuseum*

What Makes Glasgow So?

THE STORY BEHIND THAT BIG PERSONALITY

Once a noisy, sweaty industrial powerhouse, Glasgow endures today as a sprawl of architectural wonder and gallus (bold, cheeky or flashy) tales. A place of hard hands and soft hearts, it's behind that toothless grin, and layer of soot, that you'll see the complex soul of this great city.

Left Glasgow Transport Museum
Middle Cloisters at the University of Glasgow
Right George Square

MEUNIERD/SHUTTERSTOCK ©

Around its epicentre on the banks of the River Clyde, Glasgow's collection of villages merged and conspired to form one of the most productive examples of industry that the world has ever seen. Revered as the Second City of the Empire in its heyday, Glasgow became synonymous with trade from the 17th to the 20th centuries as tobacco, cotton, sugar, ships and slavery combined to put a once-insignificant settlement on every sailor's map. It was capitalism in its most impressive form, and Glasgow was open for business.

Turning opportunistic eyes firstly to tobacco, by the mid-18th-century Glasgow was the main port of entry into Britain, as the city's canny tobacco lords took full advantage of Scotland's new-found membership of the productive British Empire and links with the American colonies in Virginia. By 1770, it had moved on to become the country's largest linen manufacturer, before then turning to shipbuilding. At its peak, Glasgow was producing as much as 50% of the world's ships. The new Victorian railway networks opened up local access to coal and iron, and the sweat-fuelled mechanics of the city grew and grew. Supported further by the likes of furniture and carpet production, brewers, cooperages and electronic manufacturing, heavy industry had made Glasgow a virtual mass factory and economic powerhouse.

Yet behind the multiplying, ostentatious stone mansions and private empires, there was another side to industrial Glasgow. In the smoggy shadows could be found a city's populous too often gripped by poverty, disease and deprivation. Glasgow became too popular for its own good as the city struggled to accommodate the population surge, with workers flocking in from the Highlands, Ireland and

SOLOVIOVA LIUDMYLA/SHUTTERSTOCK ©

PK289/SHUTTERSTOCK ©

further afield. The 19th and 20th centuries saw the development of slums within limited parts of the city, as a lack of sanitation, overcrowding and malnutrition took hold. It's a desperate image that has lingered long in the minds of the people.

It is in these extremes combined that today's visitors can see the enduring identity of Glasgow. The sandstone mansions remain, in almost-majestic leafy neighbourhoods, and its hauntingly evocative, century-spanning architecture stands forever testament to head-spinning wealth generation and mercantile entrepreneurship. The universities – with Glasgow among the first in existence thanks to an early embrace of education – have gifted extraordinary minds to the worlds of engineering, economics, electronics and the arts. But just as important as its successes – and in addition to the grit, earthiness, directness and wicked sense of humour that visitors are sure to encounter – know that its people are still compulsive checkers of their moral compass, valuing fairness above all else. This shows in its politics as a long-standing socialist hub, in its ownership of history (impressive and abhorrent) and its track record in speaking up, often loudly, against injustice.

> Revered as the Second City of the Empire in its heyday, Glasgow became synonymous with trade from the 17th to the 20th centuries...

Glasgow has never been one for standing still. Through centuries it has adapted to progressing politics, new horizons and changing markets. It has pioneered and learned, endured and prospered. And through it all, that cheeky smile remains.

A City Made for Entertainment

Glasgow has shone on the world stage in recent decades, winning numerous prestigious awards for its culture, architecture and design.

It was the hosting of the 2014 Commonwealth Games, though, that really endeared the city to the watching world in a new way. The largest event of its kind ever to come to Scotland, Glasgow had a word with the weather forecaster and gleefully welcomed visitors from across the globe to create a carnival atmosphere across town.

With the annual World Pipe Band Championships, Celtic Connections and hundreds of diverse music events each month, the vibe goes on and on.

10 Footsteps of LEGENDS

HISTORY | CASTLES | VISTAS

While few today would associate Glasgow with castles and medieval mystery, there are numerous ruins and former strongholds with long stories to tell dotted around the surrounds of the city. None can better Dumbarton Castle for depth of history and an evocatively dramatic setting, impossibly lodged within a plug of volcanic basalt.

TREASUREGALORE/SHUTTERSTOCK ©

How to

Getting here Dumbarton is 15 miles northwest of Glasgow and can be reached by car, train or bus from the city centre.

When to visit The castle is open daily (except Sunday and Monday) from April to September and daily (except Thursday and Friday) from October to March.

Imagine... The castle was where a captive and betrayed William Wallace spent some of his final hours on Scottish soil before being sent south to London for execution in 1305.

MARIUSZ GOLEBIEWSKI/SHUTTERSTOCK ©

MARIUSZ GOLEBIEWSKI/SHUTTERSTOCK ©

A famous guest list The Romans, the Vikings, the Luftwaffe, Merlin, William Wallace and Mary Queen of Scots, just to name a few, have all set foot here – and you'll feel the presence of legends in the air as you ascend **Dumbarton Rock**. Tucked within a divide in the rugged stone sits its castle, one of Scotland's most formidable and ominous defensive structures.

An ancient settlement Dating to the 5th century, this was likely to have been the seat of power of the Kingdom of Strathclyde. The site of a ferocious four-month Viking siege in 871, the castle also witnessed much more clandestine activities. Both a discreet hiding place for royalty and a grim prison, the 73m Dumbarton Rock held no shortage of whispers and prayers. Modern-day adventurers can self-guide their way around the castle's multiple buildings and fortifications, navigating the steep and foreboding stairways between them.

Reinvented as a garrison fortress British Government forces installed themselves here in the 18th century as a strategic base to keep local Jacobites under a watchful eye, and the more modernised version we see today started to take shape. Take a cannon's-eye view from one of the gun batteries and imagine frantic preparations for a naval attack, contemplate devious schemes hatched from within the Governor's House to doom the Jacobites, or look up and picture WWII German bombers dropping their payloads from high above.

Far left Dumbarton Castle and Dumbarton Rock
Below left Stairway at Dumbarton Castle
Left The view from Dumbarton Rock

Take in the Views

The summits of Dumbarton Rock offer some of the best vantage points in Central Scotland. Its town is backed by the promise of Loch Lomond and the Highlands to the north, while the mighty River Clyde flows by to the immediate south. Traders, warriors and royalty have come and gone, sailing past Glasgow's Gateway for centuries and, for the imaginative, you can just about create the chilling scene of 200 attacking Viking longboats coming screaming up the river. Ascend, passing the castle's primary buildings, to the White Tower Crag for spectacular panoramas.

Listings

BEST OF THE REST

Surprising Tours

Glasgow Central Tour

Delve underground for the story of Glasgow's great Central Station. A wonderful insight into eerily forgotten Glasgow-by-rail under the care of Paul Lyons and Jackie Ogilvie, some of the best guides in the business.

City Chambers

Take a free tour of the decadent interior of the City Chambers on George Sq and surprise yourself with the staggering opulence on display – it's said to have 'more marble than the Vatican'.

Glasgow Museums Resource Centre

An overspill of the many cultural treasures of Glasgow that are not on current museum display, this is a head-spinning Aladdin's cave of over a million objects. Tours available by contacting Glasgow Life.

Legacies, Icons & Relics

Gallery of Modern Art

Set in the city-centre town house of a former tobacco lord, you'll find Glasgow's dynamic hub of bold, contemporary art.

House for an Art Lover

The immaculate implementation of Charles Rennie Mackintosh's 1901 design is a must-visit for all his fans. Set in Bellahouston Park.

Bothwell Castle

The cragged, deep-red ruins of this 13th-century relic are among the most evocative in Central Scotland. Nestled within a curve in the River Clyde near Uddingston, to the southeast of the city.

Paisley Abbey

A rare Gothic masterpiece, founded in 1163. The stained-glass windows and sentinel cloisters give the magnificent interior a tangible atmosphere. In Glasgow's southwest, by the airport.

Glasgow Women's Library

The only accredited museum in the UK dedicated to the history, stories and achievements of women. As well as lending books, Glasgow Women's Library has exhibitions and extensive collections, and hosts tours and events.

Live Music & Performances

Barrowland Ballroom

An East End institution and historic local favourite that is unapologetically all about the music. Well suited to larger gigs, it has hosted a plethora of household names since the 1930s.

Glad Café

A hipster hub and fantastic all-rounder for an evening in the South Side. Good grub and drinks menu, and an eclectic mix of up-and-coming artists.

City Chambers

Hug & Pint

A relaxed, cosy place where promising young bands are frequently hosted downstairs. The menu has some excellent vegan options.

Celtic Connections

A world-famous, two-week music festival that always lifts the January blues. There's a focus on traditional Scottish, but also how Celtic music has connected with cultures across the world.

Whisky

Pot Still

A mouth-watering collection with over 1000 malts plus a classic Glasgow pub feel – a successful combination since the 1800s.

Ben Nevis

Traditional folk sessions are hosted several times per week at this snug bar in Finnieston.

Clydeside Distillery

Sitting proud on the banks of the Clyde and constructed in 2017, this new-to-Glasgow distillery offers tours – and now tastings – of the first drops of liquid gold to flow from the casks.

Refreshments

Inn Deep

With vaulted roofs and a subterranean, cellar-like feel, this is an excellent, laid-back hang-out alongside the River Kelvin. Superb and extensive beer selection.

Òran Mór

A characterful converted church bar that pulls in the many faces of the West End, from student to pensioner. Also a theatre venue for plays, and a nightclub downstairs.

Brel

A specialist in Belgian beer, it's one of many bars on and around Ashton Lane. Spills out into a beer garden when the opportunity arises.

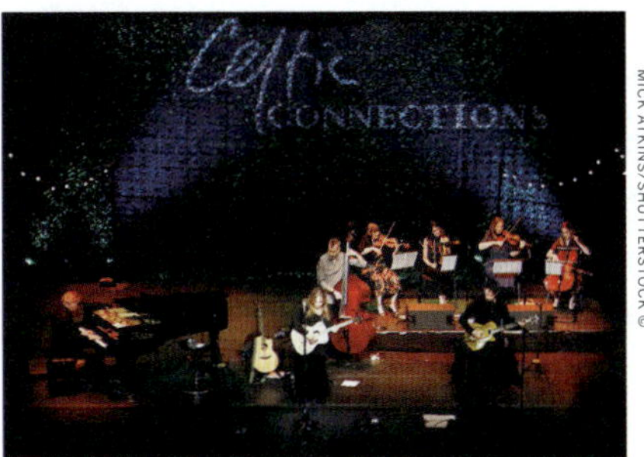

MICK ATKINS/SHUTTERSTOCK ©

Gretchen Peters performing during Celtic Connections

Mackintosh at the Willow

Break up your shopping marathon with a supremely sophisticated afternoon tea at another classy Mackintosh recreation. Book ahead.

Scottish Grub

Cail Bruich £££

One of Scotland's finest restaurants features local, sustainable food, often with some backup from France. The head chef recently collected a Michelin star.

Gannet ££

Fine dining without pretension in Finnieston; the season-led menu delves into the best of Scotland's natural larder with impressive results.

Café Gandolfi £££

At this institution of the Merchant City, the founding gentle influence of the Hebridean islands still lingers despite the bustle. Seafood fans take special note.

Stravaigin ££

For more casual dining with loads of atmosphere, this popular option on Gibson St is another West End hub to delight drinkers and diners alike.

SOUTHERN SCOTLAND

EVOCATIVE | SERENE | HISTORIC

- **Trip Builder** (p78)
- **Practicalities** (p79)
- **Immersion in the Lowlands** (p80)
- **Majestic, Stately Homes** (p82)
- **Land of Sieges & Raids** (p84)
- **Ride to the Sea** (p86)
- **Listings** (p88)

SOUTHERN SCOTLAND
Trip Builder

Seemingly far from the summer crowds, the southern regions of Ayrshire, South Lanarkshire, Dumfries, Galloway and the Scottish Borders hold endless, nature-dominated corners built for quiet reflection and historical exploration. Spectacular ruins meet decadent stately homes, and stretching lowland landscapes call for hiking, cycling and wildlife spotting.

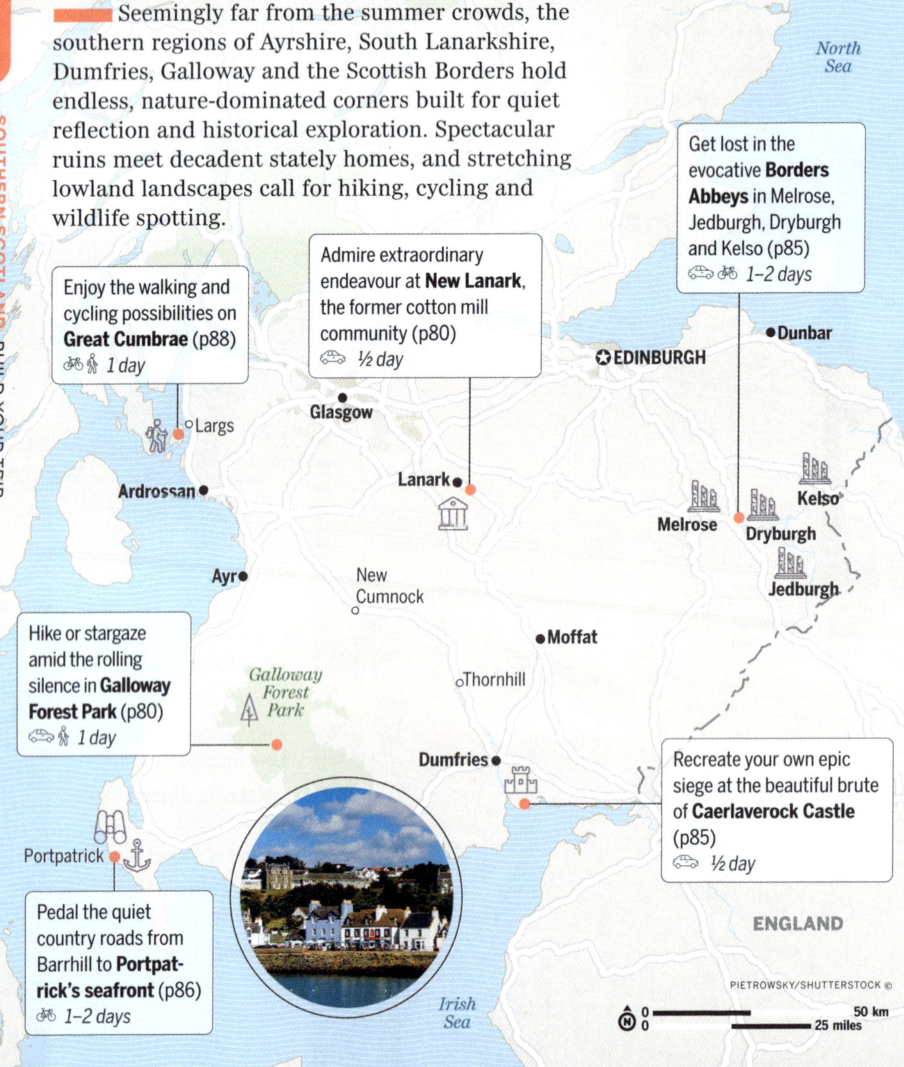

North Sea
Get lost in the evocative **Borders Abbeys** in Melrose, Jedburgh, Dryburgh and Kelso (p85)
1–2 days
Admire extraordinary endeavour at **New Lanark**, the former cotton mill community (p80)
½ day
Enjoy the walking and cycling possibilities on **Great Cumbrae** (p88)
1 day
Dunbar
EDINBURGH
Glasgow
Largs
Lanark
Ardrossan
Kelso
Melrose
Dryburgh
Jedburgh
Ayr
New Cumnock
Moffat
Hike or stargaze amid the rolling silence in **Galloway Forest Park** (p80)
1 day
Galloway Forest Park
Thornhill
Dumfries
Recreate your own epic siege at the beautiful brute of **Caerlaverock Castle** (p85)
½ day
Portpatrick
Pedal the quiet country roads from Barrhill to **Portpatrick's seafront** (p86)
1–2 days
ENGLAND
Irish Sea
0
50 km
0
25 miles

PIETROWSKY/SHUTTERSTOCK ©

Practicalities

ARRIVING

Train Hub towns can be accessed by direct trains from Glasgow or Edinburgh.

Bus Other sizeable towns are interconnected to each other and the cities by daily bus routes.

CONNECT

Phone signal can be sporadic in the more rural locations, but wi-fi is generally available at accommodation providers.

MONEY

Quality B&B stays cost upwards of £80 per night. ATMs are available in all sizeable towns, but it's still wise to carry some cash.

WHERE TO STAY

Place	Pro/Con
Melrose	Arguably the most picturesque of the Border towns, with good road access and facilities.
Kirkcudbright	Quaint and timelessly appealing, with proximity to the south coast.
Dumfries	The most accessible and practical base for exploration in the southwest.

GETTING AROUND

Car The easiest mode for a thorough exploration of the south. For public transport, visit scotland startshere.com.

Long-distance walking and cycling Increasingly popular, with terrain and landscapes that are well suited to them. The Southern Upland Way (a little over 200 miles) and the 65-mile trail between the Borders Abbeys are options.

TOP: SNAPTPHOTOGRAPHY/SHUTTERSTOCK ©
BOTTOM: BARMALINI/SHUTTERSTOCK ©

EATING & DRINKING

Local produce and pub grub Produce from surrounding farmlands dominates at all ends of the cost spectrum, with lamb, beef and game featuring heavily. Good-quality 'pub grub' can be found in almost all towns.

Milk and cookies Galloway is particularly famous for its dairy products, while Border Biscuits, based in South Lanarkshire, are among the nation's favourite companion for a cup of tea.

Must-try icecream
Cream o' Galloway

Best whisky
Annandale Distillery (p89)

DEC–MAR
Cold and rainy weather in the tourism quiet season.

APR–JUN
Refreshing and mild spring air with plenty of sunshine.

JUL & AUG
Stretching days, warmer temperatures and some rainfall.

SEP–NOV
Crisp days with beautiful colours blanketing the lowland valleys.

Immersion in the LOWLANDS

HIKING | NATURE | WILDLIFE

Serenity rules in the south and nature is permitted centre stage. From crashing waterfalls to secretive wildlife spotting, spend a few days immersed in the highlights.

How to

Getting around Road travel by car is lengthy but straightforward and beautifully scenic across the southern regions.

When to visit Southern Scotland is a blissful escape during the bustling height of the summer tourism season, while the warming colours of autumn also hold a strong pull.

More choice The plethora of activities, accommodation, restaurants and organised events across the south of Scotland are helpfully explored in more depth on the Scotland Starts Here app and website.

From the Stars to the Earth

Take an evening stargazing tour with ranger Elizabeth Tindall in Galloway Forest Park, the first designated Dark Sky Park in the UK; or learn forest bushcraft skills, including foraging, while reducing stress at Garlieston with Christy Miles from Way of the Wild.

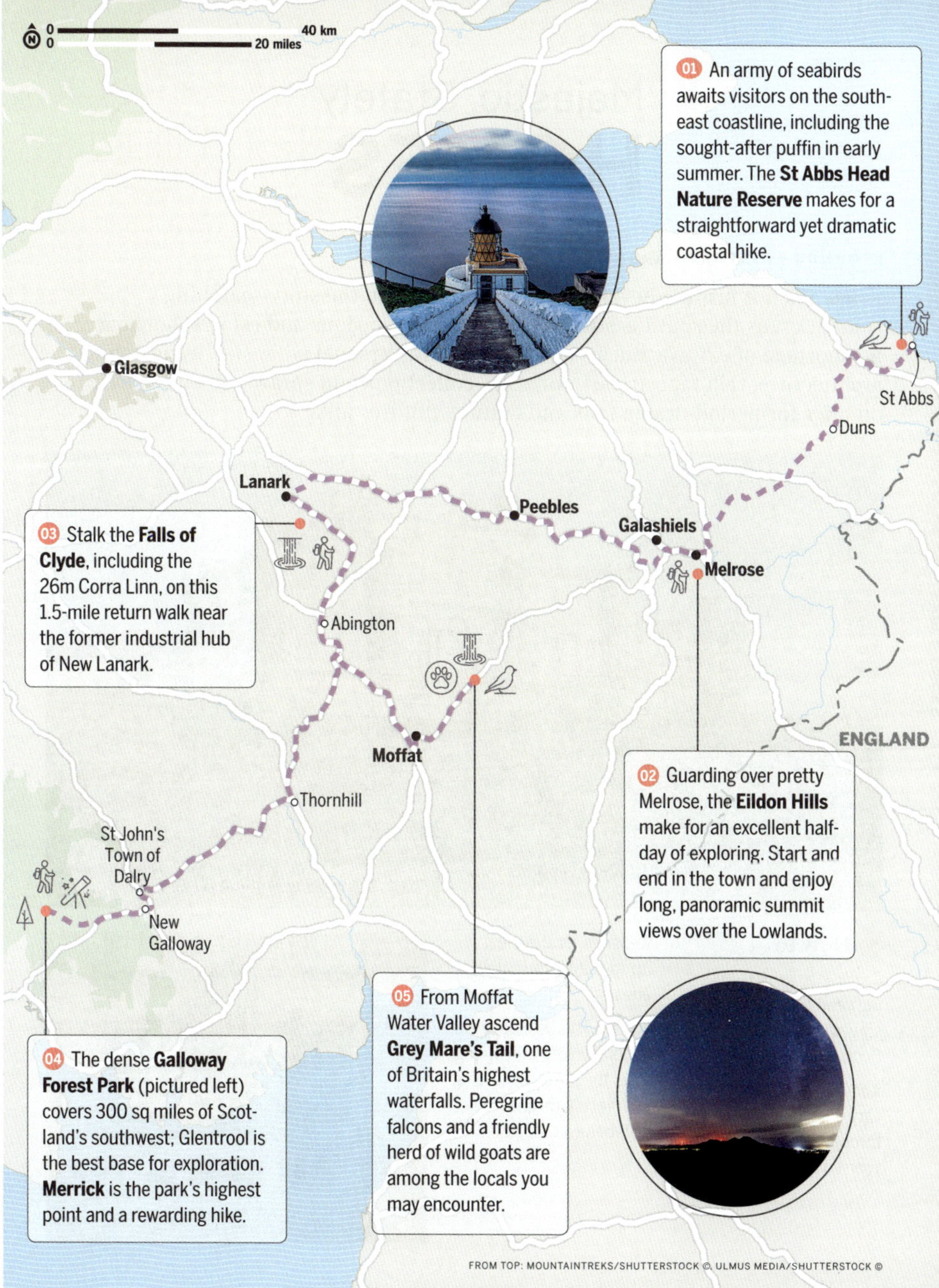

0
0
40 km
20 miles
N
Glasgow
Lanark
Peebles
Galashiels
Melrose
Duns
St Abbs
Abington
Moffat
Thornhill
St John's Town of Dalry
New Galloway
ENGLAND
01 An army of seabirds awaits visitors on the south-east coastline, including the sought-after puffin in early summer. The **St Abbs Head Nature Reserve** makes for a straightforward yet dramatic coastal hike.
02 Guarding over pretty Melrose, the **Eildon Hills** make for an excellent half-day of exploring. Start and end in the town and enjoy long, panoramic summit views over the Lowlands.
03 Stalk the **Falls of Clyde**, including the 26m Corra Linn, on this 1.5-mile return walk near the former industrial hub of New Lanark.
04 The dense **Galloway Forest Park** (pictured left) covers 300 sq miles of Scotland's southwest; Glentrool is the best base for exploration. **Merrick** is the park's highest point and a rewarding hike.
05 From Moffat Water Valley ascend **Grey Mare's Tail**, one of Britain's highest waterfalls. Peregrine falcons and a friendly herd of wild goats are among the locals you may encounter.

FROM TOP: MOUNTAINTREKS/SHUTTERSTOCK ©, ULMUS MEDIA/SHUTTERSTOCK ©

12

Majestic, Stately HOMES

LEGENDS | HISTORY | ARCHITECTURE

It's not just medieval history that appeals to the story-searching romantics, as the south is studded with grand mansions and estates, housing no shortage of extravagancies and melancholy. Personal whimsies, eye-catching architecture, rich tapestries, impressive collections and sprawling gardens are on offer for period-drama fans and culture vultures alike.

ECOS/SHUTTERSTOCK ©

How to

Getting around Getting between the estates, spread across Southern Scotland, is easiest by car.

Access Opening times vary considerably through the calendar year, so consult the websites for the most up-to-date information ahead of visiting.

Top tip The estates are generally very welcoming to all the family, including energetic kids and well-behaved dogs.

CLAUDINE VAN MASSENHOVE/SHUTTERSTOCK ©

Grand family homes The legendary 19th-century writer and inventor of the historic novel, Sir Walter Scott, built the grand stately home of **Abbotsford**, which sits at the centre of various Scott-themed attractions in the region, including Dryburgh Abbey where he is buried. The house, on the banks of the River Tweed, is packed with Scott's personal collections. Romantically steeped in Jacobite melancholy, serene **Traquair** is the oldest continually occupied house in Scotland. The wonderfully musty interior holds a playground for the imagination as secret staircases hide behind delicate, centuries-old furniture. There's an on-site chapel, garden maze and brewery selling their highly acclaimed Jacobite Ale.

Architectural excellence and extraordinary wealth Sitting precariously on the Ayrshire coast amid a vast and luscious country park is **Culzean Castle**. Visionary 18th-century architect Robert Adam had fun with this one, as the palatial exterior is surpassed by a stunning interior oval staircase. Robert Adam learned much from his father, William, and it was the latter who was most responsible for the now-extravagant **Floors Castle**, just outside Kelso. Tours at the long-standing home to the Duke of Roxburghe reveal richly decorated interiors, with a walled garden and various woodland walks on the grounds. Similarly grandiose, **Drumlanrig Castle** in Dumfriesshire is an alluring glowing sandstone structure, with summer tours available. The grounds feature salmon fishing and mountain-biking opportunities and were one of many Scottish filming locations used in the successful TV show *Outlander*.

Left Culzean Castle
Below left Drumlanrig Castle

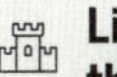

Life Behind the Walls

I feel incredibly privileged to be the 21st generation of the same family living in Traquair – it really is a family home and this is what makes it so special. People often comment on the atmosphere here and I think this comes from having been a continually lived-in house for over 900 years. You can literally feel and touch its history.

The surrounding Borders is a region of Scotland with so much more to discover. Incredible and varied landscapes from a wild coastline to rolling hills and lochs; timeless small towns; extraordinary history and heritage. And a warm welcome wherever you go.

Local insight from Catherine Maxwell Stuart, *21st Lady of Traquair*

13 Land of Sieges & RAIDS

RUINS | CASTLES | HISTORY

Haunted by historic turbulence thanks to long, bloody conflicts between Scotland and England, the Southern Scotland of today has taken on a contrastingly calm air. Breathe it in and let your imagination run loose chasing medieval ghosts as you explore some of the country's most dramatic and evocative ruins.

JAMES MCDOWALL/SHUTTERSTOCK ©

How to

Getting around Southern Scotland is a vast area, and getting to and between these attractions is most easily achieved by car, although there are fantastic opportunities for long-distance cyclists.

When to go April to September; most attractions close down over the winter months.

How much All but unstaffed Dunure Castle on this list are owned by Historic Scotland. Tickets range in price but if planning on visiting several of its properties, it's worth purchasing the Explorer Pass.

ESPEDAIR CREATIVE/SHUTTERSTOCK ©

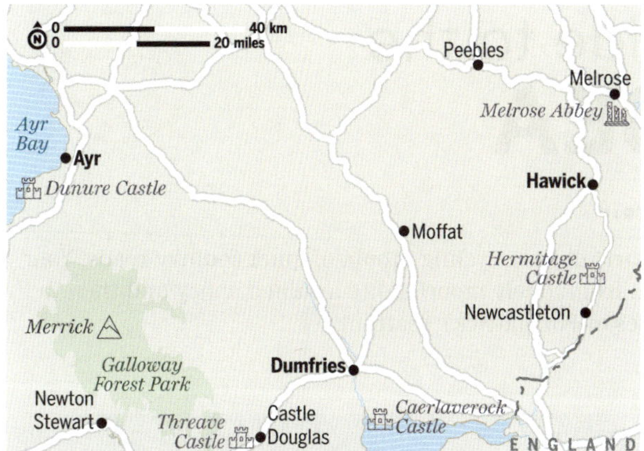

Prepare for attack That a site as idyllically beautiful as **Caerlaverock Castle** should have fallen victim to numerous brutal sieges seems inappropriately far-fetched as you approach the unusually triangular ruin on the Solway coast. Artists and photographers will love its visual romance and rare moat, while kids can play out swashbuckling fantasies in the stone interior. Despite its hard life within 'debatable lands', **Gilnockie Tower**, ancestral home of the Armstrong Clan (of 'man on the moon' fame), hosts regular events and tours.

A clandestine rendezvous Visit the exposed cliff-top ruins of **Dunure Castle** on the Ayrshire coast and the isolated **Hermitage Castle** on the Scotland–England border and eavesdrop on the past. Dunure was the meeting point, in 1429, of the long-adversarial clans of Campbell and MacDonald. Only the Campbells emerged alive. Follow in the footsteps of Mary Queen of Scots, through remote valleys to Hermitage Castle, who met her wounded soon-to-be husband in 1566 to plot their doomed future together.

Take a tranquil moment It's not all fury, scheming and backstabbing. **Threave Castle**, set in a wildlife haven near Castle Douglas, involves a short walk to capture that iconic photo (the castle itself is currently closed). The Gothic remains of **Melrose Abbey** are among the most serenely romantic in Scotland, set under the rolling Eildon Hills, this is the final resting place of Robert the Bruce's heart.

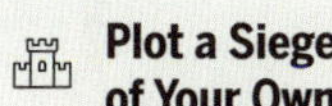
Left Dunure Castle
Below left Melrose Abbey

Plot a Siege of Your Own

Southern Scotland offers so much dramatic history coupled with unspoilt beauty, in an area known for its rich variety of cultures and heritage. Caerlaverock Castle is one of many perfectly unique ruins not to miss. Like so many strongholds in the area, it required sturdy defences from the many English raids during the Scottish Wars of Independence. It's as a result of those nervous times that the incredible atmosphere and unique splendour are still clearly tangible as you wander the staircases and rooms of one of Scotland's most beautiful castles.

Recommended By Mark Turner, *tour guide at Solway Tours*

Ride to the SEA

CYCLING | SEASIDE | DAY TRIP

Hop on a train to Barrhill for a cycling utopia of quiet country roads. Your pedal strokes will take you from lonely moorland to a ruined abbey and then to the pastel-coloured cottages of Portpatrick's seafront.

JENNYT/SHUTTERSTOCK ©

Trip Notes

Getting here Trains from Ayr to Barrhill take 50 minutes; bicycles are carried free, with no reservation required.

When to go Avoid winter as there are few options for shelter.

Cycling details Recommended for experienced cyclists. The 36-mile route is mainly flat on good-quality roads. The Old Military Rd to Portpatrick avoids the busier A-roads. To rejoin the train, head to Stranraer station, 7 miles from Portpatrick.

Bike-friendly Southern Scotland

The region is the spiritual home of Scottish cycling and was designated a UCI Bike Region in 2023. Kirkpatrick Macmillan invented the 'Velocipeded' a forerunner to the modern bicycle. Visit **Stranraer** where a sculpture of the world's first pedal bike marks the start of the Kirkpatrick C2C cycle route and check out the region's cycle trails at www.scotlandstartshere.com, or hop across to **Cumbrae**, the Island of 1000 bikes.

01 Get transported to a different era at **Barrhill**. This countryside station and signal box is surrounded by wide open spaces and you will probably be the only person getting off.

02 After 12 miles of moorland, **New Luce** offers a tranquil riverside location, a village shop in a white cottage and woodland walks where you might spot red squirrels.

04 Lose yourself in the 75 acres of **Castle Kennedy Gardens**. Discover two lochs, a monkey puzzle tree avenue and rhododendrons galore. The tea room serves local ice cream and picnic hampers.

05 After the final 10 miles celebrate your ride with fresh seafood at the Crown Hotel in **Portpatrick** (pictured left). Its outdoor terrace is perfect for soaking up the harbour views.

03 Four miles south are the ruins of **Glenluce Abbey**. Founded around 1190, the abbey was once home to 15 white-robed monks who wandered the cloisters in silent contemplation.

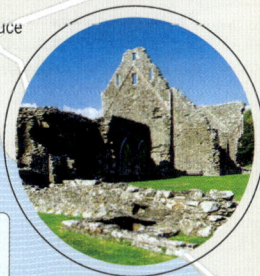

FROM TOP: CAROLE MACDONALD/SHUTTERSTOCK ©, PIETROWSKY/SHUTTERSTOCK ©

Listings

BEST OF THE REST

Relics of the Borderlands

Thirlestane Castle
Bed down for the night in the historic 16th-century home of the Duke of Lauderdale, or book a tour, go riding or shooting or sit down to afternoon tea.

William Wallace Statue
One of several statues of the 13th-century freedom fighter, William Wallace. He spent much of his hard life hiding in the southern forest, and he now enjoys a fine view a short drive from Melrose.

Dundrennan Abbey
To the east of Kirkcudbright you'll find another of Scotland's most reflective hideaways. The 12th-century Cistercian abbey was where Mary Queen of Scots spent her last night in Scotland, and her melancholy lingers.

Mellerstain House
A Robert Adam architectural masterpiece, the house and gardens make for a grand day out on a sunny day. Look up: the ceilings are particularly impressive. Located south of Gordon.

Outdoor Adventures

Go Ape
A treetop adventure course set deep within Glentress Forest, near Peebles. Fantastic for adventure seekers, groups and cyclists; the thrilling 325m zipline is the highlight.

Logan Botanic Gardens
One of Scotland's most exotic corners in the (relatively) mild far southwest near Stranraer. Palms and eucalyptus will have you imagining yourself in warmer climes.

Mull of Galloway
Head to Scotland's most southerly point for superb views over the Irish Sea and birdwatching opportunities. The lighthouse is perched atop a 79m cliff and is worth the 115-step ascent.

Great Cumbrae
A 4-mile-long island off the Ayrshire coast, this is a popular day trip for west-coast walkers and cyclists. Access is by frequent, 10-minute ferry from Largs; hire bikes in the town of Millport.

Coldingham Bay
One of the east coast's nicest beaches, the sandy bay is suited to surfing (the hotel has a surf shop). There's a lovely 3-mile coastal trail to the beach at Eyemouth, too.

Ailsa Craig
There's a blue hue to the eye-catching island and gannet colony off the Ayrshire coast that has the distinction of producing world-class curling stones. Sea tours depart from Girvan.

Farm Experiences
Take a Highland Cow Safari at Kitchen Coos and Ewes or join an Alpaca Walk in Kelso, Peebles or the Cheviot Hills. Jacksons at Jedburgh offers fun for all the family on a working farm.

William Wallace Statue

Local Heroes & Tributes

Jim Clark Motorsport Museum

A touching tribute to the racing legend and multiple Formula 1 champion. The museum in Duns features an extensive trophy cabinet, car displays and a driving simulator for kids.

Museum of Lead Mining

A surprisingly family-friendly and fascinating look at the harsh reality of mining in the 18th century, including an eerie tour of an actual mine. Find it in Wanlockhead near Sanquhar.

Devil's Porridge Museum

Just short of the Scotland–England border, this curiously named spot, fuelled by very passionate locals, provides a touching commemoration to the largest munitions factory in the world during WWI.

Festivals & Legacies

Book Festivals

That Scotland's two most celebrated scribblers hailed from the south is surely no coincidence, and modern-day readers and writers flock to the excellent annual festivals in Melrose and Wigtown. Visit festival websites for event dates.

Common Ridings

Summer in the Scottish Borders sees several horse-led festivals celebrating the equestrian tradition of sending riders to town boundaries to check for thieving raiders. Head to Jedburgh and Hawick for the biggest ones and join the townsfolk in cheering on the costumed cavalcades.

Scotland's Bard

Robbie Burns was born in Alloway, the epicentre of Burns-mania. Visit the Birthplace Museum and Burns Cottage via spooky Alloway Auld Kirk. Follow his footsteps to Dumfries where he is buried.

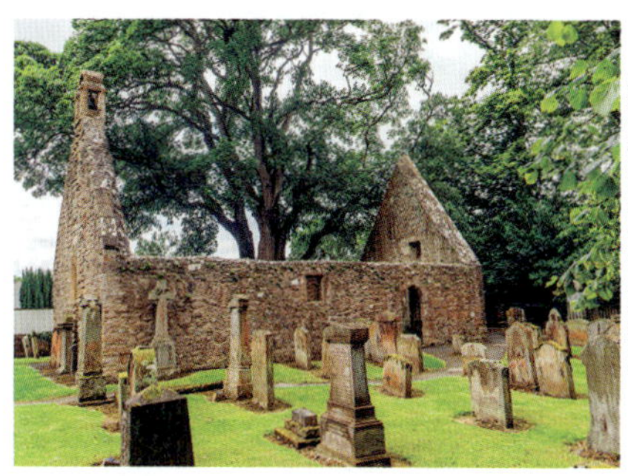

Alloway Auld Kirk

Local Food & Drink

Hoebridge £££

Top-drawer seasonal dining with great attention to detail. Located in Gattonside, just across the river from the excellent Borders hub of Melrose. Book far (very far) in advance.

Limetree Restaurant ££

Locally sourced meat, game and fish dominate a minimal menu that wins for quality and value in a cosy setting within the Hartfell Guest House in Moffat.

Auld Alliance ££

In the quaint, coastal setting of Kirkcudbright, local produce is given a supporting hand here from France. Friendly service, big flavours.

Annandale Distillery ££

Annandale Distillery produces very interesting single malts. Book tours in advance. The distillery also owns the Globe Inn, serving food and drink – Robbie Burns' favourite pub.

Gather Laggan ££

New to the foodie scene – enjoy good food and views that nourish the soul in their glass-fronted bistro.

STIRLING, FIFE & PERTHSHIRE

OUTDOORS | FOOD | HISTORY

- **Trip Builder** (p92)
- **Practicalities** (p94)
- **Seafood & Sea Views** (p96)
- **The Road to Rannoch** (p98)
- **The River Tay** (p100)
- **Kings, Queens & Castles** (p102)
- **A Castle Glossary** (p106)
- **Listings** (p108)

CATUNCIA/SHUTTERSTOCK ©

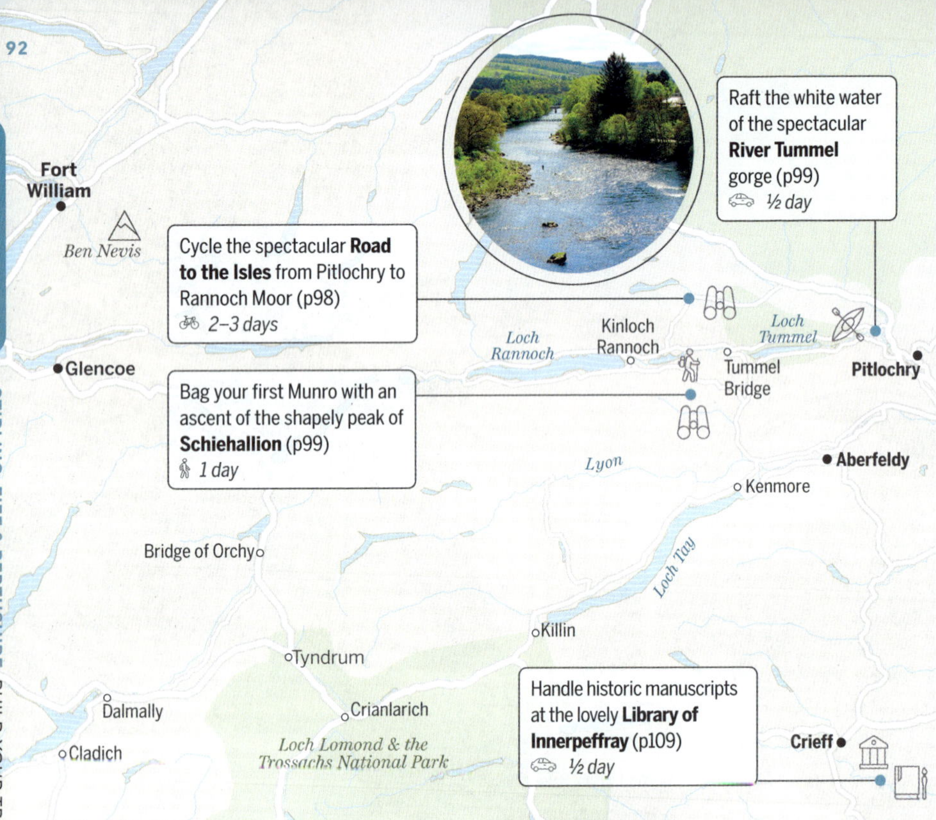

STIRLING, FIFE & PERTHSHIRE

Trip Builder

Straddling the Highlands and the Lowlands, Perthshire is the true heart of Scotland. Along with its close neighbours Stirling and Fife, it was once the playground of Scottish monarchs. Today it's a focus for serious foodies and outdoor enthusiasts.

Raft the white water of the spectacular **River Tummel** gorge (p99)
½ day

Cycle the spectacular **Road to the Isles** from Pitlochry to Rannoch Moor (p98)
2–3 days

Bag your first Munro with an ascent of the shapely peak of **Schiehallion** (p99)
1 day

Handle historic manuscripts at the lovely **Library of Innerpeffray** (p109)
½ day

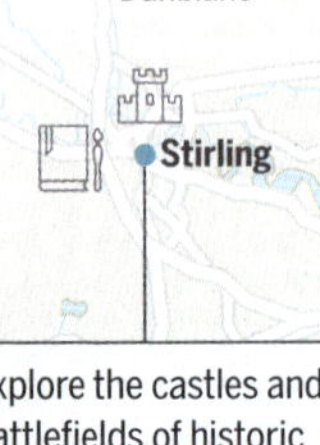

Explore the castles and battlefields of historic **Stirling** (p104)
1 day

Fort William
Ben Nevis
Glencoe
Loch Rannoch
Kinloch Rannoch
Loch Tummel
Tummel Bridge
Pitlochry
Lyon
Aberfeldy
Kenmore
Bridge of Orchy
Loch Tay
Killin
Tyndrum
Dalmally
Crianlarich
Cladich
Loch Lomond & the Trossachs National Park
Crieff
Auchterarder
Dunblane
Stirling

0 25 km
0 15 miles
Cairngorms National Park
Seek out the elusive Tayside beavers at **Bamff Ecotourism** (p109) ½ day
Enjoy a picnic on the banks of the River Tay at lovely **Dunkeld** (p100) ½ day
Inverbervie
Brechin
Montrose
Kirriemuir
Forfar
North Sea
Alyth
Blairgowrie
Dunkeld
Isla
Coupar Angus
Arbroath
Dundee
Methven
Scone
Perth
Firth of Tay
Indulge in a feast of local produce in the restaurants and farm shops of **St Andrews** (p97) 1 day
Delve into Scottish history at **Moot Hill** and visit the Stone of Destiny at **Perth Museum**. (p103) ½ day
Newburgh
St Andrews
Cupar
Crail
Anstruther
Kinross
Yetts o'Muckhart
Loch Leven
Kirkcaldy
Hike between seafood stops on the scenic **Fife Coastal Path** (p96) 2 days
Dunfermline
Culross
Aberdour
Firth of Forth
EDINBURGH

Practicalities

CHRISTIAN MUELLER/SHUTTERSTOCK ©

ARRIVING

Stirling and Perth are easily reached from Edinburgh by bus or train (one hour). Stirling train and bus stations are in the centre, within walking distance of the castle and other sights. Perth train and bus stations are on the south side of the centre, about 3 miles from Scone Palace (a one-hour walk); various local buses run past Scone Palace – ask for details at the bus station. An hourly bus service from Edinburgh to St Andrews (two hours) passes through the East Neuk fishing villages.

HOW MUCH FOR A

Takeaway fish and chips £10.50

Lobster dinner from £28

Pint of local IPA £4.25

WHEN TO GO

JAN–MAR

Colder and wetter, but quieter. Salmon fishing starts.

APR–JUN

Woods are carpeted with bluebells. Perth Festival of the Arts in May.

JUL–SEP

Busy period of school holidays. Best weather for hill walking.

OCT–DEC

Autumn colours in Perthshire. Good conditions for canoeing.

GETTING AROUND

Driving Driving is the best way to visit out-of-the-way places if your time is limited. There are restrictions on parking in certain popular areas. For info: pkc.gov.uk/ruralclearways

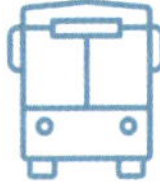

Buses Buses link most towns and villages in the region. The main operators are Stagecoach East Scotland, First Scotland East, Elizabeth Yule Coaches and Moffat & Williamson. Stagecoach's East Scotland Dayrider ticket (£8.50) gives unlimited bus travel for one day in Perthshire and Fife.

Bike A good network of cycle routes, including minor roads, cycle lanes and tracks; check out sustrans.org.uk for more detailed routes. Perthshire Gravel offers a wide range of off-road adventure trails.

EATING & DRINKING

Seafood The East Neuk of Fife – from Elie around the coast through Anstruther and Crail to St Andrews – is famous for its concentration of seafood restaurants, from humble fish-and-chip shops to Michelin-starred restaurants – don't miss the local lobster.

Regional produce Inland is some of the richest farmland in the country, and fresh regional produce – including beef, lamb, asparagus, carrots, potatoes and soft fruits – are best sampled at farmers markets, farm shop cafes and country pubs.

Must-try lobster
Shellfish Shack (p108)

Best fish and chips
Crail Fish Bar & Café (p108)

CONNECT

Wi-fi Easy to find in towns like Perth, Stirling and St Andrews. However, in more rural areas, especially in Highland Perthshire (eg around Loch Tummel and Loch Rannoch), public wi-fi in cafes, hotels and B&Bs can be very slow. Outside towns and away from trunk roads, 4G coverage can also be patchy; 5G in main towns and cities.

WHERE TO STAY

Popular with tourists, with a good range of accommodation from hostels and B&Bs to luxury country house hotels. Best to book ahead in summer. Consider travelling in quieter spring and autumn.

Town/Village	Pro/Con
Stirling	The region's biggest city has a choice of good-value hotels and B&Bs within walking distance of the castle.
St Andrews	A university town and the home of golf, loaded with upmarket guesthouses and luxury hotels.
Pitlochry	Lively and picturesque, with backpacker hostels, traditional guest houses and hotels.
Aberfeldy	Attractive Highland town, with a campsite, good B&Bs and self-catering cottages.
Perth	Centrally located Perth is a UNESCO City of Craft with an excellent museum.

HISTORIC SITES

If you plan on visiting a number of properties owned by Historic Scotland, especially as a family, consider buying an annual membership to save money (family membership £101).

MONEY

There are charges (£2 to £3) for using car parks at tourist hot spots (including Queen's View on Loch Tummel and Braes of Foss at Schiehallion), so keep a supply of £1 coins handy for the ticket machines.

15 Seafood & SEA VIEWS

FOOD | HIKING | VILLAGES

Stretch your legs on the East Neuk segment of the Fife Coastal Path, which strings together a chain of photogenic fishing villages, packed with places to enjoy the harvest of the sea, from simple fish-and-chip shops to Michelin-starred restaurants.

Trip Notes

Getting around You can hike along the Fife Coastal Path from Elie to St Andrews (total distance 25 miles) over two or three days, or link the stops by road, using bike, bus or car, along the signposted Fife Coastal Tourist Route.

When to go Best hiking weather is May to September.

Need to know Check with St Andrews tourist office about the condition of the footpath and tides; sections are sometimes closed due to erosion or high tides.

Fife Foodie Hot Spots

Salt & Pine, Tentsmuir Forest Perfect spot for a walk and a bite to eat.

Jannetta's Gelateria, St Andrews Favourite place to take the family for an ice cream.

Balgove Larder, St Andrews Love the farm shop, and you can get lunch at the same time.

Cupar Market Great local produce, especially the Arbroath smokies!

Recommended by Dean Banks, *chef-proprietor of Haar restaurant, St Andrews @haarrestaurant*

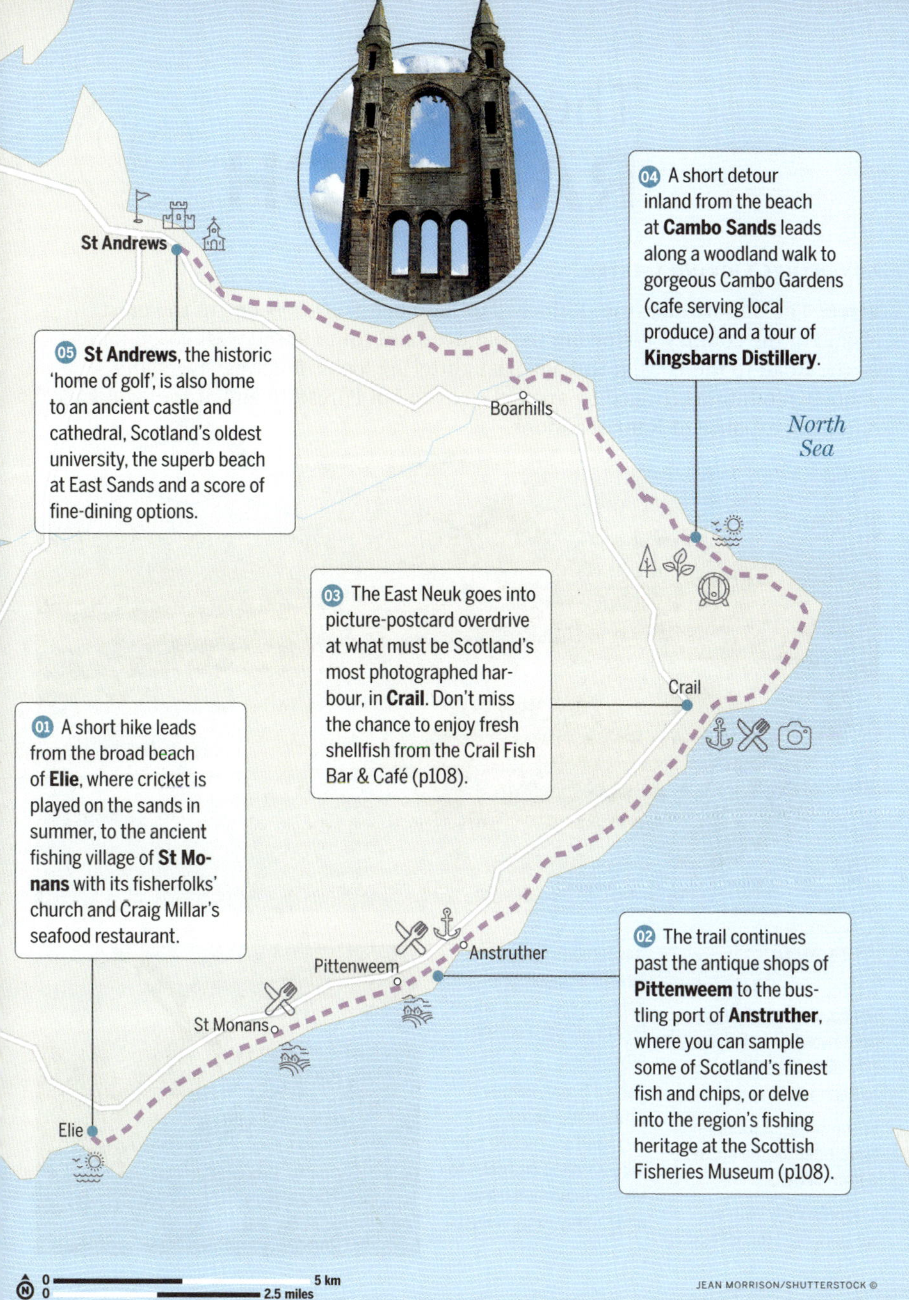

05 **St Andrews**, the historic 'home of golf', is also home to an ancient castle and cathedral, Scotland's oldest university, the superb beach at East Sands and a score of fine-dining options.

04 A short detour inland from the beach at **Cambo Sands** leads along a woodland walk to gorgeous Cambo Gardens (cafe serving local produce) and a tour of **Kingsbarns Distillery**.

03 The East Neuk goes into picture-postcard overdrive at what must be Scotland's most photographed harbour, in **Crail**. Don't miss the chance to enjoy fresh shellfish from the Crail Fish Bar & Café (p108).

01 A short hike leads from the broad beach of **Elie**, where cricket is played on the sands in summer, to the ancient fishing village of **St Monans** with its fisherfolks' church and Craig Millar's seafood restaurant.

02 The trail continues past the antique shops of **Pittenweem** to the bustling port of **Anstruther**, where you can sample some of Scotland's finest fish and chips, or delve into the region's fishing heritage at the Scottish Fisheries Museum (p108).

16 The Road to RANNOCH

ADVENTURE | HIKING | WATER

The minor road from Pitlochry to Rannoch Station is one of the most scenic in the country. Following the old overland route to the west coast, known as the Road to the Isles, it threads past glittering lochs, foaming rivers and shapely mountains fringed by ancient Caledonian Forest, to end at the wild and daunting expanse of Rannoch Moor.

ROBERT HARDING VIDEO/SHUTTERSTOCK ©

How to

Getting around A pleasant day trip by car, or a superb two-day cycling tour (35 miles from Pitlochry to Rannoch Station).

When to go October and November for the finest autumn colours.

Queen's View With a car park (£2) for access, this famous viewpoint boasts a classic photo of Schiehallion rising above Loch Tummel. Facilities now closed.

Take a break Rannoch Station Tearoom, Scotland's remotest cafe, serves coffee and cake to hikers, mountain bikers and railway excursionists.

BINSON CALFORT/SHUTTERSTOCK ©

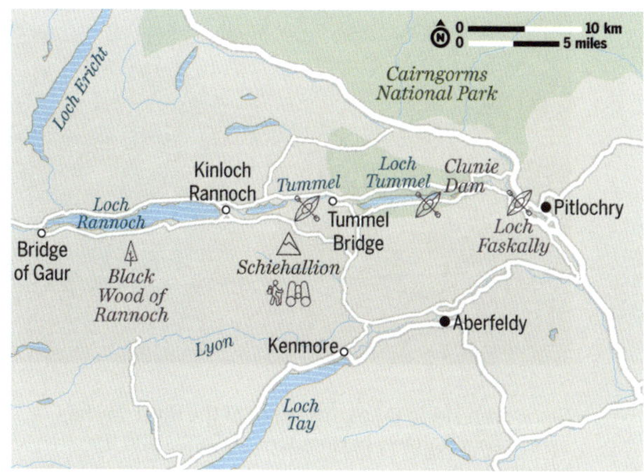

Left Black Mount and Rannoch Moor
Below left Red deer

Hike a hill Gaelic for the 'Fairy Hill of the Caledonians', **Schiehallion** is one of Scotland's most-prominent peaks, seen as a perfect pyramid when viewed from the northern shore of Loch Rannoch. It is also one of the easiest Munros (hills of 3000ft/914m in height or over) to climb. A well-made footpath leads from Braes of Foss car park (on the road from Tummel Bridge to Aberfeldy) to the broad, rocky summit ridge, where you'll be rewarded with panoramic views across Rannoch Moor to the peaks of Glen Coe (6.5 miles total; allow four to six hours).

Wander in woods On the southern shore of Loch Rannoch, between Camghouran and Dall, lies the **Black Wood of Rannoch**, a remnant of the ancient Caledonian pine forest. Here in this enclave of native woodland you can lose yourself amid a tangle of twisted moss-draped boughs and gnarled russet bark, a haven for deer, red squirrel, pine marten and rare birds such as Scottish crossbill and capercaillie.

Raft a river The **Clunie Dam** at the east end of Loch Tummel was built in 1950 as part of a hydroelectric power scheme. Regular releases of water from June to September mean that the 2 miles of the **River Tummel** from the dam down to **Loch Faskally** provide some of the most exciting and reliable white-water rafting in Scotland. The river cascades through a rocky, wooded gorge, over Grade II and III rapids to the grand finale – a 6m white-knuckle drop down the Grade IV Linn of Tummel waterfall (p109).

Rannoch Moor

The motor road ends at Rannoch Station, a lonely outpost where civilisation fades away and Rannoch Moor begins. This is the largest area of moorland in Britain, stretching west for 8 barren, bleak and uninhabited miles. Despite the appearance of desolation, the moor is rich in wildlife, with curlew, golden plover and snipe darting among the tussocks, black-throated diver, goosander and merganser on the lochs, and – if you're lucky – osprey and golden eagle overhead. You can take the train to Corrour Station and hike the 11 miles back to Rannoch (allow five hours).

The River Tay

RICHARDJOHNSON/SHUTTERSTOCK ©

SCOTLAND'S MIGHTIEST RIVER

Rising on the slopes of Ben Lui near the Highland village of Tyndrum, barely 20 miles from Scotland's west coast, and flowing for 117 miles to meet the tide at Perth, the Tay is Scotland's longest and mightiest river – more water flows from its mouth than from the Thames and Severn combined.

Left Loch Tay
Middle An osprey fishing
Right Kinclaven Bluebell Wood

Since prehistoric times, the valley of the River Tay has served as a highway between the lowlands and the Highlands. It's a route now followed by the main road and railway to the north, and by the River Tay Way, a 50-mile walking and cycling route that links Perth to the village of Kenmore at the northeast end of Loch Tay.

Loch Tay – at 15 miles long, the sixth-largest loch in Scotland – was already a centre of population 4000 years ago, when prehistoric people built a series of crannogs – timber-built roundhouses supported on piles driven into the loch bed – along its shores. You can visit a recreation of one of these ancient dwellings at the Scottish Crannog Centre near Kenmore.

For today's canoeists and kayakers, the Tay is a classic river descent, but for thousands of years before roads were built, the river was an important waterway. A log canoe found buried in the mud at Carpow, east of Perth, has been dated to around 1000 BCE (it is now on display in Perth Museum & Art Gallery).

Roman ships sailed up the Tay and legions marched to a line of forts defending the northernmost border of Empire. Ardoch (at Braco, near Stirling) is the best preserved of these, but Inchtuthil, built around 83 CE on the banks of the Tay near Spitalfield, is famous for its 10-tonne hoard of iron nails. They were buried when the Romans abandoned the fort, and only rediscovered in 1960 – samples are held by Perth Museum, and the Royal Scottish Museum in Edinburgh.

The Tay breaches the Highland line at the picturesque village of Dunkeld (whose name means 'Fort of the Caledonians'), a strategic point where the valley narrows.

ANGHARAD TREASURE/SHUTTERSTOCK ©

DALE KELLY/SHUTTERSTOCK ©

Jacobite clans fighting for the restoration of the Stuart monarchy clashed with Cameronian soldiers, who supported William of Orange, at the Battle of Dunkeld in 1689. This event, along with the Battle of Killiecrankie a few weeks earlier, signalled the beginning of 60 years of conflict that only ended with the defeat of Bonnie Prince Charlie at Culloden in 1746.

In an attempt to control the Jacobite clans, General George Wade was charged in the 1730s with building a network of military roads from the lowlands into the Highlands. The first of these followed the valley of the Tay from Dunkeld as far as Ballinluig and is still the route followed by the modern A9 motor road. A second military road crossed the Tay at Aberfeldy via Wade's Bridge (built in 1734), the oldest surviving bridge over the river.

Of course, the river is not just a highway for humans, but also for wildlife.

Of course, the river is not just a highway for humans, but also for wildlife. Eels migrate downstream to the sea to breed, freshwater pearl mussels cling to the river bed, otters forage along the banks, and the European beaver – hunted to near extinction in the 16th century – has returned. But the river's most famous wild inhabitant is the Atlantic salmon, whose arduous journey upriver to spawn is the stuff of legend.

Today all salmon fishing on the Tay – one of Europe's premier salmon rivers – is by rod and line, and all fish are carefully released alive after being caught. Old traditions persist, and the opening of the salmon-fishing season on 15 January is marked by ceremonies up and down the river, notably at Kenmore, where a pipe band leads a procession of anglers to the river.

Top Tayside Wildlife Experiences

Beaver safari See the amazing wetlands beavers have created, and watch a beaver family swimming, feeding, playing and grooming near their lodge.

Osprey-watching at Loch of the Lowes A webcam ensures you get excellent views of what's going on in the nest.

Dragonflies at Polney Loch, Dunkeld On a hot summer day the edges of the loch come alive with dragonflies and damselflies.

Walk Kinclaven Bluebell Woods Arguably one of the most beautiful bluebell woods in Scotland, full of bird song in spring and summer.

Recommended By Danièle Muir, *owner of Perthshire Wildlife*

@PerthshireWildlife

17

Kings, Queens & CASTLES

CASTLES | HISTORY | ARCHITECTURE

Explore dramatic crag-top castles, elegant aristocratic palaces, romantic island fortresses and the atmospheric ancient crowning place of Scottish monarchs, as you journey around the historic royal heartland of the Scottish nation.

JULIETPHOTOGRAPHY/SHUTTERSTOCK ©

How to

Getting around A car will make the most of your time, as outside Perth and Stirling most sights are poorly served by public transport.

When to go Many smaller castles are closed November to March. Avoid crowds at Stirling Castle by visiting weekdays outside of school holidays (July to mid-August).

Top tip Book lovers shouldn't miss the Library of Innerpeffray (p109). Founded in 1680, it houses a huge collection of rare and interesting books, some of them 500 years old.

AWE INSPIRING IMAGES/SHUTTERSTOCK ©

Scotland's Birthplace & Royal Roots

Climb the ancient mound of **Moot Hill**, which stands beside the lavish 19th-century Scone Palace (p108), and sit on a replica of the **Stone of Destiny**. This is the birthplace of Scotland as a kingdom, where Scottish monarchs – from Kenneth MacAlpin in 843 to Charles II in 1651 – were crowned.

Long before Edinburgh became the Scottish capital, **Dunfermline** was the favoured royal residence. Wander the ruins of the abbey guesthouse, converted in 1500 into a palace for King James VI whose son, Charles I, was born here in 1600, and visit the abbey church, founded by David I in 1128, which houses the tombs of three princes, two queens and seven kings, including Robert the Bruce.

ROBERT COLONNA/SHUTTERSTOCK ©

The Stone of Destiny

Legend has it that the ancient coronation stone of Scottish kings was brought to Scone in the 9th century. In 1296 it was captured by Edward I of England who took it to Westminster Abbey, where it remained for 700 years. It is now on display in the fantastic Perth Museum which opened in 2024 after a £27 million redevelopment.

Top left Scone Palace (p108)
Left Dunfermline
Top right The Stone of Destiny

Set in the lush rural heart of Fife, 16th-century **Falkland Palace** was the country residence of the Stuart monarchs. Explore the gardens where Mary Queen of Scots is said to have spent the happiest days of her life, and pop into the world's oldest surviving real tennis court, which dates from 1539. Kings James V, James VI and Charles II all stayed here too on various occasions.

Access by boat trip adds atmosphere to **Lochleven Castle**, whose 14th-century tower house is one of the oldest in the country. It was visited by Robert the Bruce in 1313 and 1323, and Mary Queen of Scots was held prisoner here in 1567 before being forced to abdicate. Combine a visit with a hike around the lovely **Loch Leven Heritage Trail**.

Who Holds Stirling, Holds Scotland...

The dramatic setting of **Stirling Castle** atop a crag commanding the broad valley of the River Forth – the ancient invasion route

History off the Beaten Track

Perthshire has a lovely selection of small churches: St Serf's in Dunning, with the magnificent Pictish carvings of the Forteviot Stone; Tibbermuir near Gleneagles; and two St Mary's, both 16th century – Grandtully with a wonderful painted ceiling, and one next to Innerpeffray Library itself. (Another amazing book collection can be found in Dunblane near the cathedral – Bishop Leighton's Library is a tiny treasure.) And then there's Abernethy Tower, south-east of Perth – a historical enigma, it's one of only two of this style in Scotland and is thought to be almost 1000 years old.

Recommended by Lara Haggerty, *Keeper of Books at the Library of Innerpeffray @Innerpeffray*

PHIL WALKER ©

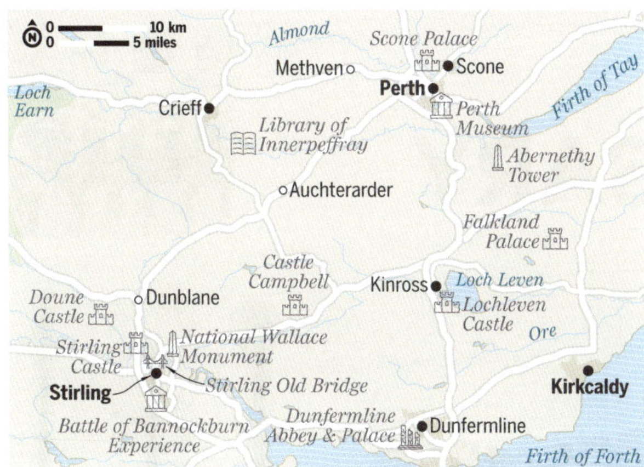

into Central Scotland – makes it arguably the country's finest fortress. Patrol the ramparts to take in the stunning views before exploring its centrepiece – the magnificent royal palace built in Renaissance style for King James V in the 1530s.

From the castle you can wander downhill to **Stirling Old Bridge**, site of a decisive battle in 1297 when William Wallace (of *Braveheart* fame) defeated an English army and set the scene for Scottish independence. Rising on another crag to the north is the Gothic tower of the **National Wallace Monument** – climb to the top for fantastic views of Stirling Castle.

Scotland's independence was clinched in 1314 at the Battle of Bannockburn, when Robert the Bruce decisively trounced the forces of England's Edward II. You can experience a digital re-enactment of the clash of armies at the National Trust for Scotland's Bannockburn Visitor Centre (p109), before taking a stroll across the actual battlefield.

More castles litter the countryside around Stirling, notably spectacular **Castle Campbell** (near Dollar), perched high on a wooded cliff (approach from the lower car park via a woodland walk), and **Doune Castle**, made famous as a film location for *Monty Python and the Holy Grail,* and more recently as Castle Leoch in the TV series *Outlander* (be sure to take the audio tour).

Left Abernethy Tower
Below National Wallace Monument

A Castle
GLOSSARY

03

04

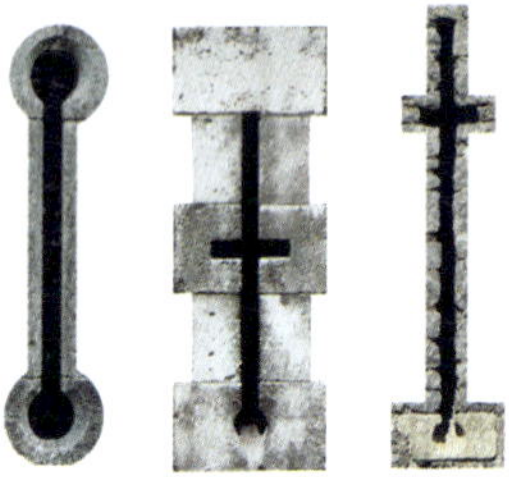

01

02

05

01 Crenellation

The tops of the walls were provided with raised sections that defenders could take cover behind while firing arrows or projectiles through the gaps.

02 Curtain Wall

The main requirement of any defensive castle was a lofty curtain wall at least 3m in thickness that wrapped around a central courtyard.

03 Machicolation

Some castles had projecting corbels, or machicolations, at the top which allowed defenders to drop rocks or boiling pitch between them onto attackers below.

04 Arrow Slit

Arrow slits were narrow on the outside, to make a small target, and widened inside to allow the archer a wide range of fire.

05 Portcullis

This was a heavy metal gate that was

hoisted up and down in parallel grooves either side of the castle entrance. It could be dropped rapidly in an emergency.

06 Sentry Post

A small tower at the corner of the castle walls, providing shelter for soldiers on lookout duty.

07 Murder Hole

A hole in the roof of the entrance passage allowed defenders to pour boiling oil or pitch onto attackers who had breached the gate.

08 Drawbridge

A bridge across an outer moat or ditch that could be raised during an attack to make the castle entrance more secure.

09 Barbican

Extra fortification built around or on either side of the castle entrance to improve its defence.

Listings

BEST OF THE REST

Seafood & Steak

Haar £££
Masterchef finalist in 2018, Arbroath-born Dean Banks has established Haar as one of Scotland's top restaurants. Don't miss his signature grilled lobster in mirin butter.

Balgove Larder & Steak Barn ££
This farm shop on the edge of St Andrews is a treasure trove of locally produced food and drink while the Steak Barn is a top spot for a barbecue lunch or dinner.

Crail Fish Bar & Café £
Join the queue that regularly forms to sample some of Fife's finest fish and chips. Go traditional and order a fish supper, wrapped in paper, enjoyed by the picture-perfect harbour.

Shellfish Shack £
Crab, lobster, razor clams, langoustines and whitefish are landed daily at this coastal gastro highlight in Anstruther, Fife's seafood capital – you can even choose your own live lobster.

Craig Millar @ 16 West End £££
Choose a sunny summer day, book a table for lunch on the outdoor terrace, and enjoy a platter of shellfish or a juicy steak with a view over St Monans harbour in this award-winning eatery.

Historical Highlights

Perth Museum
Home to the Stone of Destiny, the museum opened in 2024, offering a cornucopia of local history; from a prehistoric log boat and a cache of Roman artefacts, to the record rod-caught salmon.

Perth Art Gallery
One of the UK's oldest collections, featuring works by influential modern Scottish artists, including Joan Eardley, Sir William MacTaggart, Calum Colvin and Alison Watt.

Crannog Centre
Explore the museum which holds ancient artefacts, and the Iron Age village, crafted with locally sourced materials, showcasing traditional craftsmanship on Loch Tay.

Scottish Fisheries Museum
Watch skilled boatbuilders at work restoring historic wooden fishing vessels, and learn about the coastal communities who earned a living from the harvest of the sea.

St Andrews Castle
This storybook castle is a great place for kids to explore, complete with bottle-shaped dungeon and countermine – an underground passage hacked through solid rock during a 16th-century siege.

Scone Palace & Moot Hill
With a beautiful setting on the banks of the Tay, this elegant aristocratic palace is one of Scotland's most impressive stately homes. Within

Scone Palace

the grounds, Moot Hill is the ancient crowning place of Scottish kings since the 9th century.

Library of Innerpeffray
Bookworms can easily spend half a day in this 16th-century library, where voluntary guides will let you leaf through 300-year-old tomes, and seek out ancient books on any subject that interests you.

Battle of Bannockburn Visitor Centre
Re-enact this pivotal 14th-century clash between Scottish and English armies on a digital battlefield.

A Drink & a Snack

Loch Leven's Larder ££
Locals take a break from hiking or biking around the Loch Leven Heritage Trail at this popular farm shop and cafe, whose family-friendly facilities include outdoor tables, a play park and a sensory garden.

Taybank ££
Top choice for a sun-kissed pub lunch by the River Tay in Dunkeld, serving ales from the local Strathbraan Brewery. Live music several nights per week, and a menu featuring local produce.

Inn at Loch Tummel ££
Tote your pint across the road and bag a picnic table in one of Perthshire's best beer gardens, and soak up the glorious views over the sheep-dotted fields to lovely Loch Tummel.

Kingsbarns Distillery
Treat yourself to a leisurely two-hour tour of this rural distillery, where your guide will lead you through the whisky-making process before conducting an in-depth tasting session.

Water & Wildlife

Splash Rafting
This outfit offers exhilarating white-water rafting on the Rivers Tummel and Tay, as well as kayaking, canyoning and stand-up paddleboarding.

Canoeing the River Tummel

Perthshire Wildlife
Join an evening walking tour or guided canoe safari to go in search of the European beavers that have spread throughout the backwaters of the River Tay system in the last two decades.

Outdoor Explore
Learn to canoe or kayak, join a guided half- or full-day canoe trip on Loch Tummel or Loch Rannoch, or go sea-kayaking in the Firth of Tay.

Bamff Ecotourism
A private estate near Alyth dedicated to rewilding, with a network of short walking trails through native woods and wetland crafted by the local beavers. The Cateran Trail long-distance footpath passes nearby.

Pitlochry Dam Visitor Centre
An architecturally stunning visitor centre perched above the dam on the River Tummel houses an exhibition recounting the history of hydroelectricity in Scotland, alongside the life cycle of the Atlantic salmon.

NORTHEAST SCOTLAND

WHISKY | CASTLES | COAST

- **Trip Builder** (p112)
- **Practicalities** (p114)
- **A Coastal Trail** (p116)
- **Whisky Tour of Speyside** (p120)
- **Dundee Design Trail** (p122)
- **Listings** (p124)

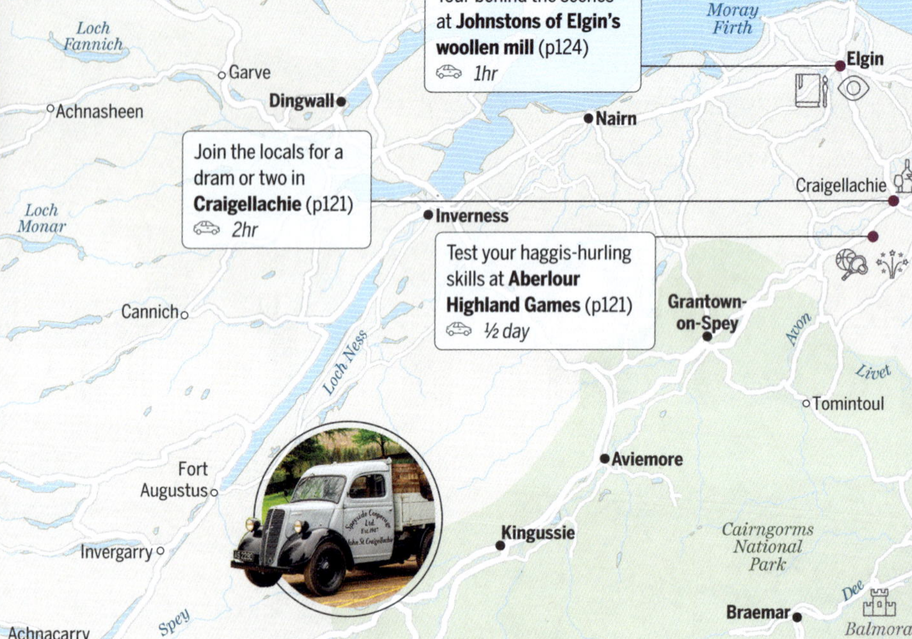

NORTHEAST SCOTLAND

Trip Builder

Inland, castle turrets and distillery pagodas jostle with verdant hills and brooding glens in a stereotypically Scottish scene. Beneath the weathered cliffs of the coastal roads, work and pleasure revolve around the sea in this region of stark contrasts.

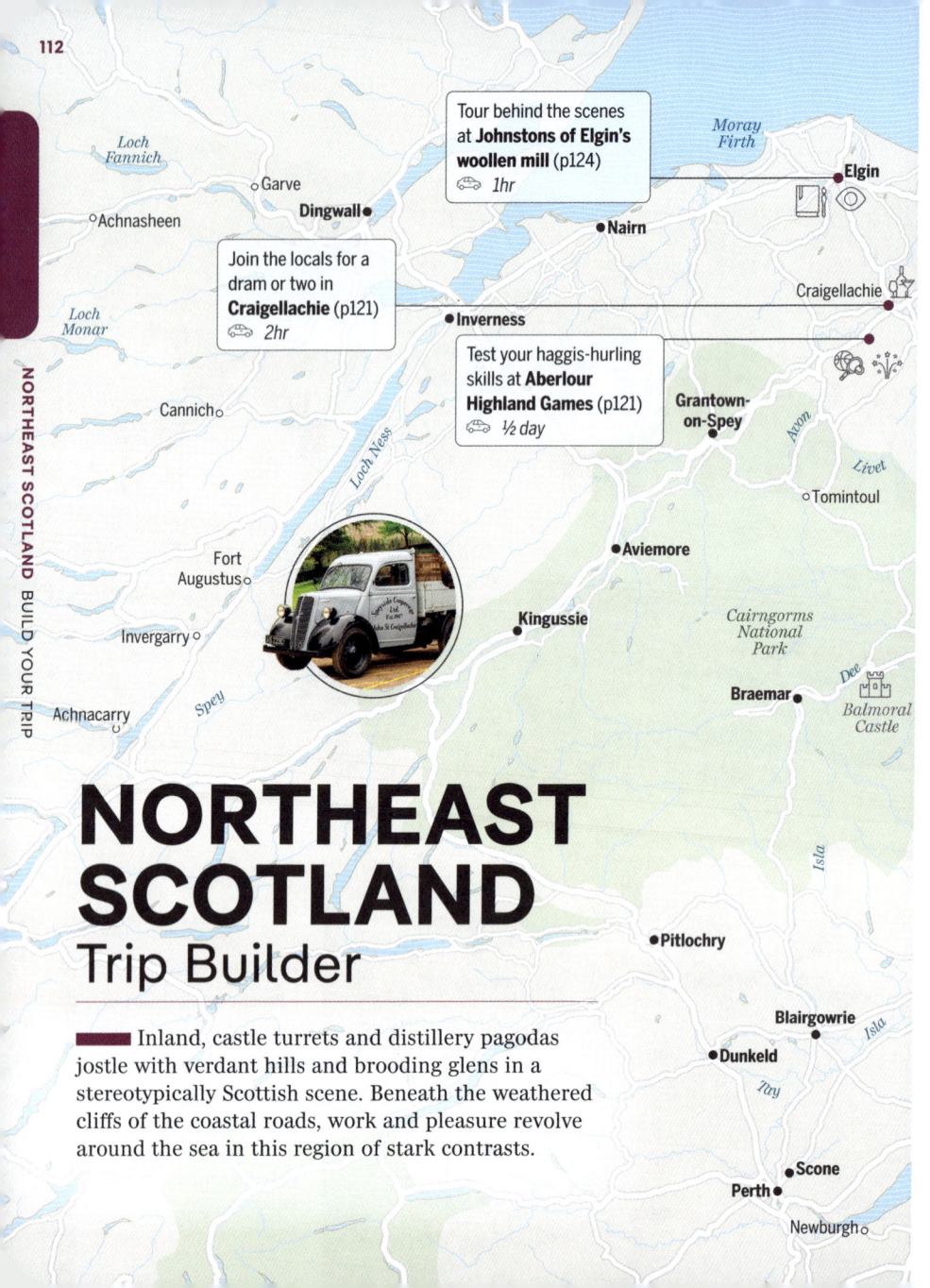

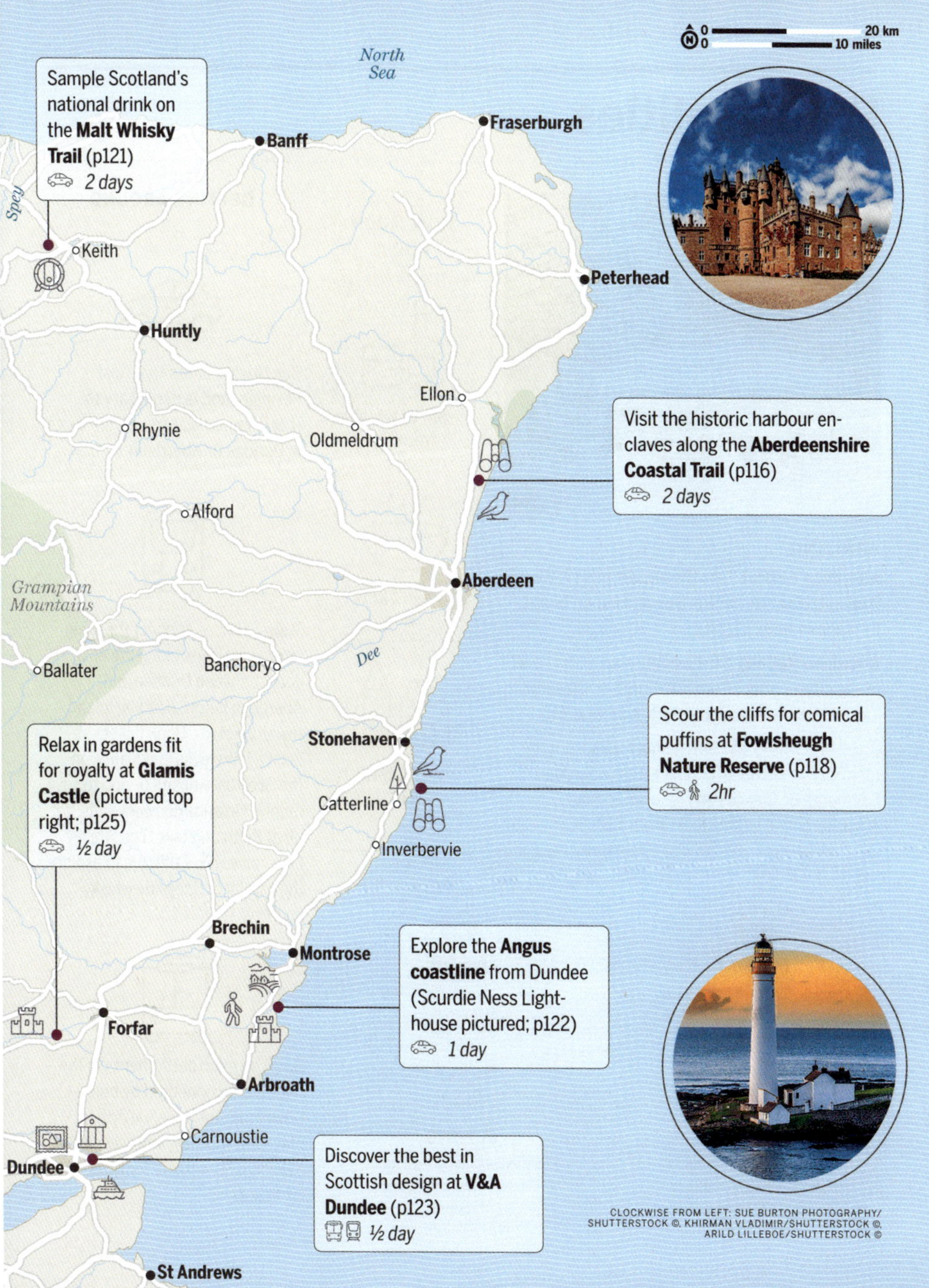
0 20 km
0 10 miles
North Sea
Sample Scotland's national drink on the **Malt Whisky Trail** (p121)
2 days
Spey
Keith
Banff
Fraserburgh
Peterhead
Huntly
Ellon
Rhynie
Oldmeldrum
Visit the historic harbour enclaves along the **Aberdeenshire Coastal Trail** (p116)
2 days
Alford
Aberdeen
Grampian Mountains
Ballater
Banchory
Dee
Stonehaven
Scour the cliffs for comical puffins at **Fowlsheugh Nature Reserve** (p118)
2hr
Relax in gardens fit for royalty at **Glamis Castle** (pictured top right; p125)
½ day
Catterline
Inverbervie
Brechin
Montrose
Explore the **Angus coastline** from Dundee (Scurdie Ness Lighthouse pictured; p122)
1 day
Forfar
Arbroath
Carnoustie
Dundee
Discover the best in Scottish design at **V&A Dundee** (p123)
½ day
St Andrews

Practicalities

MICHAEL715/SHUTTERSTOCK ©

ARRIVING

Aberdeen Airport Take the airport bus (727) 7 miles to the city centre. Buy a ticket on board for approximately £3.70.

Aberdeen Railway Station Situated in the heart of the city, connect from Edinburgh or Glasgow. Tickets purchased online start at around £15.

Dundee Railway Station A short walk from the main city attractions, connect from Aberdeen, Edinburgh or Glasgow in just over an hour. Advance online tickets start from £12.

HOW MUCH FOR A

Dram of whisky from £4

Cullen Skink £6

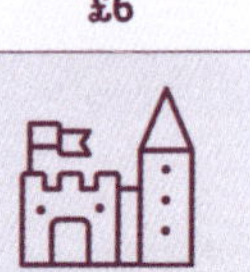

Castle tour £16

WHEN TO GO

JAN–MAR
Cold with the possibility of snow; attractions are at their quietest.

APR–JUN
Milder temperatures and seabirds return.

JUL–SEP
Temperatures are at their highest; perfect for outdoor activities and beach walks.

OCT–DEC
Chilly temperatures; keep warm at winter festivals and Christmas markets.

GETTING AROUND

Car Driving offers the most flexibility and is necessary to reach some rural areas. Hire a car in Dundee or Aberdeen.

Train Services connect the main cities and towns along the east coast between Dundee and Aberdeen before heading inland towards Forres. Book tickets at least a few weeks in advance on the ScotRail website or app to save money. On summer weekends, get off at Keith and take 'The Whisky Line' railway to Dufftown to explore the capital of Speyside whisky country.

Bus The main settlements in the region are connected by bus. Download the Traveline app to plan your journey, and search the Stagecoach website for discounted tickets.

EATING & DRINKING

Arbroath Smokie Only haddock smoked in the east-coast town using traditional methods can be called an Arbroath Smokie. Best eaten with your fingers, hot from one of the local smokehouses.

Cullen Skink Originating in the fishing village of Cullen, smoked haddock, potatoes, onions and milk are combined to create a hearty soup. Ideal as a lunchtime filler or a winter warmer.

Aberdeen Rowies/Butteries A savoury snack with a unique consistency similar to a croissant; pick up this local speciality from any Aberdeenshire bakery.

Must-try local treat
Portsoy Ice Cream (p124)

Best Cullen Skink
Rockpool Cafe (p124)

TOP: CLAIRE FRASER PHOTOGRAPHY/SHUTTERSTOCK ©
BOTTOM: BARMALINI/SHUTTERSTOCK ©

CONNECT & FIND YOUR WAY

Wi-fi Usually available for free at cafes, restaurants and hotels. Although fast and reliable in urban areas, it can be slow in rural settings.

Navigation Generally easy as major routes and attractions are well signposted. In countryside locations, enter the exact address on a navigation device as postcodes often cover large areas.

WHERE TO STAY

There are accommodation choices for every budget, from inexpensive hostels to luxury castles. City and sea-view properties command the highest prices; head to smaller towns for cheaper options.

Town/Village	Pro/Con
Dundee	A good range of options within walking distance of city attractions and nightlife, but less convenient as a regional base.
Aberdeen	Widest range of accommodation and the main transport hub for the region but it's quite industrial and the centre can be noisy at night.
Portsoy	The historic fishing village is ideal for exploring picturesque coastal enclaves; evening entertainment is limited, however.
Dufftown	Whisky lovers are spoiled for choice with numerous distilleries and pubs on the doorstep; not all advertised accommodation is in town.

WHISKY DISTILLERIES

Find out which of the 50 Speyside whisky distilleries are open to the public and their locations on VisitScotland's interactive map.

MONEY

Buy a Northern Highlights Pass online for up to 50% discounted entry at selected attractions and activities throughout northeast Scotland. A three-month pass costs £20.

18 A Coastal TRAIL

BEACHES | VILLAGES | WILDLIFE

Packed with whitewashed lighthouses, pristine beaches and cliff-hugging fishing villages, the Aberdeenshire Coastal Trail weaves through 165 miles of gratifying saltwater scenery. But expect a few surprises along the way – touring a Victorian prison is one of the top attractions.

STEVE ALLEN/SHUTTERSTOCK ©

How to

Getting around A car is essential for this trip from St Cyrus to Cullen. Hire a car in Dundee, a one-hour drive from the start of the trail. A map of the route can be downloaded from the VisitScotland website.

When to go Seasonal attractions open May to September.

Puffin stop From April to mid-August, head to Fowlsheugh or Troup Head for a chance of spotting puffins.

WILLIAM GALE/SHUTTERSTOCK ©

Unspoilt Beaches

A striking offshore lighthouse and miles of immaculate powdery sand dominated by giant dunes have established **Rattray Head** as a frontrunner for the standout beach on the route. However, a worthy rival can be found at the expansive golden sands of **St Cyrus**, bordered by grassland that brims with wildflowers and butterflies in the summer.

Newburgh is a popular location for quietly observing hundreds of local seals resting along the shore, while surfing lessons offer a more energetic beach experience at **Fraserburgh**.

BERNI0004/SHUTTERSTOCK ©

Historic Fishing Villages

The cottages of **Crovie** are hemmed in so tightly between the cliffs and the sea that the waves are almost within touching distance of their front doors. With no room for a road

Traditional Boat Building

The art of traditional boat building is kept alive in the coastal town of Portsoy, home of the annual **Scottish Traditional Boat Festival**. Throughout the year, visitors are welcome to watch volunteers creating wooden vessels by hand at **The Boatshed**, or view their time-honoured designs in the 17th-century harbour.

Top left Portsoy harbour
Top right Rattray Head
Bottom left St Cyrus beach

or cars, it has preserved a real sense of bygone times. Just along the coast is **Pennan**, Crovie's movie star neighbour. Photogenic white- and pastel-painted homes line the water's edge, although it is the red telephone box made famous by the film *Local Hero* that draws the most attention. **Gardenstown** completes this string of picturesque villages.

Dramatic Viewpoints

Perched theatrically on a rocky outcrop, **Dunnottar** is one of Scotland's most iconic castles. The approach path reveals a heart-stirring panorama of the romantic ruin burdened by a turbulent history.

During summer, the cliffs at **Fowlsheugh Nature Reserve** are transformed into seabird citadels. Observe the spectacle from vantage points along the coastal path. At **Bullers of Buchan**, a deep chasm and natural archway created by a collapsed sea cave are visually impressive.

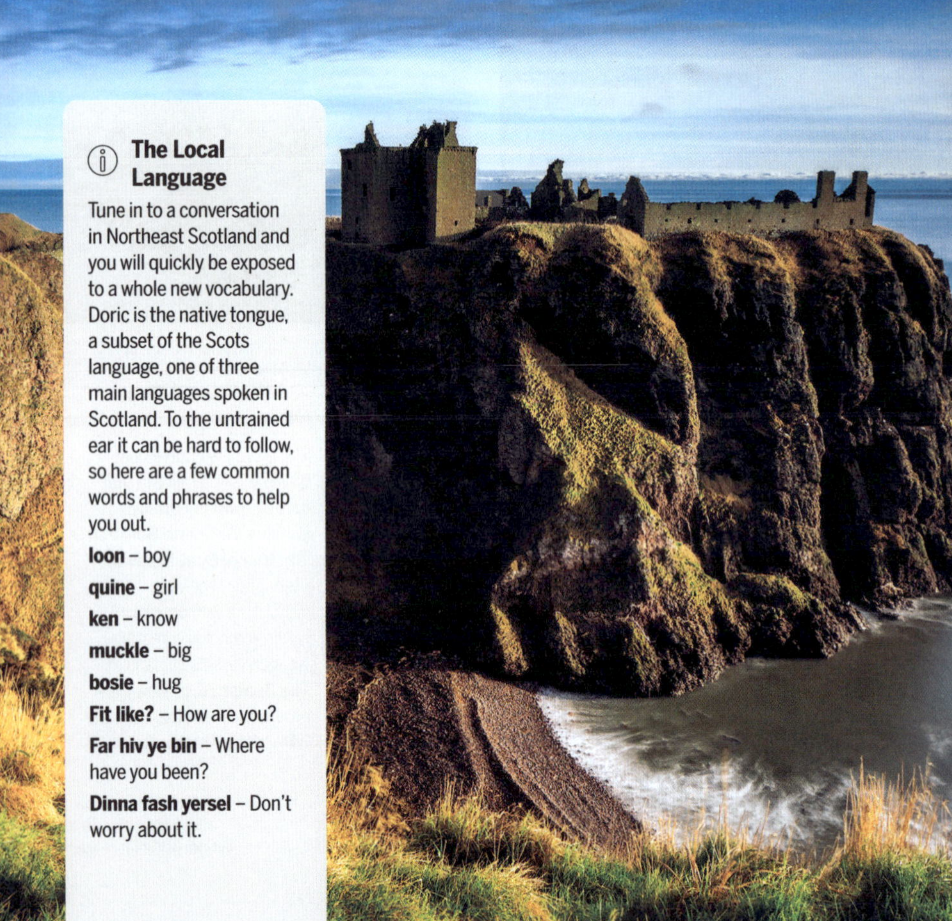

The Local Language

Tune in to a conversation in Northeast Scotland and you will quickly be exposed to a whole new vocabulary. Doric is the native tongue, a subset of the Scots language, one of three main languages spoken in Scotland. To the untrained ear it can be hard to follow, so here are a few common words and phrases to help you out.

loon – boy

quine – girl

ken – know

muckle – big

bosie – hug

Fit like? – How are you?

Far hiv ye bin – Where have you been?

Dinna fash yersel – Don't worry about it.

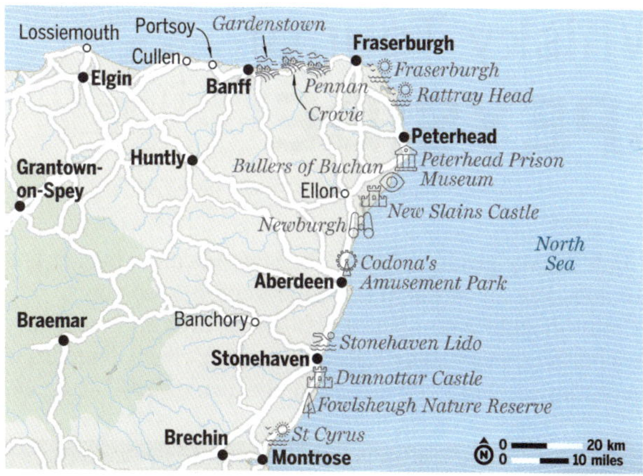

Left Dunnottar Castle
Below Razorbill, Fowlsheugh Nature Reserve

Surprising Stops

The crumbling hulk of **New Slains Castle** is far removed from the stereotypical Scottish fairy-tale dwelling. In fact, if local legend is to be believed, it is the setting for a far more sinister story. After visiting the area, Bram Stoker is said to have used the spooky structure as inspiration for his *Dracula* novel.

This isn't the only building on this stretch of coast with a dark past. Notorious as one of Scotland's toughest jails, **Peterhead Prison** has reinvented itself as a top tourist attraction. The inmates have been moved out and the cell doors permanently opened to allow self-guided tours of the Victorian establishment, which was once stormed by the SAS.

You will be glad you packed a swimming costume when you are floating in the toasty warm seawater at **Stonehaven Lido**. The Olympic-sized open-air pool is heated to a very pleasant 29°C and feels more like the Mediterranean than Scotland.

The 30.5m-high big wheel at **Codona's Amusement Park** affords a unique perspective of Aberdeen Beach. If this sounds too sedate, thrill-seekers are catered for with a range of adrenaline-inducing rides and a state-of-the-art 4D motion theatre.

19 Whisky Tour of SPEYSIDE

DISTILLERIES | HISTORY | CULTURE

The sweet aroma of malt whisky production fills the Speyside air, a bucket-list destination for Scotch aficionados and an excellent introduction for those new to Scotland's national drink. A mind-boggling number of distilleries, over half those in the country, are nestled between the green rolling hills and snaking rivers. Numerous scenic hikes and captivating castles will keep you occupied between drams.

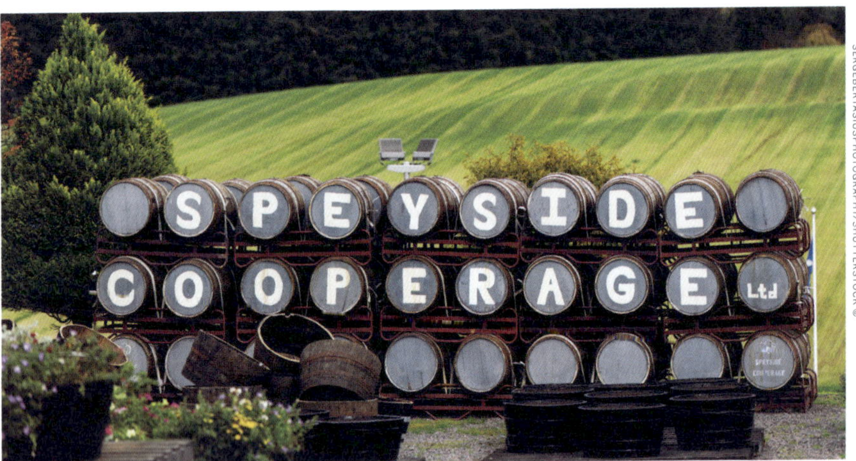

SERGEBERTASIUSPHOTOGRAPHY/SHUTTERSTOCK ©

How to

Getting around Buses serve the main Speyside towns but a car is necessary to reach rural distilleries. Car hire is available in Aberdeen. Beware, drink driving is not tolerated; many distillery tours will provide a tasting kit to take away, and it's worth considering hiring a driver guide.

When to go Most distillery tours run year-round, and it's worth considering planning your trip in the quieter off-season months.

Ride the Whisky Line The 11-mile-long heritage railway runs between Keith and Dufftown.

TRAVELLING TOURIST/SHUTTERSTOCK ©

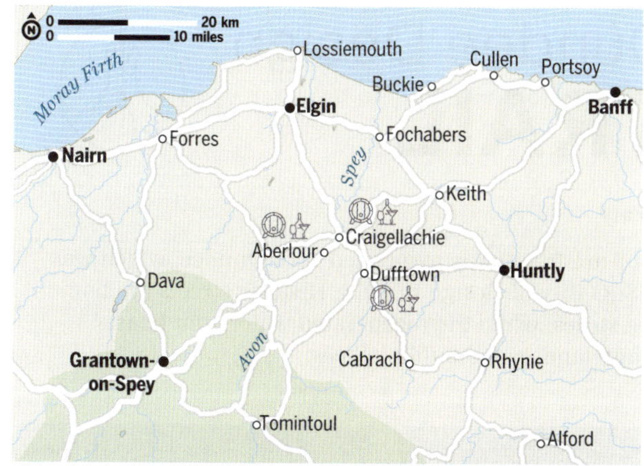

Top left Speyside Cooperage
Bottom left Glenfiddich Distillery

Malt Whisky Trail If the choice of whisky-themed options leaves you feeling intoxicated, this curated trail narrows it down to nine locations. Visit notable names like **Glenfiddich** or lesser-known labels like **Cardhu**, the only distillery pioneered by a woman. Blend your own malt at **Strathisla Distillery**, home of Chivas Regal. The **Speyside Cooperage** makes and repairs over 100,000 casks annually. Take a tour from acorn to cask and discover the importance of the humble whisky barrel.

Spirit of Speyside Festival Each May, whisky fans from around the world descend on Speyside for a celebratory gathering of Scotland's water of life. Village halls, whisky bars and even historic castles open up to welcome the public to an eclectic mix of experiences. For the best part of a week, hundreds of events take place across a wide range of venues. Book tickets online in advance.

Whisky bars Join Craigellachie locals for a dram at the **Highlander Inn** or **Quaich Bar**; ask for recommendations if you're struggling to choose from the extensive malts on offer. In Aberlour, the **Mash Tun** holds exclusive Glenfarclas casks among its ample collection, while **The Still** is lined from floor to ceiling with bottles from every whisky region of Scotland. Order a whisky flight at the **Seven Stills** in Dufftown to compare and contrast a range of malts.

Highland Games

Pair whisky with a day out to one of the region's Highland Games for an iconic taste of Scotland. From the swirling of the bagpipes to the swishing of the kilts and the tossing of the caber, these competitive historic gatherings have been a part of Scottish culture for centuries. Four local communities stage events during July and August that welcome participation from international visitors in a variety of unique events. Compete in uphill whisky-barrel rolling at Tomintoul, race on an old message bike in Forres, hurl a haggis in Aberlour or test your speed in the overseas race in Dufftown.

20 Dundee Design TRAIL

HERITAGE | DESIGN | DAY TRIP

'Innovative' and 'cool' are frequently associated with Dundee, which was named the UK's first UNESCO City of Design in 2014. Historic streets are home to quirky cafes and vintage stores, while the regenerated waterfront boasts 21st-century architecture and landscaped public spaces.

ROBERT MULLAN/SHUTTERSTOCK ©

Trip Notes

Getting around Dundee is a compact city, best explored on foot. Dundee railway station is located opposite V&A Dundee – arrive in under 90 minutes by a direct connection from Edinburgh, Glasgow or Aberdeen. If arriving by car, download a map of public car parks from the Dundee City Council website.

When to go Attractions are open year-round.

Top tip Buy a combined ticket for RRS *Discovery* and Verdant Works to save money.

Explore the Angus Coastline

Explore the historic fishing village of Auchmithie and call in at the But n Ben Restaurant for their signature Smokie Pancake. Shake down lunch with a coastal walk with Arbroath Cliff Tours. Stroll the sands of Lunan Bay or walk to the Scurdie Ness Lighthouse in Montrose before exploring the wildlife at the Montrose Basin Visitor Centre and Wildlife Reserve.

04 Less than a mile away is **Verdant Works**, a refurbished 19th-century textile mill. Watch historic machines at work and learn about the city's jute industry that once employed over 50,000 people.
05 Finish at the **McManus Art Gallery & Museum** (pictured left), encompassing eight galleries and covering a period of 400 million years. The Gothic building is a city-centre landmark.
01 Start your day by the waterfront with a visit to **V&A Dundee** (pictured above). The cliff-like building showcases Scotland's design achievements over the centuries in its permanent gallery and temporary exhibition space.
03 A short walk away is **Dundee Contemporary Arts**, a cultural hub in the city. The modern space houses art exhibitions, a shop featuring local crafts and a popular cafe.
02 Berthed next door is the Dundee-built ship, **RRS Discovery**. Famed for transporting explorer Captain Scott and his crew on their Antarctic expedition, it is now part of an award-winning museum.
W Henderson's Wynd
Blinshall St
Douglas St
Brown St
Miln St
West Marketgait
Constitution Rd
Bell St
Panmure St
West Bell St
Euclid Cres
Ward Rd
Meadowside
Barrack St
Bank St
Reform St
North Lindsay St
Session St
Hawkhill
West Port
South Tay St
West Marketgait
High St
Nethergate
Union St
Thomson Ave
Riverside Esp
S Crichton St
Earl Grey Pl W
S Union St
South Marketgait
Tay Sq
Greenmarket
Perth Rd
Dundee
Firth of Tay
0 200 m
0 0.1 mile
N

HAZEL PLATER/SHUTTERSTOCK ©

Listings

BEST OF THE REST

 Seaside Cafes & Ice-Cream Parlours

Sweetpea Cafe £
Artisan food served in a rustic setting close to Broughty Ferry train station. Tasty gluten-free and vegan choices are a speciality.

Aunty Bettys £
Join the beachfront queue at this iconic ice-cream parlour in Stonehaven for an Instagram-worthy creation. Pile up the scoops before topping them off with an array of colourful embellishments.

Miele's of Lossie £
For the best ice cream in Lossiemouth, head to Miele's. Your ice cream is best enjoyed on the sweeping golden sands of Lossiemouth East Beach.

Portsoy Ice Cream £
Experimental concoctions are the flavour of the day in this award-winning ice-cream shop near the harbour in Portsoy. Previous headliners include hot cross bun, unicorn and cranachan laced with real whisky.

Rockpool Cafe £
Cullen is famous as the home of Cullen Skink, a Scottish smoked fish chowder. Rockpool Cafe is a popular option in the village to sample this local delicacy.

 Local Art & Crafts

Logie Steading
The 1920s farm buildings at Logie Steading near Forres have been repurposed as an artisan shopping village. Offerings include secondhand books, local art and whisky.

Johnstons of Elgin
For over 200 years, local craftspeople in Elgin have been turning raw fibre into fine wool and cashmere clothing. Visit the shop and historic mill for a tour.

Hand Pict
A group of Angus crafters and artists have banded together to form a cooperative with a gallery in Letham that showcases their work. A truly local and authentic experience.

The Barn
High-quality contemporary Scottish pieces by both up-and-coming designers and established artists sit side by side in a dedicated retail space within this multi-arts venue near Banchory.

 Historic Abbeys & Cathedrals

Arbroath Abbey
In 1320 the Declaration of Arbroath paved the way for Scottish Independence. Sent from the abbey, a copy of the symbolic document is on public display.

Pluscarden Abbey
A scene unchanged for centuries can be found at Britain's only medieval monastery still serving its original purpose. Monks tend to bees and sit in prayer below rainbow glass windows.

Arbroath Abbey

Elgin Cathedral

For fantastic landscape views, climb the tower of the ruined 13th-century cathedral known as the 'Lantern of the North'. A collection of intricately carved stones is a highlight.

 Garden Escapes

Glamis Castle

The childhood home of the Queen Mother boasts ornamental gardens fit for royalty. Spooky sculptures depicting scenes from *Macbeth* lurk in the woodland shadows.

Langley Park Gardens

Lovingly nurtured by the current owners, views extend across the wildflower meadow towards Montrose while a heady scent fills the air in the colourful walled gardens.

Pitmedden Garden

Wander through the recreated Scottish Renaissance garden, inspired by 17th-century designs. The extravagant layout features almost 6 miles of box hedging and over 200 fruit trees.

Gordon Castle Walled Garden

Designed to be as productive as it is beautiful, everything in this 200-year-old kitchen garden in Fochabers is grown with purpose. From gin to beauty products, the home-grown range is inspired.

Johnston Gardens

This small oasis in the west end of Aberdeen is a photographer's dream. The varied palette of colours and textures provides the perfect backdrop for a tumbling waterfall and Japanese-style bridge.

 Craft Beer & Gin Tours

Brewdog

Infamous for its irreverent marketing, Brewdog reveals some of their behind-the-scenes secrets in a tour of the original brewhouse and Lone Wolf Distillery in Ellon. The 90-minute 'DogWalk' includes four tastings.

DIANA REBENCIUC/SHUTTERSTOCK ©

Johnston Gardens

Brew Toon

This microbrewery with heritage and provenance at its heart has revived a defunct tradition in the east-coast fishing town of Peterhead. Appreciate handcrafted beers in the taproom.

71 Brewing

Street art, industrial architecture and rustic decor are befitting of Dundee's cool city vibe. Sip on a welcome beer before walking through the brewing process and savouring a few more samples.

City of Aberdeen Distillery

A historic railway arch in the city centre provides an unexpected venue for this hip distillery. Take a tour or create your own gin while trains rumble overhead.

Glenrinnes Distillery

View the Highland landscape of the organic estate surrounding the distillery from a mountaintop before a tutored tasting of gin and vodka in a fully immersive half-day experience.

SOUTHERN HIGHLANDS & ISLANDS

ADVENTURE | COAST | HISTORY

- **Trip Builder** (p128)
- **Practicalities** (p130)
- **Inner Hebrides Hopscotch** (p132)
- **Whisky Island Discovery** (p134)
- **Meet the Master Distiller** (p136)
- **From Sea to Plate** (p138)
- **Secret Coast Road Trip** (p140)
- **Enter the Ancient Kingdom** (p142)
- **Treasures of Kilmartin Glen** (p144)
- **Listings** (p146)

Go stargazing on the Dark Sky Island of **Coll** (p133)
3 days
Isle of Coll
Experience famous beaches, boat trips and water sports in **Tiree** (p133)
2 days
Isle of Tiree
Treshnish Isles
Ulva
Go puffin spotting on **Staffa** and the Treshnish Isles (p133)
½ day
Staffa
Isle of Mull
Iona
Fionnphort
Island-hop from **Mull** to **Iona** and **Ulva** (p133 & p139)
3–4 days
ATLANTIC OCEAN
Isle of Colonsay
Tour the famous whisky distilleries in **Islay** (p134)
2–3 days
Isle of Jura
Isle of Islay
North Channel

SOUTHERN HIGHLANDS & ISLANDS

Trip Builder

Feel the calm of the west coast and the rush of adventure; immerse yourself in idyllic isles, native forests and prehistoric ruins. Slow down, breathe it in, then toast this stunningly diverse region in a cosy pub with a peaty dram.

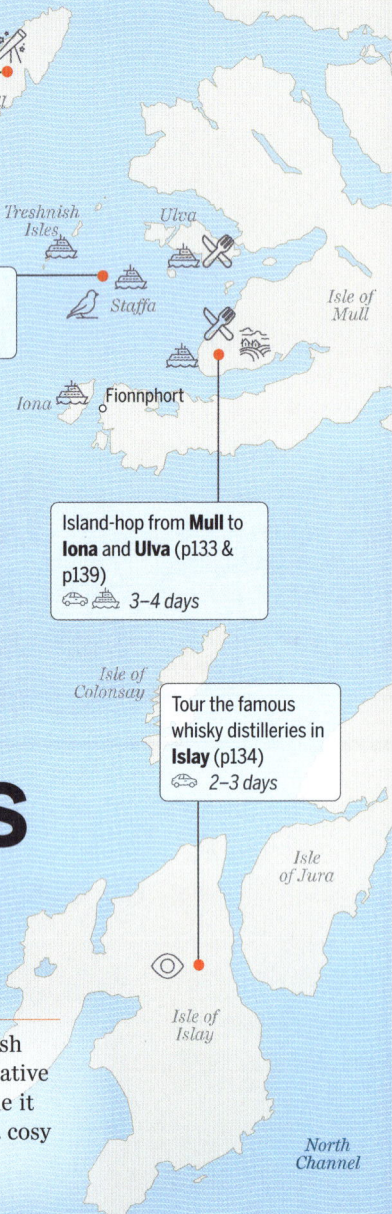

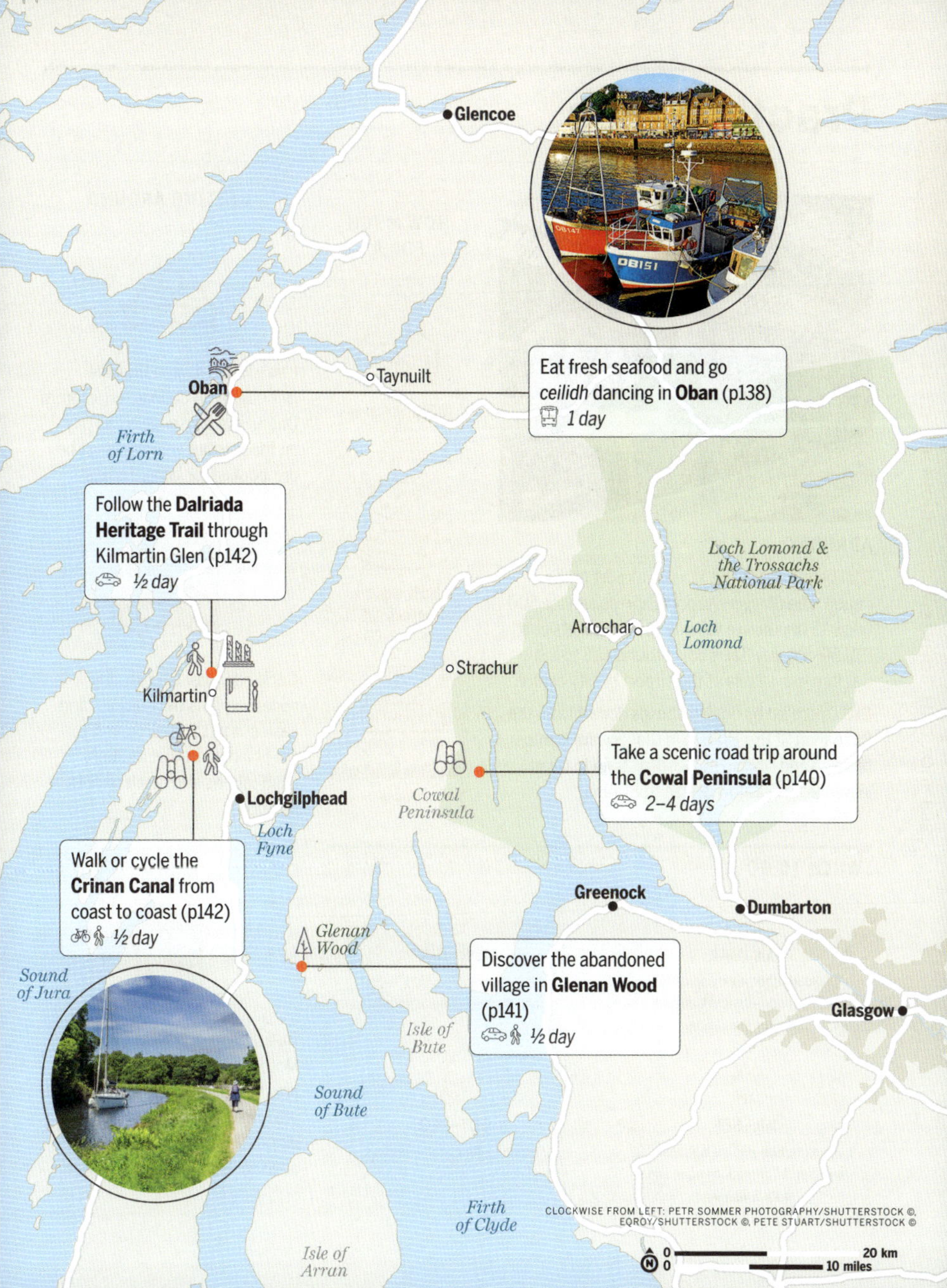
Glencoe
Eat fresh seafood and go *ceilidh* dancing in **Oban** (p138)
1 day
Oban
Taynuilt
Firth of Lorn
Follow the **Dalriada Heritage Trail** through Kilmartin Glen (p142)
½ day
Loch Lomond & the Trossachs National Park
Arrochar
Loch Lomond
Strachur
Kilmartin
Take a scenic road trip around the **Cowal Peninsula** (p140)
2–4 days
Lochgilphead
Cowal Peninsula
Loch Fyne
Walk or cycle the **Crinan Canal** from coast to coast (p142)
½ day
Greenock
Dumbarton
Glenan Wood
Discover the abandoned village in **Glenan Wood** (p141)
½ day
Sound of Jura
Glasgow
Isle of Bute
Sound of Bute
Firth of Clyde
Isle of Arran
0 20 km
0 10 miles

Practicalities

EDINBURGHCITYMOM/SHUTTERSTOCK ©

ARRIVING

Glasgow Airport The closest airport to the region. The Glasgow Airport Express service 500 takes 15 minutes to the city centre; tickets cost £10.50 one way. Taxis cost around £25 to £30. Car hire is available at the airport or city centre.

Bus Operated by Citylink, buses depart from the Buchanan St Bus Station in Glasgow for Campbeltown and Oban. The ScotRail train to Oban leaves from Glasgow Queen St Station.

HOW MUCH FOR A

Distillery tour £20

Half dozen oysters £12

Wildlife boat trip £60

WHEN TO GO

JAN–MAR
Cold weather, wintry scenery and not busy with tourists. Dark skies for stargazing.

APR–JUN
Flowers, longer daylight hours and the best puffin spotting.

JUL–SEP
Peak season and the warmest weather. All attractions open and lots of visitors.

OCT–DEC
Autumn colours, fewer visitors and drams of whisky by the fire.

GETTING AROUND

Ferry Hop between the Inner Hebrides with CalMac ferries from Oban. Foot passengers can pay on the day, but vehicles must be pre-booked for larger ferries.

Car While a car isn't strictly necessary, it is the quickest and easiest way to get around if you are planning to visit multiple destinations and reach remote locations.

Bus Citylink and West Coast Motors operate the bus services around the region. Some services are infrequent so advanced planning using the timetables is advised. Book seats in advance.

EATING & DRINKING

Seafood The west coast is famed for its fresh seafood and Oban is known as the 'Seafood Capital of Scotland'. Order a seafood platter to try a bit of everything. For something hot and more budget-friendly, you can't beat fish and chips by the sea.

Whisky Sample Islay's smoky single malt whiskies straight from the source at one of the distilleries or in a cosy local pub.

Must-try seafood platter
Skipness Seafood Cabin (p138)

Best coffee & cake
Brambles of Inveraray (p147)

WHERE TO STAY

This region has a wide range of accommodation options to suit all budgets: hostels, glamping sites, B&Bs, guesthouses and hotels. Choose one or two base locations and explore from there.

Place	Pro/Con
Tighnabruaich	A peaceful village on Argyll's Secret Coast, perfect for exploring the Cowal Peninsula. Quiet at night and not touristy.
Oban	Busy port town with great pubs and dining options. Excellent transport links.
Arinagour	Beautiful bay and main settlement in Coll: ferry port, local shop, post office, community centre and hotel-bar are here.
Bowmore	Ideal central base on Islay with shops, restaurants and a distillery. No evening public transport.
Tobermory	Colourful harbour town on Mull with boat trips to Staffa and the Treshnish Isles. Quality accommodation can be expensive.
Iona	Small and serene island, easy to explore on foot. Busy during the day in peak season, always quiet at night.

CONNECT & FIND YOUR WAY

Wi-fi Most hotels, bars, cafes and restaurants have guest wi-fi, and there is free wi-fi on CalMac ferries and at ferry ports. The connection can be slow and temperamental in some locations.

Navigation The region is easy to navigate using road signs, local maps and Google Maps. Do research and download your route in advance in case you can't get online.

TRAVEL DISCOUNTS

Save money with the Citylink Explorer Pass and CalMac Hopscotch tickets. The best ScotRail train fares go on sale 12 weeks in advance.

MONEY

Card payments are widely accepted but it is always advisable to carry cash (including coins) for the honesty boxes and small businesses that only take cash. ATMs can be found in the main towns.

21 Inner Hebrides HOPSCOTCH

FERRIES | BEACHES | WILDLIFE

Feel the buzz of boarding the ferry from Oban, 'Gateway to the Isles', to the dreamy Inner Hebrides. Embrace the slow pace and discover each island's unique traits: the energising activities, postcard villages and paradise shores with a rugged Scottish edge.

FELIX LIPOV/SHUTTERSTOCK ©

Trip Notes

Getting around CalMac operates ferries between Oban and the islands, while Staffa Trips and Staffa Tours sail to Staffa and the Treshnish Isles. Ulva ferry is operated by Rhuri Munro. Walkers and cyclists are well catered for; to cover more ground, take a car.

When to go Spring for wildflowers; May to July for puffins; August for heather; and autumn for dark skies, vibrant landscapes and fewer crowds.

Top tip Save money with CalMac's Hopscotch tickets.

Eagle Eye

Sea eagles are often spotted around the sea lochs on Mull's west coast. Look out for their broad plank-like wings and white tails (adults only). They can soar for long periods without flapping their wings and can be seen circling high overhead.

Local tip from Martin Keivers, *owner and skipper at Mull Charters @mull_charters*

05 Choose from multiple water-based adventures that showcase the famous waves and divine coastline of **Tiree**. During summer, hire a SUP or kayak and paddle the Gunna Sound in search of basking sharks.
Sea of the Hebrides
04 Book a stargazing weekend at **Coll Bunkhouse** in March and October or wrap up warm on a clear night and discover why the island secured its designated 'Dark Sky' status.
Coll
Tobermory
Tiree
Treshnish Isles
Salen
Ulva
Ben More
Craignure
Mull
Oban
03 **Staffa** and **Lunga** are where colourful, comical puffins go on their summer holidays. Observe their cute antics and classic crash landings up close on a boat trip with Staffa Tours or Staffa Trips.
Carsaig
Fionnphort
Firth of Lorn
01 Summit Mull's volcanic remains and only Munro, **Ben More**, all the way from sea level to 996m, starting from Dhiseig on the shores of Loch na Keal.
02 Tucked away in a secluded, sheltered bay on the west side of **Iona**, with pure white sand and turquoise sea, **Port Ban** is a hidden oasis and treat for wild swimmers.
Jura
0
20 km
0
10 miles
N

FROM TOP: SUSANN GUENTHER/SHUTTERSTOCK ©, SCORSBY/SHUTTERSTOCK ©

22 Whisky Island DISCOVERY

DISTILLERIES | TOURS | TRADITIONS

If there was ever a place to be voluntarily stranded, it's Scotland's 'whisky island'. Boasting 10 whisky distilleries, with more under way, Islay is heaven for whisky lovers, and a fast-track ticket for those who are yet to be charmed. Soak in the stories, traditions and unique quirks of each whisky on a series of distillery tours with a twist.

RUSSELL OUELLETTE IV/SHUTTERSTOCK ©

How to

Getting here & around CalMac runs ferries from Kennacraig and Oban; Loganair flies from Glasgow. Most distilleries can be reached by bus (Islay Coaches operates Monday to Saturday), local taxi, e-bike or by walking the Three Distilleries Pathway and the Bruichladdich to Port Charlotte route.

When to go The distilleries are open year-round. September for festivals; winter for drams and cosy fires.

Drivers drams Distilleries provide takeaway samples for drivers and cyclists to enjoy later. The perfect nightcap! (Remember: Scotland has a zero-tolerance policy for drink driving.)

OLGA MILTSOVA/SHUTTERSTOCK ©

From the cask Start the day with the Warehouse Experience at **Lagavulin Distillery**. This intimate tasting session includes a series of exclusive drams drawn straight from the cask. **Bunnahabhain** offers a similar, highly acclaimed Warehouse 9 Tasting Experience. This distillery has a stylish visitor centre that commands breathtaking views of Bunnahabhain Bay and the wild Paps of Jura beyond. For lovers of whisky and gin, visit **Bruichladdich Distillery** and try their single malt whisky and famous Botanist gin.

On the beach Settle into the sand at Machir Bay and learn all about Islay's only farm distillery on a beach tasting with the team at **Kilchoman**. Taste four whiskies from the core range, including a wonderfully fitting dram of Machir Bay. At low tide, watch a shipwreck emerge on the horizon.

The full works Experience the end-to-end journey of **Laphroaig** on an immersive tour: hike to the water source and cut the peat, sample single cask whisky in the warehouse and hand pour your own souvenir bottle. Claim your own plot of peat by becoming a 'Friend of Laphroaig'.

Best of the rest Experience the incredibly swish and stylish **Ardbeg** or enjoy a dram at the serene **Caol Ila Distillery**, tucked away on Islay's east coast, overlooking the Paps of Jura, or pop into **Ardnahoe**, the baby of the distilleries, and sample their newly aged single malt, distilled in 2018.

Top left Lagavulin Distillery
Bottom left Ardbeg whisky

Eat & Explore

We love whisky here at **Glenegedale**, particularly the warehouse experience and tasting at **Lagavulin**, who always serve up lots of fun and the best of drams.

Our favourite 'go-to' walks are at **Machir Bay**, or visit the RSPB Nature Reserve for a refreshing stomp up to the American Monument on the **Mull of Oa** then watch the sunset at **Kilnaughton Bay** with pizza from Peatzeria or SeaSalt Bistro.

Join **Islay Sea Adventures** for a wildlife boat tour, or hire a bike from **Islay e-bikes**.

Tips from By Emma Clark, *owner at Glenegedale House, Islay @glenegedalehouseislay*

Meet the Master Distiller

JIM MCEWAN, MASTER DISTILLER, ISLAY

Introducing Jim McEwan, the 'cask whisperer' and all-round whisky mastermind, who has dedicated more than 50 years of his life to the industry. From peeking through the windows of Bowmore Distillery as a child, to running the whole operation and putting Islay whisky on a global stage, Jim is a man who certainly knows his drams.

Left Whisky barrels at Bowmore Distillery
Middle Bowmore Distillery
Right Bruichladdich Distillery

13THREEPHOTOGRAPHY/SHUTTERSTOCK ©

A Dream Come True

Growing up in the village of Bowmore on Islay, Jim spent his childhood playing around the harbour and shoreline, and being chased away from the distillery by the manager. 'The distillery was like a theme park to me; it was so exciting. I always wanted to work there.'

Jim's aspiration was realised in 1963, when he secured his first job in the warehouse at age 15, which later led to an apprenticeship as a cooper, taught by Scotland's longest-serving cooper, David Bell. 'It was a dream come true to build casks; I loved the smell of the oak, the whisky, the burning of the charcoal.'

Never one to stop learning, Jim moved to Glasgow to train as a blender, and after three years was creating perfect blended whiskies for export around the world. He returned to Islay, this time as the manager of Bowmore Distillery, which was an honour for Jim, having started there as a boy.

His next big adventure was as Global Brand Ambassador for Bowmore, during which time he travelled the world extensively, introducing countries to Islay single malt for the first time – heavily peated single malts at that! 'In Asia they thought there was something wrong with the whisky because of the smoky flavour,' he laughs.

Jim thrived on the opportunity to educate people about whisky and his home island. 'When you love a product like whisky, as I do, and you love Islay, it doesn't feel like work. It was a great opportunity and a privilege.'

Bestowed Upon Us

Back permanently on home soil, Jim continued working his magic in the industry, and in 2001 moved to

DAVID FALCONER/SHUTTERSTOCK ©

MARTIN M303/SHUTTERSTOCK ©

Bruichladdich Distillery, where he was appointed as Master Distiller. He played a significant role in the revival of this distillery and is responsible for the famous Octomore range, said to be the world's peatiest whisky.

Following his retirement in 2015, Jim was tempted back into the industry to lend his expertise to Islay's newest distillery, Ardnahoe. Now, aside from selling some of his own personal casks, he has stepped back from the business and pursues a quiet life. He enjoys walking with a local group on the island and spending time with his family, including four grandchildren on the mainland.

> There is a great friendship between all the distilleries; it's a spiritual family.

Talking about the industry on Islay today, Jim says, 'I was born and raised here and the island has never been better, nor has the quality of the whisky. There is a great friendship between all the distilleries; it's a spiritual family. Whisky is our global success story and it's a credit to those working in the industry.'

When asked why Scotland is so great at making whisky, Jim answers without a second thought: 'I think whisky reflects our character perfectly: it's warm, comforting, genuine and sincere. It's as if whisky was bestowed upon us. We've cherished it and looked after it, treated it with respect. We've done that as a nation, and that's something to be proud of.'

Quick Facts about Scotch Whisky

Single malt is whisky that has been produced at a single distillery using only malted barley. Blended whisky combines various whiskies from different distilleries and can include grain whisky.

The five main whisky regions in Scotland are the Highlands, Lowlands, Islands, Speyside and Islay. They each have their own unique characteristics.

Whisky is matured in pre-used casks and the type of cask influences the colour and flavour. The most common casks are bourbon and sherry.

Islay is famous for its smoky whisky. This comes from the peat that is used to dry the barley.

23 From Sea to PLATE

SEAFOOD | CULTURE | LOCAL

Serving up some of the finest seafood in the world, Scotland's dazzling west-coast waters are much more than just a feast for the eyes. Follow the Seafood Trail through Argyll on a culinary quest, from bustling harbours and lesser-known islands to sprawling lochs and secluded spots, in search of fresh catch, seafood shacks and high-end hospitality.

How to

Getting around Road-trip the region or take public transport to locations served by bus (westcoastmotors.co.uk) or ScotRail between Glasgow and Oban.

When to go Fresh seafood is available year-round. Some restaurants and eateries close during low season: always best to check.

Top tip If you see squat lobster on the menu, go for it. Not actually lobster, this quirky crustacean is sweeter than prawns and is a lucky find for seafoodies.

Seafood shacks The rustic-green **Oban Seafood Hut** is a pier-side seafood institution. Budget-friendly seafood is dished out on paper plates, to the sound of seagulls and ferry engines; alternatively, take your prawn-packed sandwich to the peaceful surroundings of McCaig's Tower.

Huddled into a corner of the remote Kintyre Peninsula, with views across to Arran, the family-run **Skipness Seafood Cabin** is where fresh seafood platters are popularly paired with sunshine and a bottle of wine.

Lochside vistas Loch Fyne is famed for its rich bounty of high-quality oysters. Try them fresh, with grilled smoked cheddar, or in crispy panko breadcrumbs at **Loch Fyne Oyster Bar** near Inveraray.

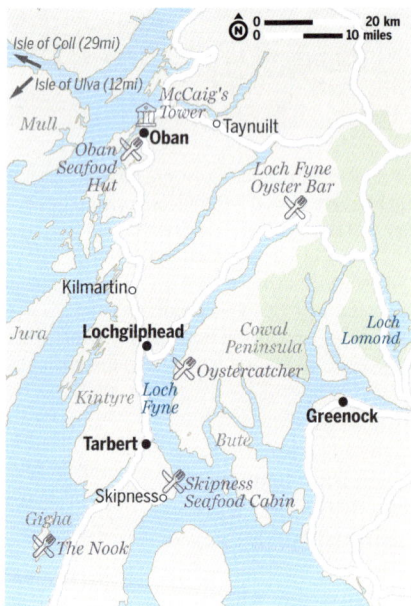

Above right Oysters
Right Oban Seafood Hut

Sustainable Shellfish

Seafood is a way of life in Argyll and sustainability is more important than ever. Most shellfish in Argyll are harvested by ethical and environmentally conscious methods, where all undersized and unwanted catch is returned to the sea alive.

Drew Stevenson, *local fisherman, Isle of Seil*

Still hungry? Head to **Oystercatcher** at Otter Ferry for award-winning, locally sourced seafood on the Cowal Peninsula. Oysters are a firm favourite, but so too are their mussels, scallops, daily specials and cosy bar.

Island eats Operate the low-tech, high-novelty system to summon the tiny ferry from Mull to Ulva for local shellfish at **The Boathouse**; fresh oysters with Guinness is a long-standing tradition. Cross to Coll to slurp on delicious homemade spaghetti with creamy lobster or chilli ginger garlic crab at **Coll Hotel** while overlooking Arinagour Bay and the small fishing boats that supplied the goods. Head to the Isle of Gigha, where **The Nook**, a tiny seafood hatch attached to the village shop, serves seafood street food, including their signature Nook Prawn Bap.

24 Secret Coast ROAD TRIP

SCENERY | PENINSULA | DRIVING

Cradled by the Kyles of Bute and Loch Fyne, Argyll's Secret Coast is just one part of the surprisingly overlooked Cowal Peninsula. Close to the central belt, yet far from the beaten track, these roads less travelled lead to magical woodland trails, hidden beaches, gastronomic gems, and all the wild charm and rich history of the Highlands, without the crowds.

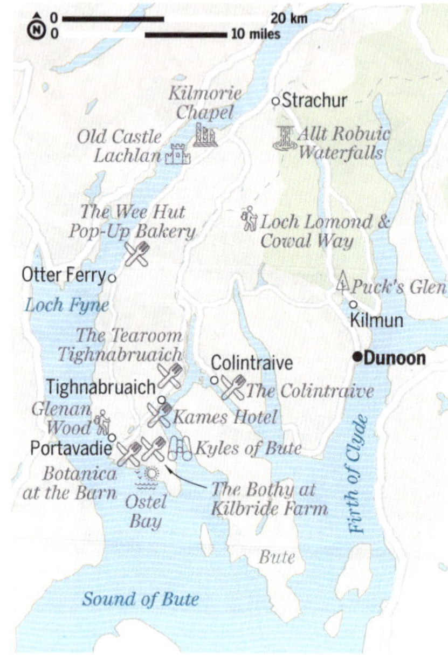

How to

Getting around Hire a car in Glasgow and take the scenic route (A83). Start in Strachur and explore the three-part peninsula.

When to visit Spring for bluebells; September for the Kyles 10 Miles road race; autumn for the beautiful colours.

Relax Finish with a soak in Scotland's largest outdoor heated infinity pool at the luxury Portavadie Spa overlooking Loch Fyne.

Scenic Stops

The enchanting, rocky gorge of **Puck's Glen** is characterised by vibrant moss, inward-slanting trees and crystal-clear pools fed by waterfalls. Tales of frolicking fairies become more believable with every step. Follow the lesser-known Waterfall Trail through Glenbranter to **Allt Robuic waterfalls**.

For jaw-dropping vistas of the undulating coastline, pull over at the **Kyles of Bute viewpoint** on the A8003 near Tighnabruaich.

Right Old Castle Lachlan

Ostel Bay is a stunning beach, arched by sand dunes at the end of a farm track. Across the sea, the shadowy layers of Arran's lofty peaks dominate the horizon.

Discover **Old Castle Lachlan** on Loch Fyne; a ruined fortress draped in ivy. Medieval **Kilmorie Chapel**, a short walk away, is where Maclachlan clan chiefs were laid to rest.

Take a break from driving and walk a section of the **Loch Lomond and Cowal Way.**

Local Eats

Fresh seafood and meat sourced from local farms are served with warm hospitality in the seaside **Kames Hotel** and the **Colintraive**, next to the ferry port for Bute.

Tearoom Tighnabruaich is famed for its mammoth slices of cake and perfect scones. For more home-baking, The **Wee Hut Pop-Up Bakery** at Evanachan Farm is a charming roadside discovery.

Try the haggis panini from the **Bothy at Kilbride Farm** and visit nearby **Botanica at the Barn** for the adventure picnic of dreams, featuring freshly baked breads, charcuterie boxes, foraged ingredients and a selection of deli goods.

The Deserted Village

Just shy of the modern marina at Portavadie, a rare patch of ancient oakland conceals the hidden remains of a village dating back to 1309. Glenan Wood is an atmospheric and evocative place, owned and protected by the local community. The woodland walk climbs through native forest on a muddy path to the abandoned village. Silence echoes around the lonely ruins, once inhabited for 600 years, and now consumed by nature; strapped into the land indefinitely, as a reminder of the village and its people. Return via the coastal path and savour the peace on the pebbly beach at Glenan Bay.

25 Enter the Ancient KINGDOM

RUINS | NATURE | WALKING

Mysterious standing stones, rock carvings, burial chambers and an ancient hillfort are scattered around Kilmartin Glen like prehistoric treasure. Follow the 7-mile Dalriada Heritage Trail on a journey through human history, spanning 5000 years in just one day.

BONOC/SHUTTERSTOCK ©

Trip Notes

Getting there Walk the full route or drive between several well-signposted car parks. West Coast Motors serves Kilmartin and the Crinan Canal on bus routes from Oban and Lochgilphead; both of which are served by train and bus from Glasgow.

When to go The area is crowd-free year-round. Come in late April or early May for bluebells, and autumn for golden light and landscapes.

Rock on Allow extra time to visit Achnabreck for incredible prehistoric stone carvings.

Britain's Most Beautiful Shortcut

Extend your adventure with a walk or cycle along the **Crinan Canal** from Ardrishaig to Crinan for 9 miles of glorious scenery. Look out for osprey, red squirrels, Highland cows and dolphins. Finish with a wander through **Crinan Wood** – a unique patch of temperate Scottish rainforest, bursting with rare plant life.

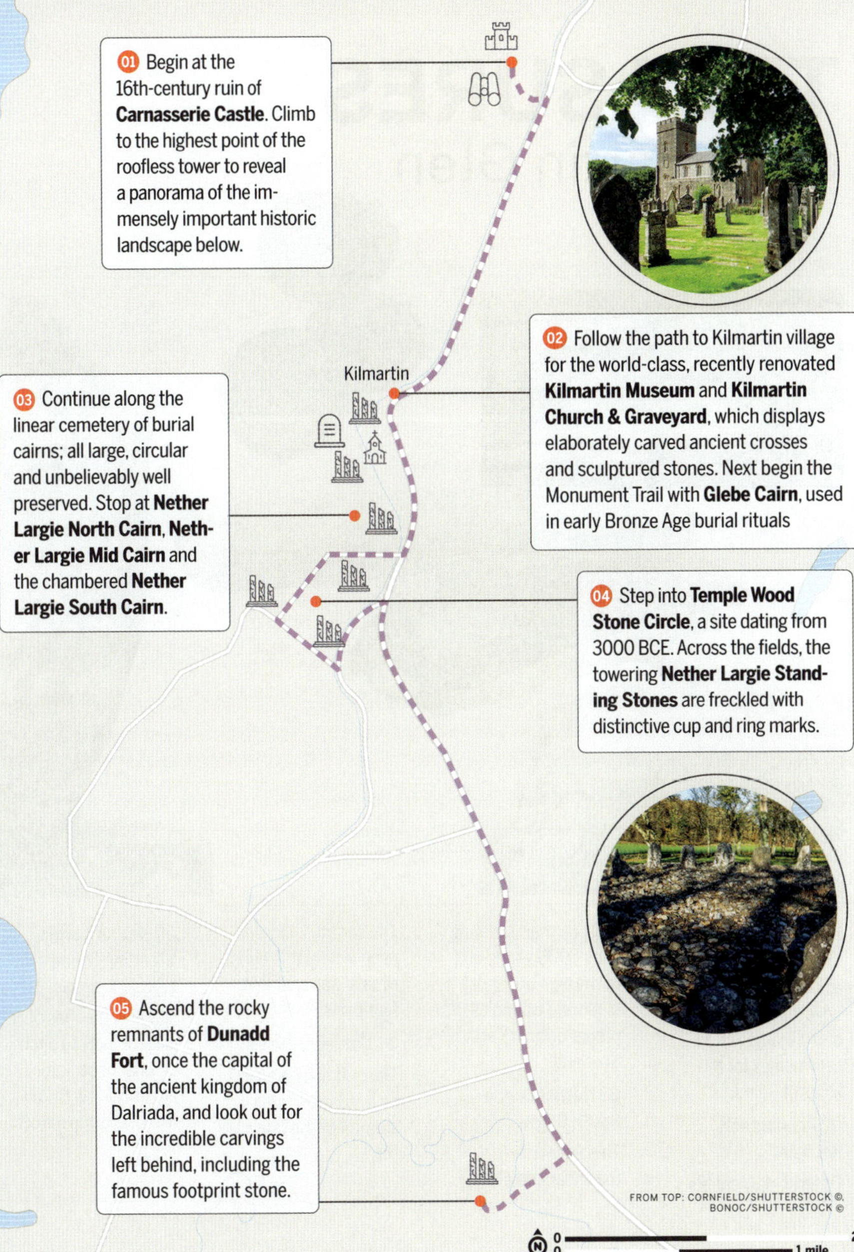

01 Begin at the 16th-century ruin of Carnasserie Castle. Climb to the highest point of the roofless tower to reveal a panorama of the immensely important historic landscape below.
02 Follow the path to Kilmartin village for the world-class, recently renovated Kilmartin Museum and Kilmartin Church & Graveyard, which displays elaborately carved ancient crosses and sculptured stones. Next begin the Monument Trail with Glebe Cairn, used in early Bronze Age burial rituals
Kilmartin
03 Continue along the linear cemetery of burial cairns; all large, circular and unbelievably well preserved. Stop at Nether Largie North Cairn, Nether Largie Mid Cairn and the chambered Nether Largie South Cairn.
04 Step into Temple Wood Stone Circle, a site dating from 3000 BCE. Across the fields, the towering Nether Largie Standing Stones are freckled with distinctive cup and ring marks.
05 Ascend the rocky remnants of Dunadd Fort, once the capital of the ancient kingdom of Dalriada, and look out for the incredible carvings left behind, including the famous footprint stone.
0
2 km
0
1 mile

FROM TOP: CORNFIELD/SHUTTERSTOCK ©, BONOC/SHUTTERSTOCK ©

TREASURES
of Kilmartin Glen

01 Footprint Stone

This carved footprint at Dunadd Fort is believed to form part of the inauguration ceremonies for the kings of Dalriada.

02 Achnabreck Rock Art

Otherworldly spirals and cup marks, dating back 5000 years; one of the best and most elaborate examples of prehistoric rock art in Scotland.

03 Nether Largie South Cairn

The oldest cairn in the linear cemetery. The central chamber, used in neolithic burial rituals, was split into four parts.

04 Carved Boar

The outline of a boar on a stone near the summit of the Dunadd Fort.

05 Nether Largie Standing Stones

The large stones, sparking theories of an ancient football pitch or lunar observatory, are freckled with 23 distinctive cup marks.

06 Poltalloch Enclosure (Kilmartin Churchyard)

A row of seven grave slabs for the Malcolm family of the Poltalloch Estate, dating from the 1300s to the 1600s.

07 Neil Campbell Tomb (Kilmartin Churchyard)

The lapidarium displays a collection of sculptured grave slabs from the 1200s to 1700s, featuring carved beasts, swords, crosses and warriors.

08 Kilmartin Cross

Kept inside the church to prevent weather damage, this incredibly detailed early Christian cross dates back to 900 CE.

09 Temple Wood Stone Circle

An artistic representation of a ritual or ceremony thought to have taken place within the stone circle.

Listings

BEST OF THE REST

Island Adventures

West Island Way

Rugged coastline gives way to a secluded bay, calm countryside and medieval chapel ruins on the 5-mile Kilchattan Bay Circular: a short and satisfying section of Bute's long-distance trail.

Discover Jura

Wild landscapes, 5000 deer, a whisky distillery, rum distillery and a gin distillery in a converted stable. Step off the ferry from Islay and straight onto this full island tour.

Kiloran Beach

A little slice of paradise on Colonsay. Cycle to the beach and hit the water on a SUP with Colonsay Bikes & Boards. Climb Carnan Eoin for the best views.

Kerrera Tea Garden £

Lunch and cake at a hidden island eatery. Five minutes on the passenger ferry from Gallanach, followed by a 2.2-mile trail of teapots and novelty signs leading to the tea garden.

Explore Lismore

Island sightseeing by Landrover with a Lismore local, including a picnic of delicious handmade treats from the Dutch Bakery.

Boats, Boards & Wildlife

Basking Shark Scotland

Mesmerising marine life encounter. Search for basking sharks and swim with them in the wild, guided by a marine biologist. Group day trips from Coll and private tours from Oban/Tobermory.

Tiree Sea Tours

Wildlife spotting and waves of excitement on a high-speed RIB ride around the waters of the Inner Hebrides. Marvel at Skerryvore Lighthouse towering above the sea on a rocky reef.

Mull Charters

Cruise the west coast of Mull for the chance to spot sea eagles swooping down to hunt fish on the surface of the water.

Seafari Adventures

Witness the famous Corryvreckan whirlpool in full spin on a tour from Easdale, or take a longer tour for whales and wildlife on the Gulf of Corryvreckan.

Castles

Castle Stalker

A picture-perfect medieval tower house, cast away from the shore on a petite tidal island in Loch Laich, near Oban. Stop at Castle Stalker View for coffee and photos.

Inveraray Castle

The ancestral home of the Dukes of Argyll, Chiefs of Clan Campbell, this fairytale castle, and *Downton Abbey* filming location, is immaculately presented with a grand interior waiting to be explored.

Inveraray Castle

Rothesay Castle
A strapping, 13th-century fortress in the middle of a Victorian seaside town on the Isle of Bute, complete with a moat and the only circular curtain wall in Scotland.

 Bars, Cafes & Cosy Pubs

Food from Argyll at the Pier £
The best comfort food in Oban. Friendly staff, a map on the wall showing where the ingredients are sourced, and the palpable buzz of preparing to board the ferry.

Reef Inn ££
Cold beers and cocktails with relaxed, straight-off-the-beach vibes in Tiree, 'Hawaii of the North'. Unwind in the casual bar and restaurant at this new luxury abode. Non-guests are always welcome.

Ben Cruachan Inn ££
Fireside drams and hearty meals at Loch Awe. Browse the extensive list of single malt whisky, craft beers and Scottish gin, and tuck into big portions of high-quality gastropub fare.

Brambles of Inveraray £
Fancy sandwiches, glorious cakes and freshly roasted coffee, produced by sister company Campbells of Inveraray. Enjoy outside in the charming Secret Garden, down the lane next to the cafe.

Puffer Bar & Restaurant ££
Fabulous fish and chips, local produce and home baking, on Easdale Island; reached by motor boat and home to the World Stone Skimming Championships. Tearoom by day, bar-restaurant by night.

The View
Party like a true Scot, overlooking the harbour in Oban. Live traditional music, Highland dancers, bagpipes and high-energy *ceilidh* dancing, guaranteed to lift your spirits and your heart rate.

Rothesay Castle

 Gifts, Crafts & Photography

Iona Craft Shop
Buy authentic Iona wool knitwear, gorgeous homewares or handmade jewellery with green Iona marble. The temptation to buy everything will hit you hard. Bike hire and takeaway coffee also available.

Ross of Coll
Colourful clothing and gifts featuring original, Isle of Coll–inspired designs, including the island's famously quirky Highland cow. Purchase from Ross and Chloe's family home in the village of Arinagour.

Whisky Island Gallery & Studio
Stunning, evocative images of Jura and beyond, available straight from the source, as prints, calendars, books and gifts. Whisky, wildlife and untamed landscapes, sublimely captured by award-winning photographer Konrad Borkowski.

CENTRAL
HIGHLANDS
ADVENTURE | OUTDOORS | WHISKY

▸ **Trip Builder** (p150)
▸ **Practicalities** (p152)
▸ **Monster Hunting** (p154)
▸ **On Screen: The Highlands on Film** (p156)
▸ **Up Ben Nevis** (p158)
▸ **Royal Road Trip** (p160)
▸ **Listings** (p162)

CENTRAL HIGHLANDS

Trip Builder

Central to the true Highlands' experience is getting outside, no matter the weather. Be it by boot, bike or boat, Scotland's wild heart is found off-road, in stag-filled forests, salmon-stocked rivers and monster-haunted lochs.

Cruise the **Caledonian Canal**, then stop at floating pubs and canal-side restaurants (p155)
2–3 days

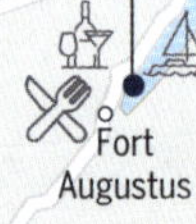

Huff and puff your way up Britain's highest mountain, **Ben Nevis** (p158)
1 day

Play spot the movie location on a cinematic trip around **Glencoe** (p156)
1 day

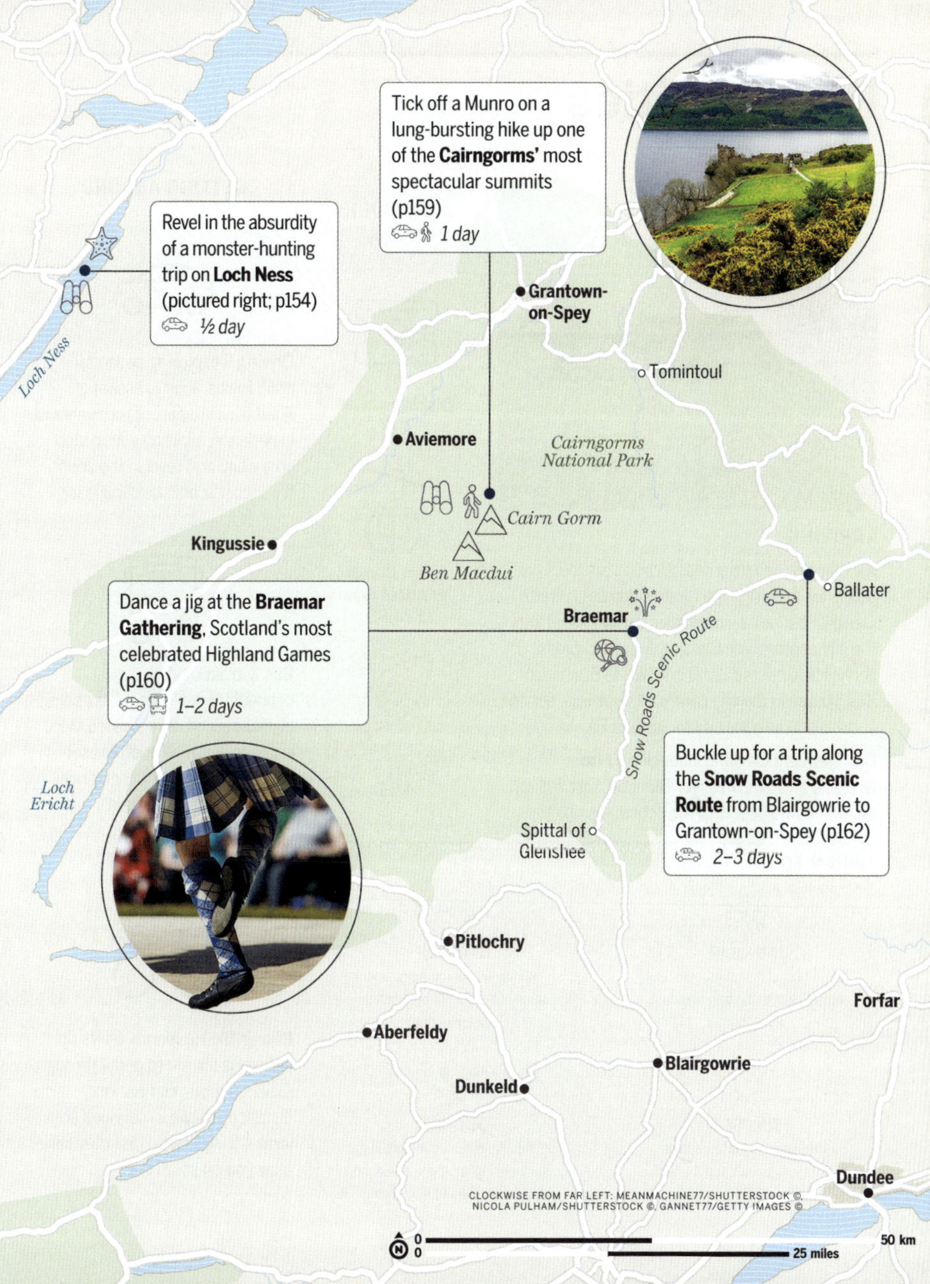
Tick off a Munro on a lung-bursting hike up one of the **Cairngorms'** most spectacular summits (p159)
1 day
Revel in the absurdity of a monster-hunting trip on **Loch Ness** (pictured right; p154)
½ day
Loch Ness
Grantown-on-Spey
Tomintoul
Aviemore
Cairngorms National Park
Cairn Gorm
Kingussie
Ben Macdui
Dance a jig at the **Braemar Gathering**, Scotland's most celebrated Highland Games (p160)
1–2 days
Braemar
Ballater
Snow Roads Scenic Route
Loch Ericht
Spittal of Glenshee
Buckle up for a trip along the **Snow Roads Scenic Route** from Blairgowrie to Grantown-on-Spey (p162)
2–3 days
Pitlochry
Forfar
Aberfeldy
Blairgowrie
Dunkeld
Dundee
0
0
50 km
25 miles

Practicalities

DANI BER/SHUTTERSTOCK ©

ARRIVING

Air Glasgow and Inverness Airports are ideal entry points for exploring the Central Highlands, with plenty of car rental companies to save travel into the city centres. The Glasgow Airport Express service 500 costs £10.50 one way to Buchanan Bus Station in the city centre. In Inverness, service 11 takes you into the city for around £5.

Bus Frequent Citylink buses depart from Glasgow and Inverness for Glencoe, Fort William, Aviemore and beyond. Find schedules online.

HOW MUCH FOR A

Distillery tour £19

Nevis Range gondola ride £24.90

Canoe hire £55

WHEN TO GO

JAN–MAR

Snow-fuzzed mountains, bracing winds, closed camping sites and few tourists.

APR–JUN

Spring brings snowmelt and some of Scotland's best midge-free weather.

JUL–SEP

The busiest time to visit the Central Highlands and the best all-round for weather.

OCT–DEC

From autumn leaves to the Northern Lights, the best season for nature without the crowds.

GETTING AROUND

Driving If exploring beyond the main towns, a car is essential. Road trips are part of the Highland experience, allowing you to stop on a whim and revel in the country's most scenic landscapes.

Bus & train Citylink buses connect the main towns, dropping passengers off at requested stops en route. ScotRail operates services throughout the Highlands: highlights include Britain's most remote station (Corrour) and the West Highland Line to Mallaig.

Biking The Highlands offers up gorgeous terrain to pedal through. Expect serious climbs, long distances between services and lorries travelling so fast they can blow you off your bike.

EATING & DRINKING

Whisky heaven The Central Highlands is awash with world-class single malt whisky. From the foot of Ben Nevis to Speyside to almost every glen in between, there's a sublime whisky experience waiting for you. The Glenlivet (p162), the country's first licensed distillery, or Royal Lochnagar (p161) are memorable starting points.

Pub grub Venison with a view, or salmon with a side of scenery, is the name of the game. The storied pubs in Glencoe and those scattered around the Cairngorms take top billing.

Must eat
A backpack picnic along West Highland Way (p163)

Best pub experience
Old Forge (p163)

WHERE TO STAY

The Central Highlands has a wide range of superb accommodation options to suit all budgets. Wild camping is allowed almost anywhere, but remember best practice: leave only footprints and take everything with you.

Town/Village	Pro/Con
Glencoe	Exceptional views are guaranteed, while adventures by boot, bike or boat are almost compulsory.
Fort William	The outdoors capital of the UK is cradled by epic mountains and sea lochs. Shame the accommodation doesn't match the setting.
Inverness	The de facto Highlands capital with the best selection of accommodation, from dingy hostels to fabulous five-star boltholes.
Aviemore	Postcard mountain town with enviable setting, souvenir shops and plenty of rustic forest lodges and campsites.
Braemar	The Cairngorms' poshest outpost, thanks to nearby Balmoral Castle.
Mallaig	Pretty harbour town with exquisite fish and chips and a ferry schedule for adventures to the Small Isles, Skye or Knoydart.

CONNECT & FIND YOUR WAY

Wi-fi Most hotels, bars, cafes and restaurants have guest wi-fi. Mobile phone signal can be hit or miss, so always tell someone your planned route before setting out on an adventure.

Navigation Buy an Ordnance Survey map if hiking, biking or planning any mountain or loch excursions; otherwise, use Google Maps.

FESTIVALS

Towns like Fort William and Aviemore see their population swell during events like the Mountain Bike World Cup and the Spirit of Speyside Whisky Festival. Book accommodation well in advance.

MONEY

Main attractions – those stunning mountains, sea lochs and heather-matted glens – are gloriously free, as is wild camping. Banks (and ATMs) are few and far between, so travel with enough cash just in case.

26 Monster HUNTING

HIKING | CYCLING | WATER ACTIVITIES

The scenery is spellbinding: rolling moorlands and pine-skirted mountains plunging into clear water where a mysterious and elusive monster hides in wait. This is Scotland's deepest and most famous loch, and whether or not you believe in Nessie – the long-necked cryptid that lurks in its depths – there are multiple ways to discover Loch Ness.

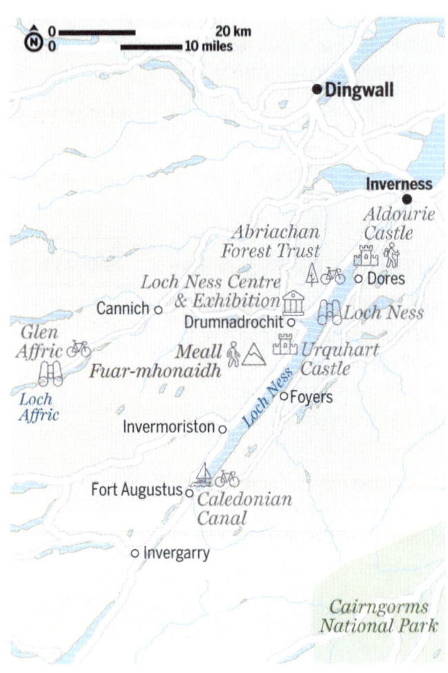

How to

Getting around The north shore of Loch Ness is home to the northernmost section of the Great Glen Way, while the opposite bank offers a mix of activity trails and a military road that make up the South Loch Ness Trail. Together they form the Loch Ness 360° Trail. To walk/cycle the 66-mile circuit takes six/three days.

When to go Year-round. Peak midge season is July and August.

More info The Loch Ness 360° website has interactive trail maps and itineraries.

Boot and backpack Hiking Loch Ness, through ancient Caledonian pine forests and along mighty rivers, offers the best of Scotland's wild terrain in microcosm. Scramble up **Meall Fuar-mhonaidh**, the lochside's highest hill at 699m, or tackle the corkscrew hike between Foyers and Dores. With a good selection of individual two- to three-hour walks, there are also plenty of options for those in a hurry: try the 4-mile **Aldourie Castle** circuit on the south bank.

Shift up a gear The Loch Ness circuit is for seasoned cyclists, but there is also plenty on offer for all ages

Above right Caledonian Canal
Right Urquhart Castle

BLO_FOTOSS/SHUTTERSTOCK ©

ALINUTE SILZEVICIUTE/SHUTTERSTOCK ©

From Loch to Lock

Fort Augustus, at the southern tip of Loch Ness, is the start of the historic, hand-dug **Caledonian Canal**, an early-19th-century waterway that cuts south for 60 miles to Corpach near Fort William. Find floating pubs and restaurants serving fresh shellfish and local single malts. Le Boat (leboat.co.uk) has a fleet of self-drive boats.

and abilities. **Abriachan Forest Trust**, 12 miles south of Inverness, has 9 miles of family-friendly loops and gnarly sections, while there are high and low roads to choose from between **Drumnadrochit** and **Fort Augustus**. Fancy a detour? Discover nearby **Glen Affric**, aka Scotland's most beautiful glen. Hire a mountain bike or hybrid at Ticket To Ride in Inverness.

Cruise power Waterfront Drumnadrochit is home to the kitsch **Loch Ness Centre & Exhibition**, and it is also the prime jumping-off point for hourly cruises to spy the world's most famous humpbacked creature. Out on the water, the gimmick is surpassed by views of crumbling **Urquhart Castle**, and there's plenty of fish in the water if you know what to look for. Two companies to sail with are Loch Ness Cruises and Loch Ness by Jacobite.

ON SCREEN
The Highlands on Film

01 02 04 05 03

01 Highlander (1986)
Christopher Lambert and Sean Connery hammed it up to the extreme when shooting in Glencoe and on the Silver Sands of Morar.

02 Skyfall (2012)
Rannoch Moor and Glen Etive saw Daniel Craig and Judi Dench escaping into the Highlands in 007's Aston Martin DB5.

03 Harry Potter (2001–11)
The Glenfinnan Viaduct was used to speed the Hogwarts Express throughout the wizarding saga, particularly in the Chamber of Secrets.

04 Braveheart (1995)
The Academy Award winner saw a face-painted Mel Gibson cavorting about in his kilt in Glencoe and Glen Nevis.

05 Monty Python and the Holy Grail (1975)
The film's notoriously silly Bridge of Death was shot near the Meeting of the Three Waters near Ballachulish.

06 No Time to Die (2021)

The latest James Bond film recasts the Cairngorms' Ardverikie Estate and Loch Laggan as the backdrop for a madcap 4x4 chase.

07 Mary Queen of Scots (2018)

The Cairngorms' Glen Feshie hosted Saoirse Ronan to film Mary's armies on the march.

08 The Queen (2006)

Glen Feshie Estate in the Cairngorms was used as a stand-in for the late Queen's real-life Balmoral retreat.

09 Rob Roy (1995)

Entirely shot in Scotland, Liam Neeson was in his element when filming around Loch Leven and at Achnacarry's Caig Falls Bridge.

10 Local Hero (1983)

As well as Burt Lancaster and former Doctor Who Peter Capaldi, Camusdarach beach near Morar was the star of this classic.

Up Ben NEVIS

HIKING | ADVENTURE | DAY TRIP

Chief among the landscapes to explore in the Central Highlands is Ben Nevis, Britain's highest mountain at 1345m. It towers above every glen, sea loch and mountain and can be tackled in a number of ways from the base-camp town of Fort William. Pack a backpack and spend a day scrambling up ridges – just be sure to treat it with the respect it deserves.

JOSEFKUBES/SHUTTERSTOCK ©

How to

Getting to the top There are two routes to the summit, both requiring a full day. Factor in covering a distance of 10 to 11 miles. Walk Highlands (walkhighlands.co.uk) has detailed A to B descriptions of both options.

When to go Snow-covered from November to April, the best season is from late May to early October. Crampons, ice axes and experience are a must for a winter ascent.

Festival The Fort William Mountain Festival celebrates mountain culture every February, with films and events.

JOHN A CAMERON/SHUTTERSTOCK ©

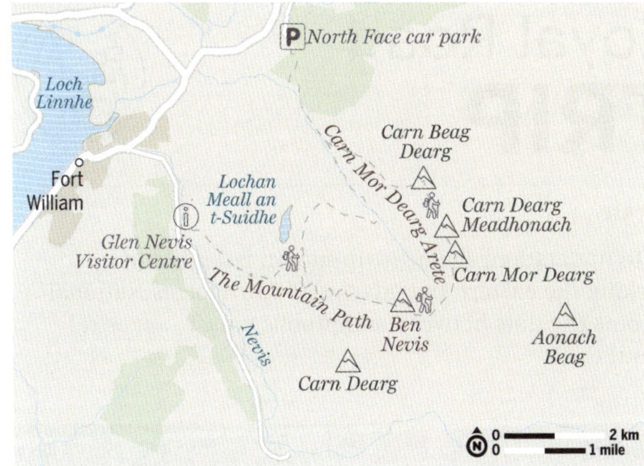

Top left Hikers scale Ben Nevis
Bottom left Highland cattle in Glen Nevis

Choose Your Route

The Mountain Path From the Glen Nevis Visitor Centre, the most straightforward ascent begins over the River Nevis bridge before heading up steep terrain with epic views of the Mamores. Further on, the path zigzags up a rocky, if well-worn, scree slope that saw a Ford Model T driven up it to the top in 1911. The summit, crowned by cairns and the ruins of a 19th-century weather station, can be reached in 3½ to 4½ hours. The route attracts around 130,000 hikers a year, so avoid weekends.

Carn Mor Dearg Arete Among Europe's finest mountain and ridge walks, experienced scramblers with a head for heights should consider this alternative. Do not attempt the ascent lightly – at 4½ to 5½ hours to the summit it is both longer and more strenuous, and involves traversing the jagged crest of Carn Mor Dearg and a last push up a steep slope of boulders. The rewards are plentiful: from the spectacular views of Ben Nevis' cliffs, buttresses and gullies to the rocky chutes on the West Face of adjacent Aonach Mor. Start at the North Face car park near Torlundy, don't forget a map and compass, and think twice about attempting the route in misty weather.

Peak Performance

Munro-bagging in the Central Highlands is an art form. Here are four other heartstring-tugging hikes.

Schiehallion, Pitlochry A broad ridge and storied summit with awe-inspiring views of Loch Rannoch (4–6hr/6 miles).

Aonach Eagach, Glencoe The narrowest ridge scramble in Britain connects Meall Dearg to Sgorr nam Fiannaidh. Not for the timid (7–9hr/6 miles).

Buachaille Etive Mòr, Glencoe The pin-up mountain's iconic rock face is as imposing as they come (7–8hr/8 miles).

Braeriach, Cairngorms Britain's third-highest summit (1296m) and one safeguarded from the crowds because of the long approach or bike in (8–10hr/16 miles).

28 Royal Road TRIP

HISTORY | WHISKY | ROAD TRIP

It doesn't take long to understand the heart-in-mouth potential of Scotland's royal route. Tracking the eastern boundaries of Cairngorms National Park, it is a road trip that joins the dots between sumptuous palace, ancestral clan homes and off-grid distilleries.

Highland Fling!

September only means one thing in Braemar: caber tossing, tug of war and highland dancing at the **Braemar Gathering**, the annual royal Highland Games. Despite the skirling and whirling, it's a sophisticated affair, attended by the royals since first enjoyed by Queen Victoria in 1848. Buy tickets in advance.

Trip Notes

Getting around This 125-mile route is best discovered over three to four days. While it can be cycled, it traverses Britain's highest public road, with the roller-coaster section between Blairgowrie and Braemar offering only essential services. Expect single-track roads, tight bends and wayward sheep.

When to go Year-round. September's Braemar Gathering draws the largest crowds.

Top tip Owned by Swiss art dealers Manuela and Iwan Wirth, the Fife Arms in Braemar brims with decadent suites, a restaurant, pub and cocktail bar themed around royal history.

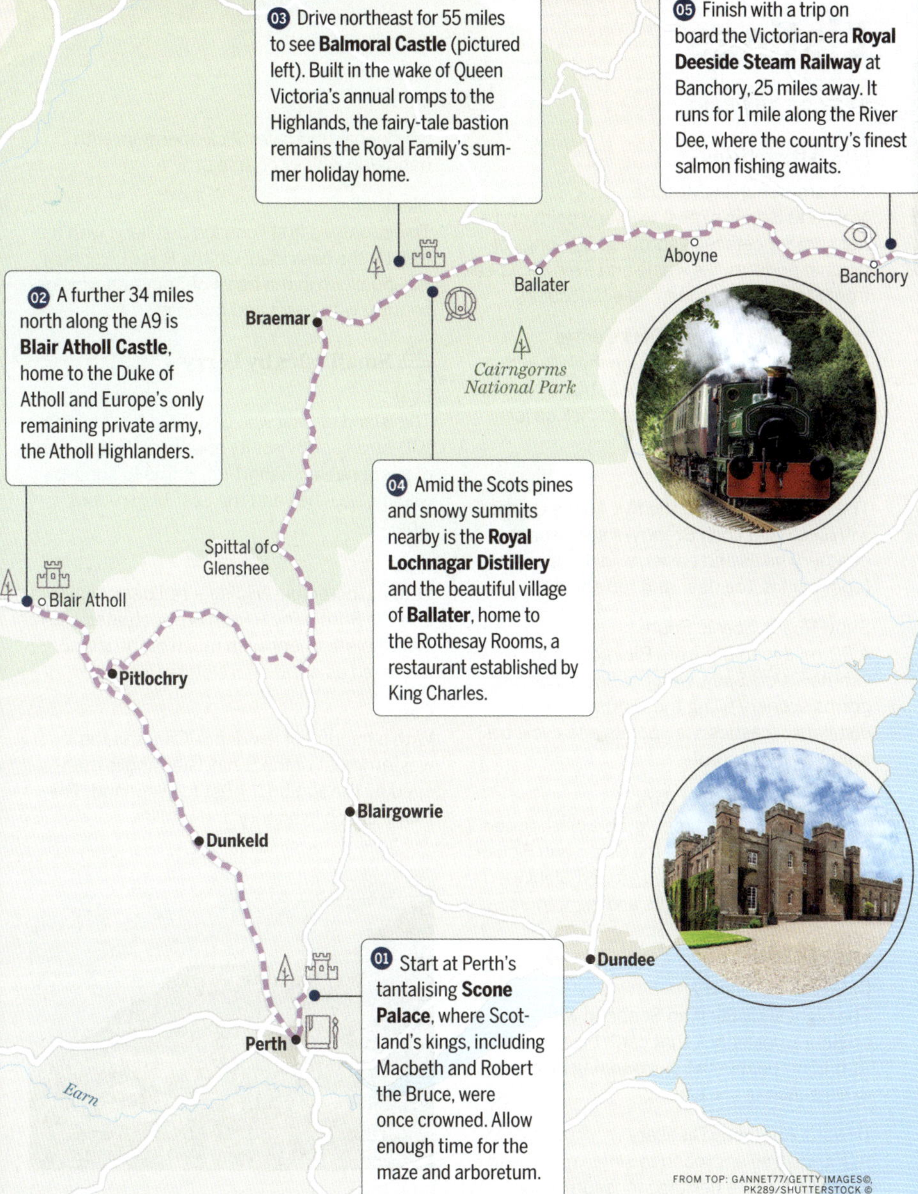

01 Start at Perth's tantalising **Scone Palace**, where Scotland's kings, including Macbeth and Robert the Bruce, were once crowned. Allow enough time for the maze and arboretum.

02 A further 34 miles north along the A9 is **Blair Atholl Castle**, home to the Duke of Atholl and Europe's only remaining private army, the Atholl Highlanders.

03 Drive northeast for 55 miles to see **Balmoral Castle** (pictured left). Built in the wake of Queen Victoria's annual romps to the Highlands, the fairy-tale bastion remains the Royal Family's summer holiday home.

04 Amid the Scots pines and snowy summits nearby is the **Royal Lochnagar Distillery** and the beautiful village of **Ballater**, home to the Rothesay Rooms, a restaurant established by King Charles.

05 Finish with a trip on board the Victorian-era **Royal Deeside Steam Railway** at Banchory, 25 miles away. It runs for 1 mile along the River Dee, where the country's finest salmon fishing awaits.

FROM TOP: GANNET77/GETTY IMAGES©, PK289/SHUTTERSTOCK ©

Listings

BEST OF THE REST

Attractions

Ardnamurchan Lighthouse
Mainland Britain's most westerly point and a hot spot for cetacean spotting. Sightings of dolphin pods, minke whale and even orca peak from May to September. Take binoculars.

Highland Safaris & Red Deer Centre
Take a Landrover tour through the hills with a safari ranger or a Loch Tay boat trip, or visit the Red Deer Centre, hire bikes and pick up local walking trails.

Glen Clova
The most beautiful of the five Angus Glens, with secluded Loch Brandy, a spectrum of heathery hikes and easier, wildlife-filled walks (spot eagles, roe deer and red squirrel).

Snow Roads Scenic Route
A 90-mile road trip from Blairgowrie to Grantown-on-Spey, with the finest Cairngorms scenery filling the windscreen and distilleries, castles, viewpoints and cycle trails found along the route.

Cairngorms Dark Sky Park
The Highlands' most memorable place to see the Northern Lights and the Gaelic and Pictish rulers of the stars. Located around Glenlivet and Tomintoul, with events and night tours.

Distilleries

Dalwhinnie Distillery
The highest distillery in Scotland with an original smokestack that can't be missed. Abundant peat in the surrounding bogs adds extra punch to the whisky.

Dewar's Aberfeldy Distillery
A 360-degree approach to single malts, with tours, tastings, a heritage museum, shop, whisky bar and cafe. Slick operation with hands-on whisky courses.

Glenlivet
The country's first licensed distillery, with history by the cask load. On the River Livet near Ballindalloch in the heart of Speyside whisky country with tours and tastings.

Small Isles by Ferry

Eigg
The island of Eigg was bought in 1997 by the 100-strong community and turned into a sort of sustainable Shangri-La. Home to superb wildlife, beaches and the Lost Map record label.

Rum
With its incredible wildlife – red deer, eagles and the Rum pony – Rum is punctuated with incredible scenery, with much of the island managed as a National Nature Reserve.

Canna
With a handful of residents, Canna is the westernmost of the Small Isles and is managed by the National Trust for Scotland. The island is rich in history and wildlife.

Glen Clova

 Brews & Views

Kenmore Hotel £
Scotland's oldest inn, dating back to 1572, with views courtesy of the River Tay. Look for a poem scrawled on the Poet's Bar chimney written by Robert Burns.

Clachaig Inn £
Storied Glencoe pub with three bars, including the outdoorsy Boots Bar, home to 400-odd whiskies, 130 Scottish gins, live music, barrel seating and a dusty fire.

Old Forge £
Mainland Britain's remotest pub in Knoydart. Reached by ferry from Mallaig, or 18-mile walk-in from Kinlochhourn. *Ceilidhs* and local ales, but also Trappist beers from the Belgian landlord.

Bike Glenlivet Cafe £
Enjoy a brew and the breakfast of champions before taking on one of the many mountain bike trails. With bike hire available, and trails for all abilities, this one is a must.

 By Boat

Knoydart
Known as Britain's last great wilderness, remote Knoydart can be accessed by foot, over hill and moor, or by ferry. Ferries are run by Western Isles Cruises several times a day from Mallaig.

Nova Spero
Once an entrenched fishing boat, now an overnight adventure cruiser with storm hatches, shipping bell and landing winch. Based out of Kinlochleven, with multi-day trips year-round.

Provident Sailing
Sail the west coast waters on *Provident,* a historic Brixham sailing trawler that has been modernised for comfortable island sailing, with trips from Oban to the Small Isles and beyond.

GWYNETH BELL/SHUTTERSTOCK ©

Isle of Rum, seen from the island of Eigg

 Great Outdoors

West Highland Way
Starting in Milngavie and winding 96 miles to Fort William through the Highlands' finest scenery. The ultimate day trip is the knee-crunching Devil's Staircase, from the Kingshouse to Kinlochleven.

Glencoe Mountain Resort
Scotland's first ski centre, with unrivalled snowsports in winter and daredevil mountain-biking trails in summer. Knockout views of Buachaille Etive Mor.

Mountain Bike World Cup
Fort William's steep slopes welcome the Mountain Bike World Cup every year – try the gnarly Witch's Trails at the Nevis Range to tackle gravity head-on.

Loch Morlich
Life-affirming loch cradled by Caledonian pine forest, with the Cairngorms' finest stand-up paddling, kayaking and canoeing from the shore. Spot osprey, red squirrel and capercaillie.

NORTHERN
HIGHLANDS
OUTDOORS | HISTORY | ADVENTURE

- **Trip Builder** (p166)
- **Practicalities** (p167)
- **Wonders of Wester Ross** (p168)
- **Cape Wrath** (p172)
- **On the Clearances Trail** (p174)
- **Gateway to the Highlands** (p176)
- **Highland Games** (p178)
- **Listings** (p180)

NORTHERN HIGHLANDS
Trip Builder

Big skies, dramatic coastlines and vast moorlands: this is the ultimate escape to the wilderness. There is so much space here that it is easy to find yourself alone on the shores of a loch or a pristine beach. And if you tire of your own company, there's the spectacle of the Highland Games.

Ride the scenic **Far North Line** from Inverness to Wick (p180)
1–2 days
Take a boat to the epic landscapes of **Cape Wrath** (p172)
1 day
Cape Wrath
Durness
Bettyhill
Tongue
Thurso
Wick
Forsinard
Latheron
The Minch
Learn about the Highland Clearances at the Timespan museum in **Helmsdale** (p175)
½ day
Enjoy mountain views and shop for local crafts in **Lochinver** (p180)
½ day
Lochinver
Loch Shin
Helmsdale
Lairg
Brora
Dornoch Firth
Visit **Culloden Battlefield** and learn about the Jacobite defeat on that fateful day (p177)
½ day
Twist and turn your way up the spectacular **Bealach na Bà** mountain road (p170)
1 day
Tain
Braemore
Moray Firth
Kinlochewe
Achnasheen
Dingwall
Nairn
Shieldaig
Applecross
Inverness
Culloden Battlefield
50 km
25 miles

Practicalities

ARRIVING

Inverness Airport Located 20 miles from Dingwall, the largest town in the south of the region.

Inverness train station Serves the Far North Line and the Kyle Line.

Inverness bus station Has connections including Dornoch and Ullapool.

CONNECT

Wi-fi in towns and villages is good, but away from settlements it is less reliable. Downloading maps or taking a paper map is recommended.

MONEY

Families can save on train travel with 'Kids for a Quid' – a £1 return ticket for children. See scotrail.co.uk.

WHERE TO STAY

Place	Pro/Con
Dornoch	Great variety of accommodation and dining, plus a beach and golf course.
Durness	Good base for Cape Wrath. Hostel, hotels, camping and B&B.
Ullapool	Accommodation to suit all budgets. Convenient for exploring the west coast.
Wick	Large choice of places to stay. Good base for Caithness day trips.

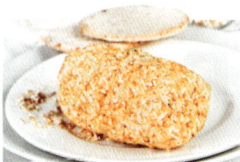

GETTING AROUND

Car Driving is the best way to explore the region's least populated areas.

Trains and buses Most towns and villages are served by trains and buses, but they can be infrequent.

Cycling A great way to discover quiet, single-track roads.

EATING & DRINKING

Crowdie cheese This creamy cheese is produced in Tain and goes great on an oatcake.

Smoked fish Fish prepared in traditional smokehouses has a distinctive taste from the wood smoke.

Highland gin distilleries Dunnet Bay and Badachro distilleries use local botanicals, such as gorse blossom and sea buckthorn.

Best hot chocolate
Cocoa Mountain (p181)

Must-try flatbread
Seafood Shack, Ullapool (p171)

MAR–MAY

Changeable weather, less busy. Spring flowers blossom.

JUN–AUG

Warmest weather; attractions can be busy.

SEP–NOV

Cooler temperatures. Less busy, trees change colour.

DEC–FEB

The coldest months. Some visitor facilities are closed.

29 Wonders of WESTER ROSS

ROAD TRIP | SCENERY | EXPLORING

To experience the beauty of the north, slow down for this stretch of the northwest, now-immortalised by the NC500. Enjoy glittering sea views, sunset beaches and soaring mountains as you weave your way south from Ullapool to Applecross.

JAROSLAV SEKERES/SHUTTERSTOCK ©

How to

Getting here and around This route is best travelled by car. If you are in a larger vehicle, note that the Bealach na Bà pass into Applecross is unsuitable – the coastal road enjoys sea views to Skye and the Outer Hebrides.

When to go Summer for seasonal opening hours and weather.

Top tip Slow down – this is a stretch of road that many people on the final stages of the NC500 rush, but is one of the most rewarding scenic drives in the country. Enjoy the views and explore the communities on the route.

MORENOO1/SHUTTERSTOCK ©

Landscapes to Inspire

Life's a beach This route has no shortage of showstopper beaches; try **Gruinard Beach**, **Mellon Udrigle Beach** or **Firemore Beach** and for that perfect sunset shot, head to **Gairloch Beach**. **Big Sand Beach** does what it says on the tin, and **Ullapool**'s tranquil shores frame one of Scotland's most picturesque towns.

Dizzying waterfalls South of Ullapool, the 46-metre **Falls of Measach** crash into **Corrieshalloch Gorge** in a spume of ice-cold water and spray, while a suspension bridge spans the gorge in a culmination of raw energy and spectacular views. **Victoria Falls** sits close to Loch Maree and is named after Queen Victoria, who visited in 1877.

D K GROVE/SHUTTERSTOCK ©

Destitution Road

The A832, linking Loch Ewe, Little Loch Broom and Loch Broom, is one of the country's most scenic road trips. Known as the Destitution Road, it was built by local labourers following the devastating potato famine that hit the highlands in the mid-19th century.

Top left Bealach na Bà pass
Bottom left Mellon Udrigle Beach
Above right Falls of Measach

A bird's eye view Enjoy incredible hikes, with fantastic routes from Ullapool into the surrounding hills, as well as some more challenging routes. Terraced sides, steep gullies and jagged summits characterise the dramatic and rugged peaks of **An Teallach**. The highest peaks are Bidean a' Ghlas Thuill (1062m/3484ft) and Sgùrr Fiona (1058m/3473ft). For a good all-rounder, **Beinn Eighe** is one of the most accessible of the Torridon peaks (1010m/3314ft). For those who want the views without the hike, drive over the famous and winding **Bealach na Bà** pass into Applecross (626m/2054ft).

Lochs Wester Ross has six main lochs – **Loch Carron**, **Torridon**, **Maree**, **Gairloch**, **Ewe** and **Broom** – which offer striking views, a smattering of islands and tranquil waters that sit beneath dizzying mountains.

Spotlight on Inverewe Garden

On the same latitude as Moscow but warmed by the Gulf Stream, **Inverewe Garden** were created by Osgood Mackenzie in 1862 and gifted to the National Trust for Scotland in 1952. Spanning 50 acres, they include over 2500 exotic plants and flowers and 2000 acres of conservation land.

At its heart is Inverewe House, now a captivating museum that plunges visitors into the mid-20th century. The gardens have a range of trails, red squirrels, otters, a heronry, golden eagles and white-tailed sea eagles.

Art exhibitions, nature-related family activities, a cafe, a visitor centre, and a shop complete the picture.

Douglas Gibson,
Visit Wester Ross
@visit westerross

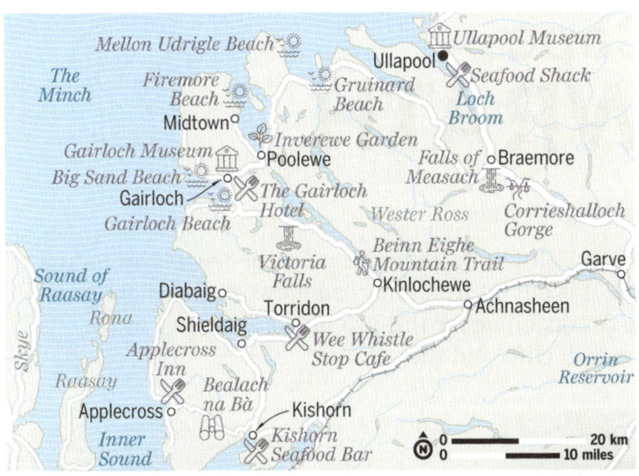

Left Beinn Eighe
Below Fish platters from the Seafood Shack

Heritage and Hospitality

Uncover the past This region oozes history. Get under the skin of the fishing communities with a trip to the **Ullapool Museum** or uncover the storied histories of the crofting communities that eked out a living in the area at the new **Gairloch Museum**. Ullapool Museum is housed within a former Thomas Telford–designed church, while Gairloch is housed in a converted Cold War facility. This region of contrasts is sure to ignite a flame of wonder.

Gastro highs Start the journey with a trip to the **Seafood Shack** in Ullapool – a local institution selling the freshest seafood – but get there early before queues form. To round off the journey, unlace your boots and prepare to cosy in for the evening at the **Applecross Inn**. Enjoy the laid-back atmosphere and perfectly presented pub grub as you swap stories with other travellers. Elsewhere along the route, enjoy a relaxed meal at the **Gairloch Hotel** with stunning views across the bay or pit-stop at the **Wee Whistle Stop Cafe** with views over Loch Torridon. Alternatively, head south to the **Kishorn Seafood Bar**, where fresh fish and shellfish are served from a little blue log cabin.

30 Cape WRATH

WILDERNESS | TOUR | ADVENTURE

The most northwesterly point of Scotland is one of the few places on the planet that feels untouched. It is cut off from the road network and there is no land between here and the Arctic. Come for the adventurous journey to the Cape Wrath lighthouse, the high cliffs and the wildlife.

WIRESTOCK, INC/ALAMY STOCK PHOTO ©

How to

Getting here and around You cannot drive on Cape Wrath. A ferry takes foot passengers from Keoldale Pier (2.5 miles from Durness) across to the cape, from where you can take the minibus onwards.

When to go The ferry operates April to October, but can sometimes be cancelled due to weather and tide conditions. Access is also dependent on the Ministry of Defence, which owns much of the land and uses it for military training exercises. See visitcapewrath.com.

Top tip Durness has plenty of accommodation options and acts as a good base if the ferry is cancelled.

MATHIAS PABST/SHUTTERSTOCK ©

Choose Your Cape Adventure

Ferry & bus Cape Wrath's road is cut off from the mainland by a stretch of water called the Kyle of Durness. **Britain's smallest ferry** crosses it in 10 minutes. A minibus meets the ferry and takes passengers on the 11-mile road to the **lighthouse**. It is a bumpy ride – the road was originally built in 1826 for horse traffic – but the entertaining drivers provide lots of insight about Cape Wrath. Before the return journey, passengers have some time to explore: walk away from the lighthouse to look out on the vast moorland and the highest cliffs in Britain, and stop in at one of the remotest cafes in Scotland, the Ozone.

By bicycle Cycling the road means you can join the **Cape Wrath Fellowship**. All you have to do is take a selfie with your bike in front of the lighthouse and send it to Cycling UK. Bikes must be carried on the ferry; there is no bike rental on Cape Wrath.

A night on the beach Hikers can head to **Kearvaig Bay**, a beautiful sandy beach with a white cottage to spend the night in. This is a bothy with no facilities and a similar experience to camping (see moutainbothies.org.uk). The minibus, by arrangement, can drop off and pick up hikers at the end of the road that leads to the bay.

Top left Kearvaig Bay
Bottom left Cape Wrath Lighthouse

Wildlife of Cape Wrath

Seeing the wildlife on Cape Wrath is a sensual and mental awakening. The remoteness, the high cliffs, the wind, the all-around light from an endless sky, the waves surging below and, of course, the sound of the seabirds and the spectacular plunging dives of many gannets.

Puffins, razorbills and guillemots fly to and from the cliffs in apparently endless succession, fulmars soar in the wind with ease and cackle endlessly from their nests. Further down the cliff face, kittiwakes gather together in separate nest colonies and below them shags dress their cluttered nests with seaweed.

Donald Mitchell, *High Life Highland Countryside Ranger*

31 On the Clearances TRAIL

ROAD TRIP | MONUMENTS | HISTORY

The human tragedy of the Highland Clearances – where thousands of families were displaced from their homes in the 18th and 19th centuries to make way for sheep farming – is brought into stark focus at several locations. Plan your Highland road trip around visits to these atmospheric and emotive places.

JOSE MIGUEL SANCHEZ/SHUTTERSTOCK ©

Trip Notes

Getting here and around Dunrobin Castle (pictured above), the first stop on this trail, is 54 miles from Inverness. Visiting all the locations requires over four hours of driving.

When to go June to August for the better weather, as the sites are mainly outdoors.

Top tip Timespan museum in Helmsdale is excellent for learning more about the Clearances. The cafe is also a great place to taste local – the herbs are from the garden, and the crab and salmon caught by local fishers.

Clearance Artefacts

A 'Sutherland Chair' can be seen in Timespan. It was handmade at the time of the Highland Clearances, deliberately designed to be close to the floor so that the sitter would be below the thick peat smoke rising from the fireplace in the thatched longhouse.

Jacquie Aitken, *Heritage Officer @Timespan*

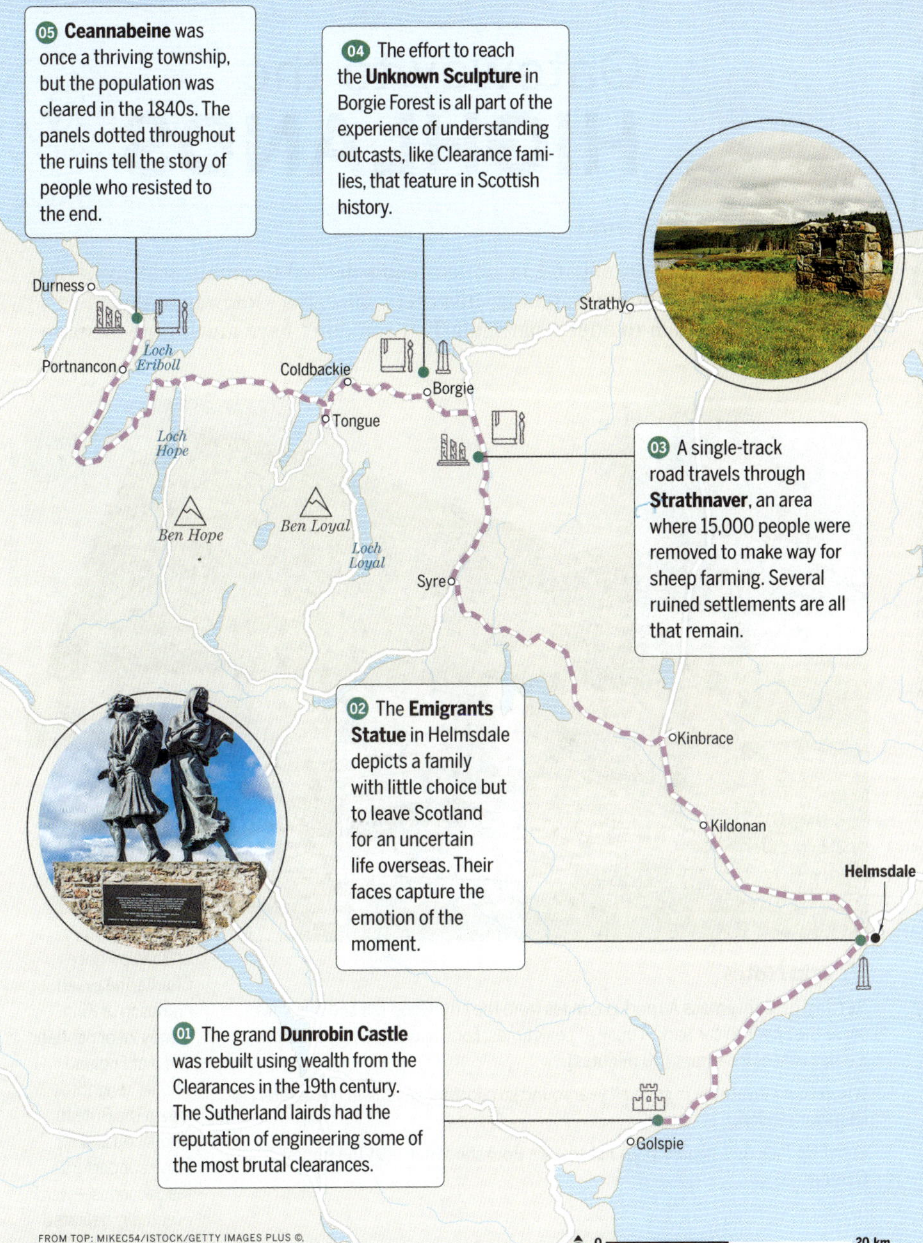

01 The grand **Dunrobin Castle** was rebuilt using wealth from the Clearances in the 19th century. The Sutherland lairds had the reputation of engineering some of the most brutal clearances.
02 The **Emigrants Statue** in Helmsdale depicts a family with little choice but to leave Scotland for an uncertain life overseas. Their faces capture the emotion of the moment.
03 A single-track road travels through **Strathnaver**, an area where 15,000 people were removed to make way for sheep farming. Several ruined settlements are all that remain.
04 The effort to reach the **Unknown Sculpture** in Borgie Forest is all part of the experience of understanding outcasts, like Clearance families, that feature in Scottish history.
05 **Ceannabeine** was once a thriving township, but the population was cleared in the 1840s. The panels dotted throughout the ruins tell the story of people who resisted to the end.
Durness
Portnancon
Loch Eriboll
Loch Hope
Ben Hope
Coldbackie
Tongue
Ben Loyal
Loch Loyal
Borgie
Strathy
Syre
Kinbrace
Kildonan
Helmsdale
Golspie
0 20 km
0 10 miles
N

FROM TOP: MIKEC54/ISTOCK/GETTY IMAGES PLUS ©, CLAUDINE VAN MASSENHOVE/SHUTTERSTOCK ©

32 Gateway to the HIGHLANDS

CYCLING | LOCHS | SOLITUDE

From political drama and Jacobite dreams dashed to prehistoric mysteries and showstopping wildlife-watching, Inverness-shire, the 'Gateway to the Highlands', has much to offer – particularly if you don't have much time to spare the region.

Trip Notes

Getting here Inverness Airport is 8 miles from the city. Good rail and bus links serve the city. The car park is busy at peak times. For Culloden, take the 27 bus 5 miles east of Inverness (30 minutes).

When to go Inverness is good all year round so consider visiting in the quieter shoulder season.

Local tip Pick up a history book in Leakey's Bookshop then visit the Botanic Gardens.

Bonnie Prince Charlie

Much of this region's history involves the captivating story of Bonnie Prince Charlie, the exiled grandson of King James VII of Scotland and II of England. Charlie sought to regain the British throne. He and his brave supporters – the Jacobites – were eventually defeated at Culloden in 1746.

01 Begin at the mouth of the Moray Firth with a visit to **Fort George**, one of Europe's mightiest forts, which was blown up by Bonnie Prince Charlie's supporters and cost over £1 billion in today's money to build!

Cromarty Firth

Black Isle

Moray Firth

Nairn

Nairn

HIGHLAND

Inverness

Ness

02 Step back in history as you explore the prehistoric mysteries of the **Clava Cairns**, an ancient cemetery set above the River Nairn.

03 Visit **Culloden Battlefield** (pictured left and right) where the last battle on British soil took place in 1746, ending Bonnie Prince Charlie's attempt to regain the throne. In an hour, 1600 Jacobites were killed or injured at this haunting site east of Inverness.

04 Orient yourself with a coffee and walk along the River Ness, which meanders through the city to **Inverness Castle**, where you will enjoy spectacular views across the Highland capital.

05 Round off your trip with a dolphin-spotting boat trip with **Dolphin Spirit** Inverness.

0 — 10 km
0 — 5 miles

Highland GAMES

01 Kilts

Game rules state that competitors in the heavy events must wear kilts. The colours and patterns on the kilt are specific to a clan.

02 Haggis Hurling

A novelty event where competitors stand on top of a whisky barrel and try to throw a haggis the furthest.

03 Highland Chieftain

An honorary role, usually undertaken by a local celebrity. They award prizes to the competitors and lead the opening and closing ceremonies.

04 Massed Pipes and Drums

One of the great spectacles of the games is the sight and sound of hundreds of bagpipers and drummers playing and marching.

05 Highland Fling

Said to be a warrior dance to celebrate victory in battle, or to mimic the antics of red deer.

06 Tossing the Caber

Athletes flip a log, called a caber. It can weigh up to 68kg. The

goal is to toss it as straight as possible.

07 Livestock Exhibitions

Displays of local breeds, like Highland Cattle, can often be seen at Highland Games.

08 Food and Craft Stalls

Highland Games are a great opportunity to try Scottish produce and street food, or buy from a local artist.

09 Tug o'War

Two teams pull against each other, with the aim of hauling the opposing team across the line. It involves lots of shouting from the team coaches.

10 Solo Piping Competitions

Musicians are judged on different styles of piping, including pibroch, which is slow and classical.

11 Hammer Throwing

Competitors whirl the hammer around their head as fast as they can and try to throw it the furthest. The hammer can weigh up to 10kg.

Listings

BEST OF THE REST

Whisky & West-coast Seafood

Balblair Distillery

This distillery, 6 miles from Tain, featured in the film *Angels' Share*. The tour ends with a dram of fruit and spice flavours.

Glenmorangie Distillery

Experience all stages of the whisky process with a tour of Glenmorangie's distillery and warehouses. Enjoy tasting some of the Highland's best-loved single malt whisky.

Shieldaig Bar & Coastal Kitchen ££

The rooftop terrace with loch views is the perfect place to enjoy a scrumptious seafood pizza made in a wood-fired oven. In Shieldaig.

Cliffs, Mountains & Caves

Lochinver

For superb mountain views, head to this town and the surrounding area. Lochinver is the starting point of the hike to Suilven, one of the most distinctive peaks in Scotland.

Duncansby Stacks

Surprisingly few people make the trip to view these spectacular sea stacks, home to vast seabird colonies. They are a 2-mile walk from John O'Groats.

Inchnadamph Bone Caves

These caves, found to contain remains of lynx, reindeer and polar bear, are a 3-mile walk. Park at the car park on the A837 between Elphin and Inchnadamph.

The Far North Line

If you're after stunning vistas and mesmerising wilderness, take the train from Inverness to Wick. Get off for a meal and a cold beer at Platform 1864.

Stac Pollaidh

Pronounced 'Stac Polly', the distinctive jagged peak 15 miles north of Ullapool makes for a fantastic hike or roadside photo.

Smoo Cave

Accessed by a long staircase to a 15m-high entrance. A covered boardwalk leads to a waterfall and there are tours to explore further. Located in Durness.

Music, Theatre & Highland Games

Ceilidh Place

Excellent program of Scottish folk music on West Argyll St in Ullapool. There is also a bookshop, art gallery, restaurant, bar and accommodation.

Dornoch Pipe Band

On Saturday evenings, May to September, the band parades in Dornoch's town square. Highland dancers perform to the music.

Lochinver

Lyth Arts Centre

The most northerly arts centre in mainland UK. The program has something for everyone: theatre, comedy, world music, dance and family events. A short drive from Wick.

Halkirk Highland Games

Kilted musclemen tossing cabers, pipe bands, dancers and much more. Held on the last Saturday of July, the Games at Halkirk can attract crowds of 5000.

Coast, Beaches & Gardens

North Coast 500

The 516-mile driving or cycling tour starts in Inverness and takes in the best of the region's coastal views.

Attadale Gardens

This subtropical, privately owned garden is open to the public who can enjoy 20-acres of serenity and a bite to eat at the Midge Bite!

Thurso-East

Surfers from around the world descend on Thurso in the winter to ride the waves. The pier at the harbour is a good place to view the action.

Sandwood Bay

One of the most beautiful and unspoilt beaches in the UK, with pink sands, dunes and cliffs. It's a 4-mile walk from the nearest car park at Blairmore.

North Coast Sea Tours

Boat tour to the 60m-tall Old Man of Stoer sea stack, then to the puffins and other seabirds of Handa Island. From Kylesku pier.

Made in the Highlands

Storehouse

A short drive from Dingwall, the Storehouse has a restaurant and farm shop selling fresh produce, local cheese and bread, plus a brilliant selection of gins, whiskies and craft beer.

Sandwood Bay

TOMMY LEE WALKER/SHUTTERSTOCK ©

Lochinver Craft Market

On selected Fridays stallholders set up in the village hall. Pottery, jewellery, clothing, art, food and more from local producers.

Alchemist Gallery

Located in a historic pharmacy building in Dingwall, this gallery has a great selection of work from local artists and designers, and hosts regular exhibitions.

Coffee, Cake & Treats

Cocoa Mountain £

Incredible hot chocolate adored by regulars, plus truffles with innovative flavours like whisky caramel cappuccino. Find cafes in Dornoch and Balnakeil Craft Village in Durness.

Secret Tea Garden £

Superb homemade scones and cakes in a gorgeous garden setting in Drumbeg.

Highland Farm Cafe £

A modern eco-building with splendid views over the Cromarty Firth. Lovely breakfasts and a great haggis burger. Around 3 miles from Dingwall.

SKYE & THE OUTER HEBRIDES

HISTORY | HIKING | BEACHES

- **Trip Builder** (p184)
- **Practicalities** (p186)
- **Hiking Trotternish** (p188)
- **Unwind in Uist** (p192)
- **Skye's Secret Sister** (p194)
- **St Kilda: Edge of the World** (p196)
- **Hebridean Island Hopper** (p198)
- **Road Trippin' Lewis & Harris** (p200)
- **Listings** (p202)

SKYE & THE OUTER HEBRIDES
Trip Builder

Adventure awaits off the west coast of Scotland. Skye's jaw-dropping landscapes, time-honoured castles and fine-dining options are popular tourist draws, while those seeking solitude – along with ancient standing stones and stunning sandy beaches – head for the Outer Hebrides.

See soaring sea cliffs and rare birdlife on remote **St Kilda** (p196)
1–2 days

Hop between gorgeous **South Harris beaches** like Luskentyre and Seilebost (p201)
1 day

Drive the winding **Golden Road** through a wild and beautiful landscape (p201)
½ day

Venture to uninhabited **Mingulay** for its seabirds, seascapes and abandoned village (p199)
1 day

Sandwood Bay
Durness
Bettyhill
Port of Ness
Tongue
Loch Hope
Loch Loyal
Laxford Bridge
Barvas
The Minch
Scourie
Syre
Isle of Lewis
Loch More
Stornoway
Kylesku
Altnaharra
Travel back 5000 years at the atmospheric **Calanais Standing Stones** (p200)
½ day
Clachtoll
Loch Assynt
Lochinver
Pick up some hand-woven Harris Tweed in the **Tarbert Tweed Shop** (p203)
½ day
Loch Shin
Knockan
Achiltibuie
Lairg
Invercassley
Shiant Islands
Ullapool
Bonar Bridge
Croick
Drumchork
Dundonnell
Melvaig
The Little Minch
Poolewe
Gairloch
Hike to the **Quiraing** through one of Scotland's most remarkable land-scapes (p189)
½ day
Uig
Loch Torridon
Rona
Torridon
Shieldaig
Brochel
Dunvegan
Inverness
Portree
Raasay
Drive **Calum's Road**, the fruit of one man's 10-year labour (p195)
½ day
Lochcarron
Skye
Inverarish
Sligachan
Sconser
Kyle of Lochalsh
Drumnadrochit
Loch Ness
Glenbrittle
Glenelg
Five Sisters of Kintail
Fort Augustus
Arnisdale
Canna
Stroll through the pretty seaside gardens surrounding **Armadale Castle** (p202)
½ day
Armadale
Rum
Mallaig
Loch Morar
Arisaig
Eigg
Muck

Practicalities

HENNER DAMKE/SHUTTERSTOCK ©

ARRIVING

Skye Easily reached by bridge from the mainland. Come by car, by train (to Kyle of Lochalsh followed by a local Stagecoach bus service) or by coach tour.

The Outer Hebrides Connected to the mainland, Skye and each other by regular car ferry services run by CalMac. Loganair operates flights to Lewis, Barra and Benbecula, with connections to Glasgow, Edinburgh and Inverness, and several inter-island flights.

HOW MUCH FOR A

Fish & chips £8

Distillery tour £22

Wildlife boat trip £50

WHEN TO GO

JAN–MAR

Expect chilly and wet conditions, with many attractions closed.

APR–JUN

Ideal time to travel, with mild weather and fewer crowds.

JUL–SEP

Bright but busy. Skye and Harris get very crowded; the Uists less so.

OCT–DEC

Wrap up warm against bracing conditions to enjoy sights all to yourself.

GETTING AROUND

Car The easiest and most convenient way to get around the islands is by car. This allows you to visit hard-to-reach spots and stop whenever you like to admire the frequently spectacular scenery. Rent a car on the mainland, in Tarbert (Skye) or in Stornoway (Lewis).

Bus Stagecoach runs regular bus services throughout Skye. A Skye DayRider ticket costs £9.20. In the Outer Hebrides, various local bus services run irregularly during the day, but rarely evenings or on Sunday.

Ferry CalMac ferries link Skye to the Outer Hebrides – and the Hebridean islands to each other. Prices range from £3.65 to £17.30 per person and £12.65 to £80.80 per car (one way).

EATING & DRINKING

Seafood No trip to Scotland's western isles is complete without tasting fresh, locally caught seafood. Try everything from salmon and scallops to langoustines and lobster.

Spirits From smooth, smoky Talisker whisky to citrusy yet sweet Harris Gin, spirit lovers will be in their element.

Sausages The country's most famous blood sausage comes from Lewis. You'll find Stornoway black pudding on menus across the region, usually as part of a full Scottish breakfast.

Best seafood
Three Chimneys (p189)

Must-try whisky
Isle of Raasay Single Malt (p194)

CONNECT

Wi-fi Wi-fi is widely available and generally reliable in hotels and restaurants throughout Skye. There's even free public wi-fi in the main town of Portree. In the Outer Hebrides, things get slower and patchier – and you can't rely on phone signal for data backup. It is worth downloading maps or carrying a paper copy.

WHERE TO STAY

Most people venture here to get closer to nature. But how close do you want to get? Choose between the comfort of a big town base and a back-to-basics rural stay.

Place	Pro/Con
Portree	Well connected with hotels, restaurants and shops. Gets very crowded in summer.
Sleat Peninsula	Skye's southern tip is green and serene, but a long drive from most of the major attractions.
Stornoway	The Outer Hebrides' main town is a convenient, comfy base, yet lacks the away-from-it-all feel.
West Coast of Harris	Stay In a B&B overlooking the spectacular sandy shoreline. Downside: hard to reach with no car.
Castlebay	From budget backpackers to hotels and B&Bs, Barra has many options, making it a great base

PREPARE FOR RAIN

It doesn't matter when you're visiting: there is always the chance of rain (and usually with very little warning). Always carry a raincoat.

MONEY

Cards are widely accepted, but carry cash to use in small businesses like cafes, independent museums and honesty boxes.

33 Hiking TROTTERNISH

HIKING | VIEWS | DAY TRIP

Strap on your hiking boots for a day in the glorious landscapes of Skye's Trotternish peninsula. Start with the spectacular and strenuous Quiraing hike, tackle the short but steep Old Man of Storr, then warm down with the easy-going Scorrybreac circuit.

WAYLEEBIRD/SHUTTERSTOCK ©

How to

Getting here Trotternish is the northernmost peninsula of Skye. The hike starting points are easiest to reach by car (drive north on the A855 from Portree), though the infrequent 57A bus will get you close.

When to go Summer is the best time for hiking. Even then, the weather can turn in an instant, so dress appropriately.

Top tip End your day with a slap-up meal overlooking Loch Dunvegan at the superb **Three Chimneys**. Book well in advance.

FRANCESCO BONINO/SHUTTERSTOCK ©

KACA SKOKANOVA/SHUTTERSTOCK ©

The Quiraing

This epic collection of craggy cliffs, rocky stacks and grassy plateaus is one of Skye's most distinctive landscapes – and one of its most popular hikes. This challenging 4-mile, two-hour loop gets busy in summer, so start as early as possible to avoid crowds and ensure a parking spot; it's particularly spectacular at sunrise. Follow signs off the A855 at Brogaig and drive for around 2 miles to reach the Quiraing car park.

The Prison

From opposite the car park, the hiking trail immediately leads up to a distant, jagged rock formation known as the Prison. The name comes from its resemblance to a fortress, which becomes clearer as you continue along

Rock & Fall

For a spectacular view without the climb, stop at the **Kilt Rock** viewpoint between the Old Man of Storr and the Quiraing. This 90m-high cliff face is made up of basalt columns that resemble the pleats of a kilt. Nearby, **Mealt Falls** elegantly plummets into the foaming ocean.

Top left The Quiraing
Top right Hiking to the Old Man of Storr (p191)
Left The Prison

the path, crossing a small stream and climbing a scree slope beside the structure.

The Needle

Continue beyond the Prison and you will come to a series of column-like rock formations, including the wizened and jagged Needle. Beyond this point, the cliff-hugging path winds down into a shallow valley, then instantly climbs back up again. Luckily, the views get better and better with each step.

The Table

As you reach the 540m summit, the view expands into a full panorama. On a clear day, you can see beyond the islands of Raasay and Rona to the mainland. More immediately, you can look down at the Table, a flat glassy plateau that was allegedly used for centuries by locals to hide sheep and cattle from invaders. When you are done, a steep and often muddy path leads back to the car park.

A Different Way Back

Head down Trotternish's attraction-packed west coast for an alternative route back to Portree.

Skye Museum of Island Life A preserved village of thatched cottages offers insight into crofting life.

Grave of Flora MacDonald Nearby is the grave of Flora MacDonald, who helped Bonnie Prince Charlie escape capture.

Fairy Glen An enchantingly strange landscape of rolling green hillocks, *lochans* (ponds) and rock formations just east from the town of Uig.

Galley Cafe Grab a takeaway snack and drive down to the charming ruins of Caisteal Uisdean for a lochside picnic.

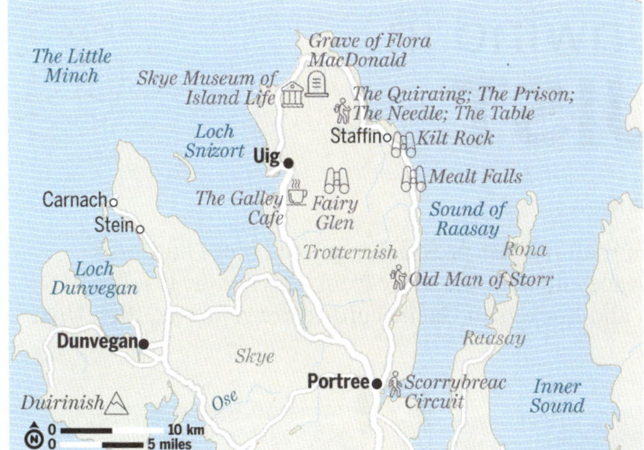

Left Modern stone circle at Fairy Glen
Below Skye Museum of Island Life

The Old Man of Storr

Another popular Trotternish hike leads to the Old Man of Storr, a 50m-high shard of rock said to be the thumb of a local giant buried in the landscape. A clear gravel path curves up the hill from a car park beside Loch Leathan, just off the A855, although the path soon turns to well-worn rock and dirt. It gets steeper, rougher and muddier as it snakes up to the top, but within just 45 minutes you will be standing at the foot of the Old Man and surveying the landscape below. Head back down the same way you came (30 minutes).

The Scorrybreac Circuit

This gentle, 45-minute shoreside loop is a fine way to round off an active day. Start at the small car park behind the Cuillin Hills Hotel. Signs will lead you past the boathouse and up the hill to the Nicolson Memorial, commemorating one of Scotland's oldest Celtic clans. A nearby viewpoint offers a lovely prospect of Portree Bay. Continue to the tidal Black Rock, a popular sunbathing spot for seabirds, and along the narrowing coastal path past a series of salmon farms. Soon enough, the path climbs inland and winds its way back to Portree.

34 Unwind in UIST

GAELIC | WHISKY | ROAD TRIP

Slow down and soak it all in. Uist provides a quieter, more laid-back option for those seeking peace and solitude away from the crowds. If miles of sandy, windswept beaches and buckets of Gaelic culture are your bag, then Uist is for you.

Trip Notes

Getting here Uist is easily accessed by CalMac Ferries from Harris to the North; Skye and Mallaig to the east; and Barra and Oban to the south and southeast. For up to date timetables and fares, check www.calmac.co.uk

When to go Summer is the best time for fair weather, but be aware that midges are at their worst in August.

Island hopper This experience takes in the inhabited islands of Berneray, North Uist, Grimsay, Benbecula, South Uist and Eriskay.

The Home of Gaelic

Gaelic remains the first language of the Outer Hebrides, and you'll hear its distinct and lyrical voice spoken in shops and cafes and written on road signs. Community spirit rings true in Uist, and visitors can join in with regular summer *cèilidhs*.

0
0
20 km
10 miles
Boreray
Berneray
Vallay
North Uist
Ceann a'Bhaigh
Lochmaddy
Clachan na Luib
Baleshare
Monach Islands
ATLANTIC OCEAN
Grimsay
The Little Minch
Benbecula
Wiay
Loch Bi
Geirninis
Loch Druidibeag
Howmore
South Uist
Loch Aineort
Milton
Dalinburgh
Lochboisdale
Polochar
Fuday
Fiaraidh
Fuday
Eriskay
Sea of the Hebrides
Barra
•Welcome to Taigh-tasgaidh Chill Donnain•
·taigh·tasgaidh· | Museum·

02 Head to Lochmaddy (pictured right) in North Uist, crossing Grimsay and Benbecula's causeways, and delve into the cultural highlights at **Taigh Chearsabhagh Museum and Arts Centre**.

03 Trace the footsteps of the young Jacobite through South Uist on the **Bonnie Prince Charlie Trail**. The Young Pretender went into hiding in Uist following the fateful Battle of Culloden.

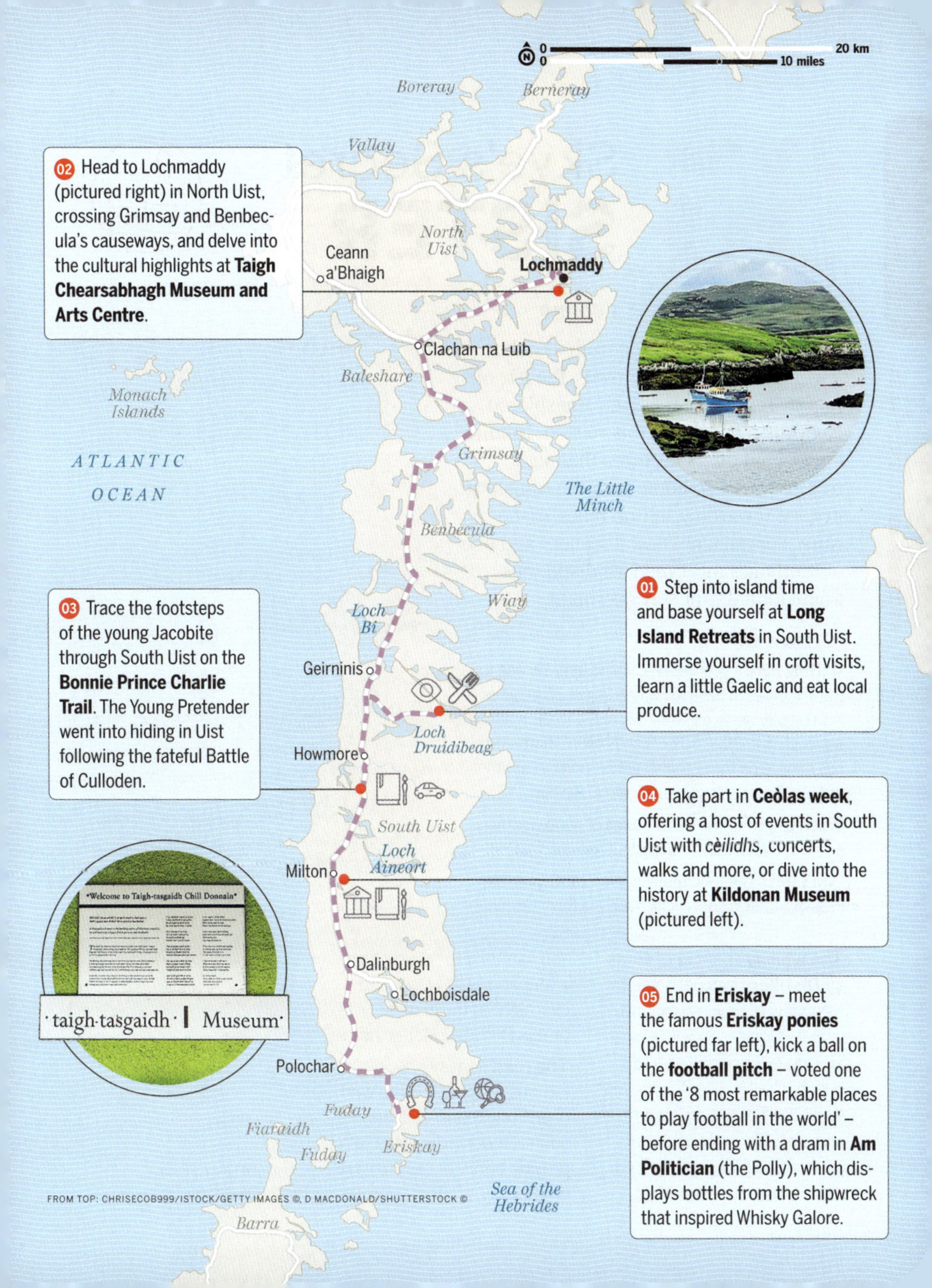

01 Step into island time and base yourself at **Long Island Retreats** in South Uist. Immerse yourself in croft visits, learn a little Gaelic and eat local produce.

04 Take part in **Ceòlas week**, offering a host of events in South Uist with *cèilidhs*, concerts, walks and more, or dive into the history at **Kildonan Museum** (pictured left).

05 End in **Eriskay** – meet the famous **Eriskay ponies** (pictured far left), kick a ball on the **football pitch** – voted one of the '8 most remarkable places to play football in the world' – before ending with a dram in **Am Politician** (the Polly), which displays bottles from the shipwreck that inspired Whisky Galore.

FROM TOP: CHRISECOB999/ISTOCK/GETTY IMAGES ©, D MACDONALD/SHUTTERSTOCK ©

35 Skye's Secret SISTER

CROWD-FREE | WHISKY | HIKING

A quick ferry ride from Skye but a world away from its crowds, the Isle of Raasay remains a relatively unexplored Hebridean jewel. But this rugged, 10-mile-long island offers far more than just respite – it's also home to fascinating local history, rewarding hilltop hikes, castle ruins, spectacular coastal scenery and one of Scotland's most modern distilleries. Come for a day or stay overnight.

How to

Getting here A year-round CalMac ferry service runs from Sconser in Skye to Raasay in just 25 minutes, with regular services every day of the week. A return trip costs £15.30/4.60 per car/person. There's no bus service on the island so get around by car or bicycle; Raasay House Hotel offers bike hire.

When to go For the best chance of good weather, come between May and September.

Don't miss The beautifully carved 1300-year-old Pictish Stone, a short walk from the ferry terminal.

The whisky The **Isle of Raasay Distillery** has perhaps the best view of any in Scotland, with its glass-covered facade looking out across to Skye's craggy Cuillin Hills. As the first legal distillery on an island once infamous for its illegal production, Raasay released its first single malt in 2021. You can try it for yourself on a tour and tasting, and stay overnight at the distillery's luxurious Borodale House hotel.

The road Raasay's most famous attraction is the work of just one man. After the council repeatedly failed to provide better access to northern Raasay, crofter Calum

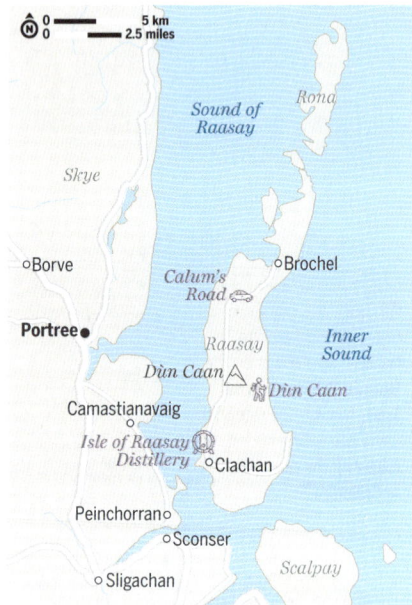

Top right Calum's Road
Right Isle of Raasay Distillery

SCOTT CH/SHUTTERSTOCK ©

ANA IACOB PHOTOGRAPHY/SHUTTERSTOCK ©

Skye in Miniature

The Isle of Raasay is a well-kept secret. We have all the great things that Skye is famous for: whisky, walks, fantastic food, beautiful beaches, breathtaking views and outdoor activities... But we have it all on this much smaller island, which makes it far easier to fit in everything you would like to do. I suppose you could say that Raasay is Skye's fun little sister.

Carol Anderson, *Raasay Tourism Group*

MacLeod decided to take matters into his own hands. Over the next 10 years, using only a pickaxe and a shovel, he converted a narrow footpath into a usable, 1.75-mile-long road. Half a century on, **Calum's Road** remains as a lovely scenic drive, starting just beyond the brooding Brochel Castle.

The hill The island's highest peak is the flat-topped **Dùn Caan**, which can be reached with a three-hour, round-trip hike from the ferry terminal. The path winds through historic mining villages, pine forests and loch-dotted moors before zigzagging up to the 443m-high summit. The final stretch is steep and rocky, but the panoramic views from the top provide ample reward.

36 St Kilda: Edge of THE WORLD

ISLAND | BIRDLIFE | DAY TRIP

The tiny archipelago of St Kilda, situated around 100 miles west of the Scottish mainland, is the most remote corner of the British Isles. It is also one of the most beautiful, thanks to its soaring sea stacks, abundant birdlife and fascinating island history. But absolute isolation doesn't come easy: you'll need money, time and a strong stomach to get here.

How to

Getting here Kilda Cruises and Sea Harris boats depart from Leverburgh in Harris (shortest journey). Alternatively, trips depart from Skye, Uist and Barra (longer journeys).

When to go Trips are scheduled most days between late April and September. Even in summer, inclement weather can frequently force last-minute cancellations; keep an extra day spare as backup.

How much Tours cost around £260 per person. Most trips will offer a two-day 'weather window' to allow better chances to get in.

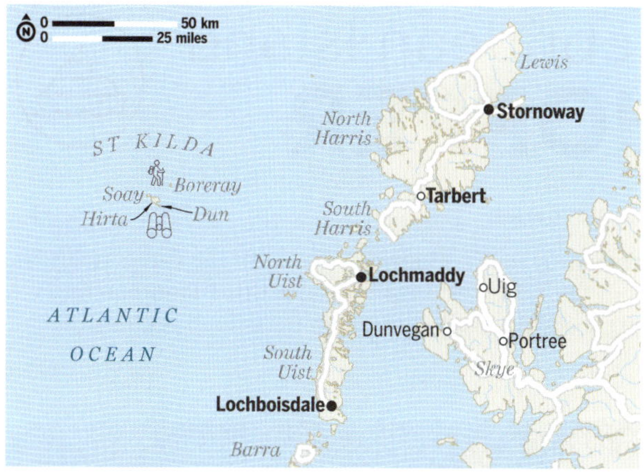

Weather-beaten The three-hour boat trip to **Hirta**, the main island in this wild Atlantic archipelago, can be a rough crossing. This 'edge of the world' place has a wild and foreboding presence as it looms from the western horizon, echoing noisily with the sound of hundreds of thousands of seabirds.

The death of St Kilda Despite its isolation, St Kilda was inhabited for 2000 years until the evacuation of the 36 remaining islanders in 1930. The gradual and steady loss of their subsistence way of life, based on harvesting and eating seabirds, made life untenable. The march of modernity had crept up on the residents of **Village Bay** and carried the people with it on a tide of change. Today, their lives can be discovered in the empty hearths and small **museum** that tell their story.

Dual World Heritage Status Without a doubt, Hirta's biggest draw is its unspoilt nature. Hike to **Ruival** or climb **Conachair's** steep face, littered with stone-built **cleits** and grazed by rare **Soay sheep**. Stand on the UK's tallest sea cliffs and gaze at the islands of **Soay**, **Boreray** and **Dun**. Offshore stacks complete the jigsaw; the most notable – and essential to the St Kildans – are the towering columns of **Stac Lee** and **Stac an Armin**.

Seabird city Hirta's birds are a sight to behold. But save some camera memory for the return boat journey when you skirt close to St Kilda's colossal sea stacks, swarming with thousands of yellow-headed gannets and clouds of puffins.

Top left Stac Lee and Stac an Armin
Bottom left Soay sheep

Stay on St Kilda

If one day isn't enough, consider camping on Hirta. A small **campsite** managed by the National Trust for Scotland offers space for six people along with basic toilets, showers and drinking water. There is no guaranteed electricity supply, wi-fi or mobile-phone signal, and you'll need to bring your own camping stove and food; pack extra in case your departure is delayed. It costs £20 per person per night, and must be booked in advance. Check long-range weather forecasts before visiting as weather can close in quickly. Email stkilda info@nts.org.uk to book.

37 Hebridean Island HOPPER

BOAT TRIPS | WATER SPORTS | CYCLING

Opt for a slice of paradise at the southernmost point of the Outer Hebrides. Barra, known as the 'Jewel of the Hebrides', is the base for this island-hopping experience. Enjoy chattering seabird colonies, uninhabited islands, glittering beaches and oodles of culture.

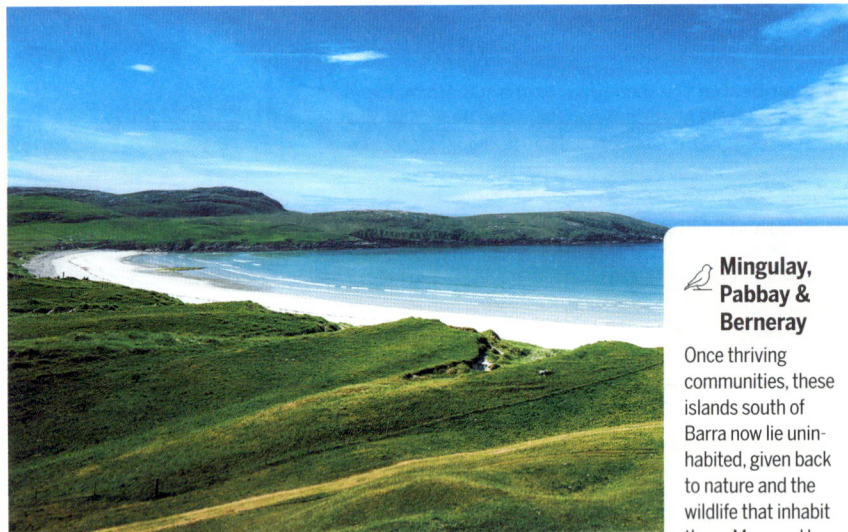

JUSTINE KIBLER/SHUTTERSTOCK ©

Trip Notes

Getting here and around CalMac Ferries sail daily from Oban and from neighbouring Eriskay several times a day. Hebridean Sea Tours operate boat trips (£65 per person) to Mingulay, Pabbay and St Kilda.

When to go Visit in May to August when boat trips are running and the seabirds are on the cliffs.

Top tip Slow down. Like a single malt, islands should be savoured slowly and enjoyed at a more leisurely pace. Soak up the sights and watch the sun set.

Mingulay, Pabbay & Berneray

Once thriving communities, these islands south of Barra now lie uninhabited, given back to nature and the wildlife that inhabit them. Managed by the National Trust for Scotland, expect soaring eagles, raucous seabird colonies, marine mammals and coastlines that will take your breath away with dizzying cliffs, stacks, arches and glistening turquoise bays.

0 5 km
0 2.5 miles
01 Plane spotting on Traigh Mhòr, where the beach acts as a runway for the world's only scheduled beach landing. Enjoy breathtaking beach views while you wait for the flight to land.
Fiaraidh
Fuday
Eoligarry
Hellisay
Ardmhor
Fuiay
05 Hire bikes in Barra and cycle the causeway to Vatersay. At only 3 miles long, Vatersay is excellent for everyone to cycle. Stop and enjoy a picnic at the twin beaches – Traigh Shiar (pictured left) and Traigh a Bhaigh.
03 Set off on a kayaking adventure with Clear-water Paddling, or join them for a wild-camping experience on an unin-habited island.
Barra
Castlebay
02 Explore Castlebay, Barra's main settlement. Kisimul Castle, home of Clan MacNeil, stands in the bay. For fantastic views, climb Heaval, Barra's highest summit (383m).
Vatersay
ATLANTIC OCEAN
Traigh Shiar
Traigh a Bhaigh
04 Book a tour with Hebridean Sea Tours and visit uninhabited Mingulay and Pabbay for the outstanding seabird colonies.
Mhaoldoniaich
Pabbay (0.7mi); Mingulay (3.5mi)

FROM TOP: RICHARD MURPHY FINE ART/SHUTTERSTOCK ©, WIRESTOCK CREATORS/SHUTTERSTOCK ©

38 ROAD TRIPPIN' Lewis & Harris

HISTORY | CULTURE | BEACHES

Lewis and Harris, divided by mountains and connected by road, are the largest islands in Scotland. Lewis is famous for its archaeology and iconic Chess Pieces, and Harris, to the south, is an island of contrasts with Alpine-like mountains and beaches to rival any Caribbean island. Together, Lewis and Harris make an unforgettable road trip.

How to

Getting here and around Loganair flies to Stornoway Airport (Lewis) from Glasgow, Edinburgh, Inverness and Benbecula. CalMac sails to Stornoway from Ullapool daily. Harris can be reached by ferry from Skye and Uist. Harris and Lewis are connected by road. Getting around is easiest by car.

When to go Summer for the weather, winter for the wild and windswept experience of the Atlantic islands. Remember: dress appropriately!

Top tip Beaches, particularly Luskentyre, get very busy – search out a quieter spot.

History Start by visiting some of the traditional blackhouses. The **Blackhouse** in Arnol and **Gearrannan Blackhouse Village** give a compelling insight into Hebridean life in the past. Head to **Dun Carloway broch**, an impressive Iron Age round tower built around 200 BCE. Finally, drive south to **Calanais Standing Stones**, which comprise 13 large stones laid out in a circle around a central monolith. From here, another 40 smaller stones radiate out in a cruciform. Erected between 3000 and 1500 BCE, Calanais is older than Stonehenge, and it offers a better view, too, overlooking pretty Loch

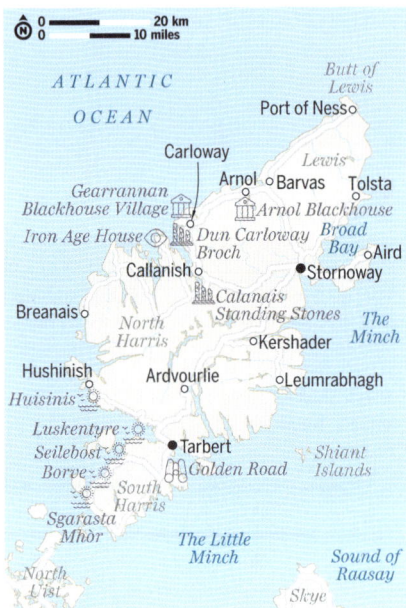

Top right Calanais Standing Stones
Bottom right Dun Carloway broch

NATALIA YATSKEVICH/SHUTTERSTOCK ©

JOE GOUGH/SHUTTERSTOCK ©

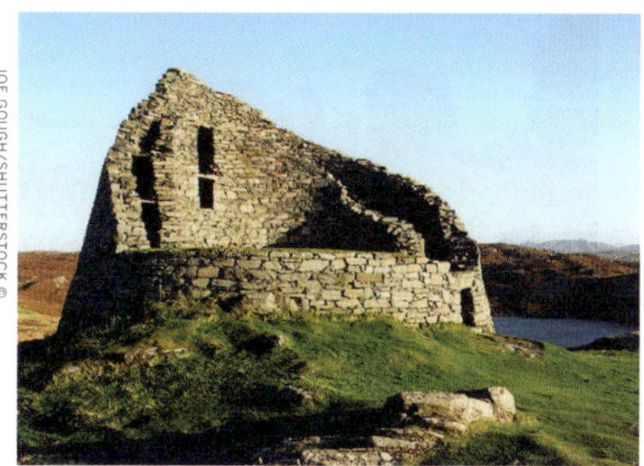

Lewis Chess Pieces

Discovered on the island in 1831, the Lewis Chess Pieces are a set of medieval gaming pieces made from walrus ivory and sperm whale tooth. Their facial expressions are full of character and a testament to the extraordinary skill of their carver(s). See them at the National Museum of Scotland in Edinburgh and the British Museum in London, as well as on long-term loan at the Museum nan Eilean (p202) in Lewis.

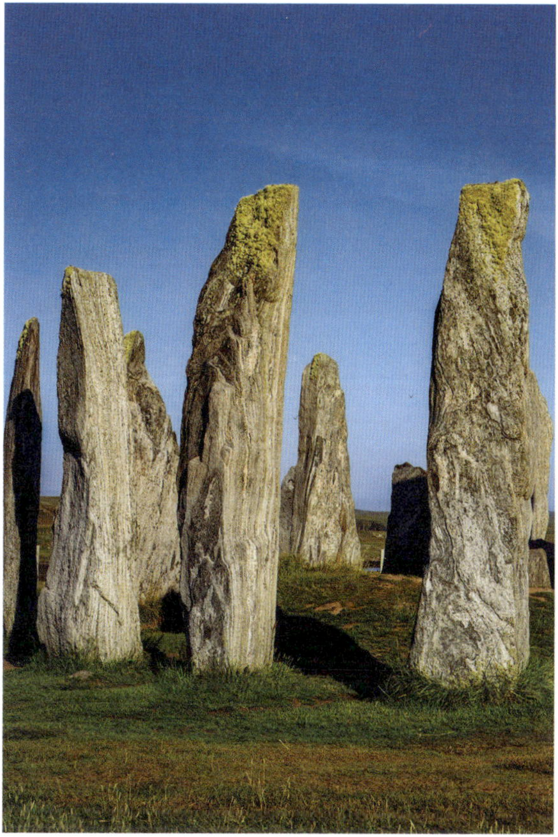

Lydia Prosser,
Curator of Medieval Archaeology and History, National Museum of Scotland @NtlMuseumsScot

Roag and Bernera island – home to Bosta **Iron Age House**, a reconstruction of one excavated on the beach.

Life's a beach Harris is famous for its landscapes and coastal roads. Drive the '**Golden Road**' down the island's southeast coast with its sweeping bends and show-stopping wildlife and scenery. Slow down and dip your toes in the turquoise waters of some of the region's best beaches. **Luskentyre** is the most famous – and busiest – so why not try **Huisinis**, **Seilebost**, **Sgarasta Mhòr** or **Borve**? There are plenty of options!

Listings

BEST OF THE REST

Outdoor Attractions

Fairy Pools

This collection of enchanting blue-green plunge pools and gentle cascades is one of Skye's most magical sights. Come early or late to avoid the day-tripping crowds.

Armadale Castle Garden

Centred around a semi-ruined 17th-century castle, these vast flower-filled gardens in southern Skye offer spectacular views across to the mainland. A ticket includes access to a fascinating museum on the Clan Donald.

Balranald Nature Reserve

With its mix of rich grassland, sand dunes and wild marshes, this rarely visited reserve on North Uist is a haven for birdlife. Keep an ear out for corncrakes and their distinctive rasping cry.

Our Lady of the Isles

This 9m-high granite sculpture of the Madonna and Child stands on South Uist as a symbol of resistance; it was built on land earmarked for a Ministry of Defence missile facility, scuppering the government's plans.

Sandy Beaches

Traigh Mhòr

Commonly known as Tolsta Beach, this stretch of soft golden shoreline within easy reach of Stornoway is known for its grassy dunes and powerful ocean swells (ideal for surfing).

Garrynamonie Beach

With an extensive flower-rich machair system and around 20 miles of white beaches reaching down the west coast of South Uist, this lesser-explored area of the Outer Hebrides offers peace, solitude and uninterrupted Atlantic views.

West Beach

Berneray's West Beach frequently scoops awards for its beauty, pristine sands and turquoise waters. It was once used by mistake to advertise Kai Bae Beach in Thailand!

History Museums

Staffin Dinosaur Museum

One of Skye's most popular family attractions, this museum (founded by local dinosaur hunter Dugald Ross) has an interesting collection of dinosaur footprints and fossils.

Museum nan Eilean

Inside Stornoway's Lews Castle, this new exhibition space showcases various aspects of Hebridean life, from island professions to the Gaelic language. It's also home to six of the famous Lewis Chess Pieces.

Seallam!

Gaelic for 'Let me show you', this visitor centre just north of Leverburgh on Harris has

Armadale Castle

CHRIS ALLAN/SHUTTERSTOCK ©

exhibits on Western Isles history and nature. There is also a genealogy centre for those tracing their Hebridean ancestry.

Dunvegan Castle

Skye's Dunvegan Castle & Garden is one of the best in the Hebrides and has been continuously occupied by the same family for 800 years. Explore this impressive castle and its extensive gardens.

Island Art Galleries

Dandelion Designs

This charming little gallery in Stein, a crofting township on Skye's Waternish peninsula, showcases a wide range of paintings, photographs and crafts by a mix of local and invited artists.

Raasay Gallery

Works by local artists are featured at this purpose-built gallery space on Skye's neighbouring isle. But the best landscape of all is outside, with spectacular views across the sea to the Cuillin Hills.

Island Darkroom

Overlooking loch-covered moorland, this photography gallery in Lewis displays beautiful prints created in the on-site darkroom. Hands-on workshops let you try analogue film processing and printing for yourself.

Skoon Art Gallery

South Harris' east coast has many fine art galleries, including Mission House, Finsbay and Holmasaig. But if you have limited time, head straight for Skoon, set within a renovated crofthouse.

Hebridean Handicrafts

Isle of Skye Candle Company

This artisan producer sells wax candles as well as reed diffusers, soaps and bubble

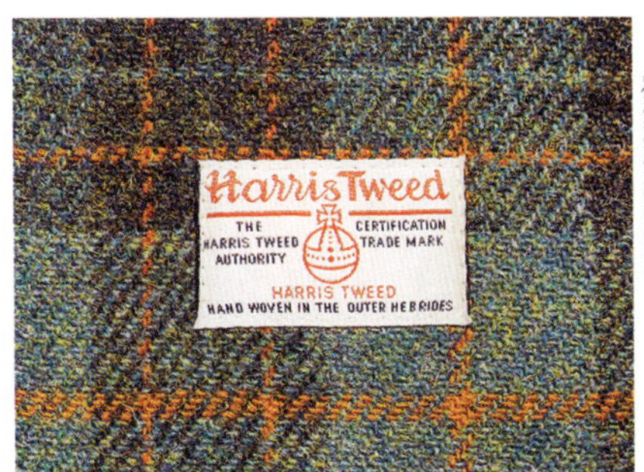

Harris Tweed

baths. Fragrances are inspired by Scotland, allowing you to take home the aromas of whisky, seaweed and heather.

Borgh Pottery

A working studio near the northern tip of Lewis selling hand-thrown ceramics inspired by the local landscape. Watch artist Sue Blair at work on her potter's wheel and take home a souvenir.

Tarbert Tweed Shop

No trip to the Outer Hebrides is complete without picking up some Harris Tweed. This Tarbert store has an array of tweed items, from suit jackets to soft furnishings, hats to handbags.

Hebridean Jewellery

Overlooking pretty Iochdar Beach on the northwest coast of South Uist, this out-of-the-way jeweller specialises in handcrafted silver and gold creations incorporating traditional Pictish and Celtic designs.

ORKNEY
CULTURE | LANDSCAPES | HISTORY

▸ **Trip Builder** (p206)
▸ **Practicalities** (p207)
▸ **Hop to Papa Westray** (p208)
▸ **Neolithic Orkney** (p210)
▸ **Creative Orkney Trail** (p212)
▸ **5000 Years of Orkney Creativity** (p214)
▸ **St Magnus Way Walk** (p216)
▸ **Listings** (p218)

PETE STUART/SHUTTERSTOCK ©

ORKNEY
Trip Builder

Visitors to this archipelago, at times more akin to Scandinavia than Scotland, are lured by islands brimful with ancient monuments and landscapes steeped in Viking sagas. Bygone eras are chronicled in stone, but it's the people who are the real preservers of the past.

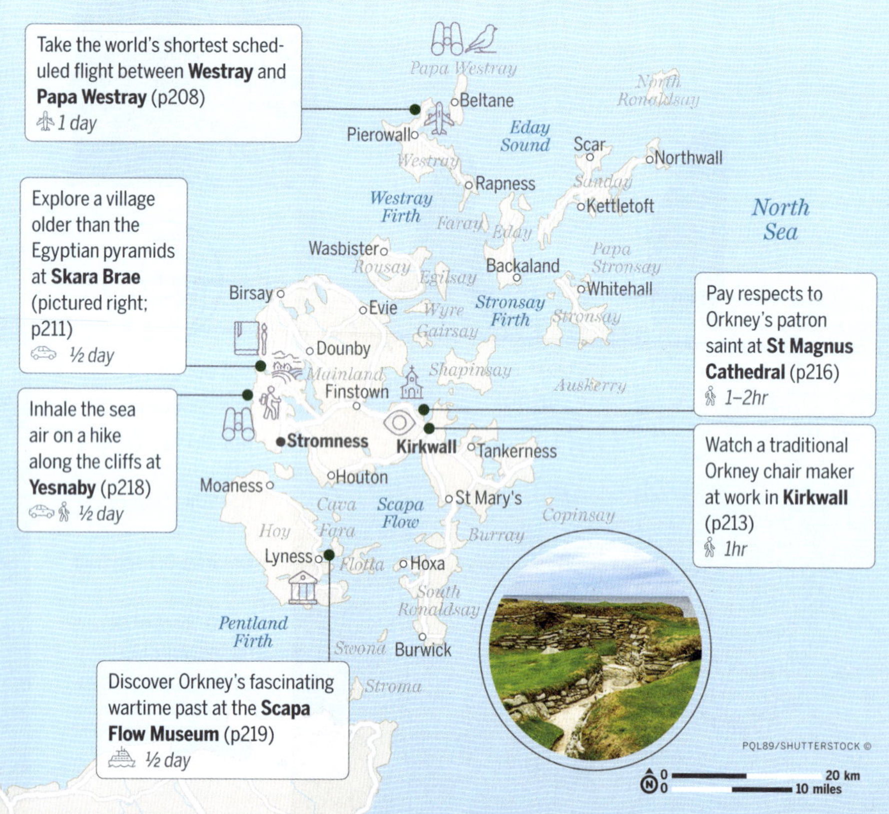
Take the world's shortest scheduled flight between **Westray** and **Papa Westray** (p208)
1 day
Explore a village older than the Egyptian pyramids at **Skara Brae** (pictured right; p211)
½ day
Inhale the sea air on a hike along the cliffs at **Yesnaby** (p218)
½ day
Discover Orkney's fascinating wartime past at the **Scapa Flow Museum** (p219)
½ day
Pay respects to Orkney's patron saint at **St Magnus Cathedral** (p216)
1–2hr
Watch a traditional Orkney chair maker at work in **Kirkwall** (p213)
1hr
Papa Westray
North Ronaldsay
Beltane
Pierowall
Eday Sound
Scar
Northwall
Westray
Rapness
Sanday
Westray Firth
Kettletoft
North Sea
Faray
Eday
Papa Stronsay
Wasbister
Rousay
Egilsay
Backaland
Whitehall
Birsay
Evie
Wyre
Stronsay Firth
Stronsay
Gairsay
Dounby
Shapinsay
Mainland
Auskerry
Finstown
Stromness
Kirkwall
Tankerness
Houton
Moaness
St Mary's
Cava
Scapa Flow
Copinsay
Hoy
Fara
Burray
Lyness
Flotta
Hoxa
South Ronaldsay
Pentland Firth
Swona
Burwick
Stroma
0 20 km
0 10 miles

PQL89/SHUTTERSTOCK ©

Practicalities

ARRIVING

Kirkwall Airport Serves direct flights from major Scottish cities. On arrival take the bus 3 miles to Kirkwall.

Ferries Boats to Orkney sail from Thurso to Stromness, Gills Bay to St Margaret's Hope or Aberdeen to Kirkwall.

CONNECT

Connect to free public wi-fi at the Orkney Library and some Mainland businesses. Access in the outer isles is very limited.

MONEY

Carry a few pounds of loose change for local honesty boxes selling eggs, vegetables, cakes, preserves and baked goods.

WHERE TO STAY

Town/Village	Pro/Con
Kirkwall	The bustling central hub of the islands; it can get busy.
Stromness	Quaint and historic maritime character, but with few evening options.
St Margaret's Hope	Close to the best spots for marine wildlife, though far from town.

GETTING AROUND

Car Necessary to explore beyond the main towns and attractions.

Bus Buses run regularly between Kirkwall and Stromness; rural buses can be infrequent.

Ferry & plane Both depart from Mainland to the outer isles, but be aware, there is no public transport on these islands.

IMAGES BY LAURIE GOODLAD ©

EATING & DRINKING

Pattie supper A local speciality of mince, potatoes and onion deep-fried and served with chips.

Fattie cutties Fruity biscuits originating from Westray; buy them in independent food stores.

Bere bannocks These flat breads are made from an ancient local barley. Top them with butter or cheese.

Must-try sweet treat
Orkney Fudge

Best local seafood
Murray Arms Hotel (p219)

JAN–MAR

Cold with short daylight hours; good chance of seeing the Northern Lights.

APR–JUN

Temperatures fluctuate between low and mild; the best time for festivals.

JUL–SEP

Warm temperatures and longest daylight hours; ideal for outdoor exploring.

OCT–DEC

Low temperatures and shorter days; few tourists, so attractions are quiet.

39 Hop to Papa WESTRAY

NATURE | BEACHES | HERITAGE

With good wind, the flight between Westray and neighbouring Papa Westray takes close to one minute and closer to two minutes on a bad day – making this the world's shortest scheduled flight, as confirmed by the *Guinness Book of Records*. Journey aside, Papay, as it's affectionately known, provided the backdrop to the blockbuster film *The Outrun* and is worthy of a deeper delve.

How to

Getting there Book a return flight from Kirkwall to Papa Westray with Loganair. Most outbound flights stop at Westray before continuing to Papa Westray, but check with the airline before booking. The island itself is walkable.

When to visit Year-round, although weather is best in spring and summer.

Top tip On return to Kirkwall Airport, collect your personalised souvenir flight certificate.

Local tip Book a tour with the Papay Ranger.

0 2 km
0 1 mile
North Hill Nature Reserve
North Hill Trail
Papa Westray
North Wick Beach
St Boniface Kirk
South Wick Beach
Holm of Papay
Knap of Howar
Kelp Store
Holland Farm
Burland Walk
Beltane
The North Sound
Papa Sound

Uncover the past Dating back to around 3800 BCE, **Knap of Howar**, a neolithic farmstead, has the oldest standing stone buildings in northwest Europe. Just along the coast, take sanctuary in **St Boniface Kirk**; Pictish stones found in the kirkyard indicate a religious site much older than the current 12th-century building. The **Kelp Store** has exhibits detailing Papay's rich history and heritage, while the agricultural museum at **Holland Farm** is a time capsule of a lost way of life.

Nature walks In spring and summer, the rare maritime heathland of **North Hill**

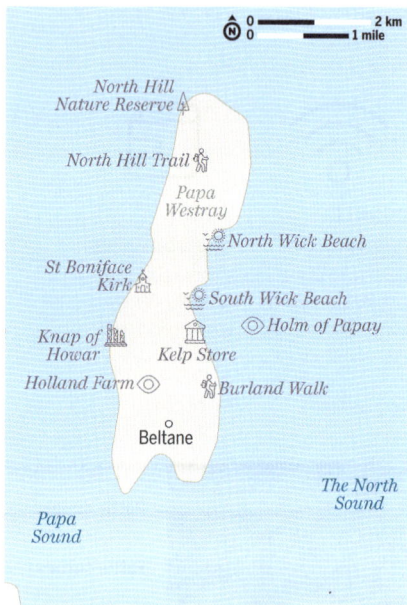

Top right Knap of Howar
Right Black guillemots, North Hill Nature Reserve

JENNYT/SHUTTERSTOCK ©

HANNAH WHEATLEY/SHUTTERSTOCK ©

An Uninhabited Island

A community-owned boat ferries visitors across to the uninhabited island of Holm of Papay, just off the east coast of Papa Westray. The best preserved and most remarkable of the three neolithic chambered cairns found here is also the largest. Modern skylights illuminate the interior, allowing you to pass through confidently. Book in advance via the Papay Ranger on Facebook.

Nature Reserve is blanketed in a vivid tapestry of wildflowers, including the rare Scottish primrose. The **North Hill Trail** skirts the coast for 4 miles and takes in the seabird nesting colonies at Fowl Craig. The cliffs bustle with guillemots, razorbills, fulmars and even a few puffins between April and August. Alternatively, head 2.5 miles along the **Burland Walk** to the wetlands around St Tredwell's Loch where wildfowl glide the calm waters and waders feed along its fringes.

Quiet beaches Amble across the fine white sands of neighbouring **North Wick** and **South Wick** beaches on the east coast where local seals are likely to be your only companions. At the south end of the island, aquamarine shallows are bordered by a serene horseshoe bay at Bothican.

40 Neolithic ORKNEY

ARCHAEOLOGY | MONUMENTS | STONE CIRCLES

Roam across Orkney and you are transported to an age when people forged communities of stone. Their legacy has left an imprint on the landscape for millennia, no more so than at the Heart of Neolithic Orkney, an epicentre of significant monuments designated a UNESCO World Heritage Site. Towering stone circles, sombre burial cairns and ancient dwellings remain shrouded in mystery.

BARBARA ASH/SHUTTERSTOCK ©

How to

Getting around A car offers more freedom (hire one in Kirkwall) or take a local Stagecoach bus from Kirkwall to the main sites mentioned.

When to visit Attractions are open year-round but can be very busy in summer, especially on cruise-ship days.

Tour tips Book in advance for entry to Maeshowe. Free tours of Ring of Brodgar and Stones of Stenness take place during summer. For tour info visit historic environment.scot.

IMAGEBROKER/ANGELA TO ROXEL/GETTY IMAGES ©

An ancient tomb The passageway of **Maeshowe** leads to a surprisingly spacious chamber where giant sandstone slabs defy gravity and Viking graffiti is scrawled across the walls. Entry to this 5000-year-old tomb includes an informative guided tour and pre-booking is essential.

Towering standing stones Nearby, the Ring of Brodgar and Standing Stones of Stenness are both huge prehistoric stone circles. The **Standing Stones of Stenness** are believed to be the oldest stone circle in the UK – even older than the famous and iconic Stonehenge – and are made of four stones up to 6 metres high. Make the short walk to **Barnhouse**, a neolithic settlement discovered in 1984. Although not as impressive as Skara Brae, Barnhouse is quieter and shares many features and dates to a similar period. At just over 4000 years old, the neighbouring **Ring of Brodgar** is a relative youngster in this ancient landscape. Set in a natural amphitheatre, the purpose of Britain's third-largest stone circle remains an enigma.

A 5000-year-old village Dig deep into the fabric of island life at the world-famous **Skara Brae**. Thanks to Skara Brae being cocooned under a layer of earth, the prehistoric village has been magnificently preserved. Stone beds and dressers stand as they would have done thousands of years ago and are equivalent to what we use today. A visitor centre and cafe houses finds from the settlement overlooking the beautiful Bay of Skaill.

Top left Standing Stones of Stenness
Bottom left Entrance to Maeshowe

Less Crowded Neolithic Sites

Unstan Chambered Cairn Distinctive pottery named Unstan Ware and human bones were found during excavations of this 5000-year-old burial monument on the Mainland.

Cuween Hill Chambered Cairn Human and dog skulls discovered here, also on the Mainland, reveal ancient burial rituals. Beware, you will need to crawl into this shadowy tomb.

Island of Rousay Make the short ferry crossing to the 'Egypt of the North', home to over 150 ancient attractions. Midhowe Chambered Cairn is one of the finest.

Island of Eday Attracting few tourists, you will likely have Vinquoy Chambered Cairn and one of Orkney's tallest standing stones to yourself.

41 Creative Orkney TRAIL

ART | CRAFTS | SHOPPING

In workshops across Orkney, artisans welcome you in while they carve, spin, engrave, turn, paint and weave. Makers enthusiastically share their techniques, inspiration and island stories with visitors. Browse their studios and leave with a unique handcrafted memento.

Orkney Chairs

For centuries, Orcadians have huddled by their firesides in a high-back or hooded Orkney chair (pictured above). Constructed from a wooden frame with a backing handwoven from local oat straw, the style is unique to the islands. Once considered simple furniture, it is now exhibited as a Scottish design icon in V&A Dundee.

Trip Notes

Getting around For flexibility, a car is recommended; hire one in Kirkwall. Reach outer islands by Orkney Ferries or Loganair. Buses run frequently between Kirkwall and Stromness but are infrequent in rural areas. Download the Traveline app to plan public transport.

When to go Several workshops only open in spring and summer.

Top tip Sanday and Stronsay have their own creative trails. Trail leaflets can be found at tourist information points.

02 Travel 3 miles south to **Harray** where Andrew Appleby's ceramics at Fursbreck Pottery and the wood-turned designs in Michael Sinclair's studio are heavily influenced by Orkney's neolithic past.
01 Visit Alison Moore's workshop in **Stromness** for gemstone jewellery that reflects her geology background. Next door, Castaway Crafts sells handmade Tweed products and items from over 100 local artists.
04 Continue on 6 miles for a lunch break at The Kirk Gallery & Café in **Tankerness**. The renovated church showcases the jewellery collections of Sheila Fleet, while the cafe serves up Orkney cuisine.
03 Ten miles further on in **Kirkwall**, the tradition of making Orkney chairs continues at Orkney Handcrafted Furniture and Scapa Crafts. Robin Palmer creates tactile ceramics, and Ortak runs tours of their jewellery workshop.
05 Finish 17 miles further south at **Hoxa Tapestry Gallery**. Established by their late mother, a brother and sister duo combine their artistic talents to produce tapestries, rugs, paintings and yarns.
Rousay
Egilsay
Westray Firth
Eday
Shapinsay
Balfour
Wide Firth
Shapinsay Sound
Finstown
Stenness
Mainland
Kirkwall
Tankerness
Houton
Foubister
St Mary's
Cava
Northtown
Burray
Hoy
Fara
Hoxa
St Margaret's Hope
Flotta
South Ronaldsay
Pentland Firth
Swona
Burwick
0 10 km
0 5 miles
N
FROM TOP: TBKMEDIA.DE/ALAMY STOCK PHOTO ©, NAT WILKINS/ALAMY STOCK PHOTO ©

5000 Years of Orkney Creativity

ISLAND DESIGNS FASHIONED BY ANCIENT ARTISANS

Contemporary crafters are just the latest chapter in Orkney's 5000-year-old story of talented islanders. Taking inspiration from the earliest inhabitants of the archipelago, they keep alive skills and traditions passed down from previous generations. A number of astonishing archaeological finds reveal the origins and progression of Orkney's creative past.

Left Neolithic bone pins
Middle Spinning wheel
Right Artisan crafting an Orkney chair

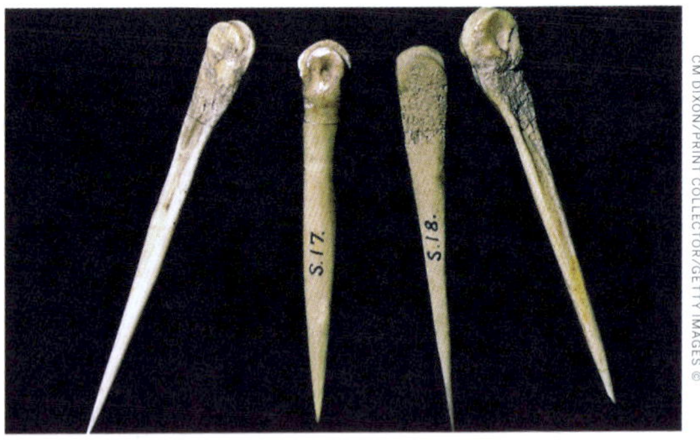

When a neolithic potter sat down to work on their latest creation, it is unlikely they could have predicted the stir their humble vessel would make five millennia later. At first glance, the pottery sherd uncovered at Ness of Brodgar is fairly unremarkable, but expert analysis of the surface has revealed a hauntingly personal link to one of Orkney's original artisans – their fingerprint. This is not the only notable impression left in clay at the site; a rare imprint of neolithic woven textile found on another pottery shard was likely left by the maker's clothing.

This era was a time of transformation with the introduction of pottery, polished stone and large-scale monuments. Despite rudimentary apparatus, there is evidence of exquisite workmanship among the New Stone Age communities, who designed objects with both function and fashion in mind. Inspiration from Orkney's prehistoric past can be found in the work of today's makers, who depict standing stones and tombs in jewellery and artwork; while others take literal inspiration from ancient discoveries by styling bowls and pots on millennia-old designs.

As the Bronze and Iron Ages rolled in, metalworkers joined the list of Orkney's skilled artisans. If there had been an Iron Age version of the 21st-century creative trail, potters, textile makers and jewellery designers would all be plying their trade much like today.

What we know about Orkney's creative past mainly comes from archaeologists sifting through murky earth, waiting for the soil to surrender another piece of the jigsaw. Now and again they strike gold, or something even better – wood. Wooden items are rare finds as organic material can deteriorate quickly, which is why the discovery

WERNER FORMAN/UNIVERSAL IMAGES GROUP/GETTY IMAGES ©

HEMIS/ALAMY STOCK PHOTO ©

of a perfectly preserved 2000-year-old carved wooden bowl at The Cairns dig site is all the more extraordinary. What makes it even more unusual are the intricate bronze repairs, showcasing a harmony of old and new craftsmanship. The recovery of an intact piece of clothing conserved in a peat bog was another scarce gift from the Iron Age. An expert study of the 2000-year-old 'Orkney Hood' has revealed masterful spinning and weaving skills.

Further innovation came when the Vikings arrived, importing a new wave of ideas, techniques and handcrafted global goods and, more significantly, a new language and culture. Treasure troves from boat burials and concealed hoards have brought to light their appreciation of highly decorative jewellery and ornate personal possessions. One of the most curious finds from Orkney is the Scar Dragon Plaque, featuring two intricately carved dragon heads. It is perhaps the Norse era more than any other that can claim the biggest influence on today's designers. Gallery windows across the islands are filled with beautifully crafted keepsakes engraved with Norse runes and mythical creatures. Just as the Viking artisans traded their goods around the world by boat, Orkney's current creatives sell their wares to international visitors travelling on ferries and cruise liners, and in some ways very little has changed, other than the boats being bigger.

> Inspiration from Orkney's prehistoric past can be found in the work of today's makers...

Learn a Local Craft

Orkney Creative Hub was set up to support and nurture a new wave of local artists and designers. Although visitors are very welcome at their weekly workshops, they are not packaged as tourist experiences. Most participants are local residents looking to learn new skills, including weaving, spinning, painting and felting. Sessions offer an authentic opportunity to join Orkney's creative movement and craft your own unique souvenir under the tutorship of a professional artisan. Introductory sessions covering a variety of artistic disciplines generally last several hours and take place at venues across Kirkwall. Workshops must be booked online in advance at orkneycommunities.co.uk/orkneycreativehub.

42 St Magnus WAY WALK

HIKING | SCENERY | PILGRIMAGE

Set foot in the story of Orkney's patron saint as you hike 58 miles from the location of his martyrdom in Egilsay to his final resting place in St Magnus Cathedral. The waymarked pilgrim trail weaves along attractive coastline, past significant historical sites, and unveils wide open vistas before arriving at the heart of the islands in Kirkwall.

Trip Notes

Getting here & around Orkney Ferries runs a regular service between Tingwall and the start of the route in Egilsay. Stagecoach buses run close to the beginning and end of each section, although they can be infrequent.

When to visit The weather is best in spring and summer.

Short on time Walk 11.5 miles from Orphir to Kirkwall taking in history and scenery.

Top tip Download the St Magnus Way app and consider hiring an e-bike from E-Tour Orkney.

The Story of St Magnus

The legacy of St Magnus continues to shape Orkney's culture despite more than 900 years passing since his martyrdom. Born Magnus Erlendsson, he co-ruled Orkney with his cousin Haakon in what started as a harmonious relationship but later severely deteriorated. During peace talks on the island of Egilsay, Haakon betrayed Magnus and ordered his murder. Initially buried where he lay, his body was subsequently transferred to Birsay where miracles were attributed to his gravesite. These wonders saw him canonised, and when his nephew founded St Magnus Cathedral in honour of his uncle, Magnus' relics were interred in one of the pillars.

02 Take the ferry back to Mainland and visit **St Magnus Church** in Birsay to view a spectacular stained-glass memorial. The current building stands on a centuries-old site of worship where miraculous healings ascribed to the saint are said to have taken place.
01 Perched close to the site where Haakon oversaw the execution of his cousin in Egilsay, the 12th-century **St Magnus Kirk** makes a poignant start to your journey.
Eday
Rousay
Egilsay
Stronsay Firth
Birsay
Evie
Tingwall
04 In Kirkwall, **St Magnus Cathedral** (pictured above and below) is the jewel in the crown among the trio of religious buildings bearing his name. A suitably ornate interior is revealed beyond the robust red-sandstone edifice.
Dounby
Mainland
Wide Firth
Yesnaby
Finstown
Hoy Sound
Stenness
Kirkwall
Shapinsay Sound
Stromness
Tankerness
Orphir
03 The remnants of Scotland's only surviving **circular medieval church** sit in a picturesque setting along the Orphir coast. Dedicated to St Nicholas, it is said to have been built by Earl Haakon in repentance for the death of St Magnus.
Hoy
0
10 km
0
5 miles
N

FROM TOP: DORSTEFFEN/SHUTTERSTOCK ©, ALANMORRIS/SHUTTERSTOCK ©

Listings

BEST OF THE REST

Distilleries & Breweries

Highland Park

For over 200 years this distillery on the outskirts of Kirkwall has been producing single malts revered around the world. Join a tour to discover its Viking origins.

Scapa

Not to be missed! Scapa produces an incredible malt whisky and has the best tasting room in their modern 'Noust' – designed like an upturned boat with enviable views across Scapa Flow.

Orkney Distillery

Sample the range of award-winning Kirkjuvagr Gin, distilled in a sleek black cafe-bar on Kirkwall's waterfront. Tour behind the scenes or craft your own gin under expert guidance.

Deerness Distillery

A friendly-family welcome awaits at this bespoke self-built distillery in the country. Award-winning gin, vodka and coffee liqueur are bottled and labelled by hand in an entirely artisan process.

Orkney Brewery

A Victorian schoolhouse provides the setting for this brewhouse and cafe. If you can't visit the brewery, pop into their Peedie Bottle Shop in Kirkwall for a dram.

Swannay Brewery

Served up in bars around Orkney, the beer brewing process takes place in a former dairy farmstead in the north of Mainland where visitors can buy bottles directly from the source.

Coastal Trails

Yesnaby

In the west, Yesnaby's striking sandstone cliffs feature weathered arches, craggy sea stacks, rare primulas and a weather-beaten appearance. For a quieter hike, head east to Deerness for the Mull Head hike.

Brough of Birsay

Cross the causeway at low tide and circumnavigate the coast of this small landmass, once home to Picts and Vikings. Explore the impressive Norse settlement, but return before the tide does.

Old Man of Hoy

A steady climb up the hillside from Rackwick reveals a panorama encompassing the north coast of Scotland before reaching one of Britain's tallest sea stacks.

Vat of Kirbister

Relax on a thoughtfully placed bench by a spectacular rock arch in Stronsay. Despite relatively little effort required to get there, the view makes this a gratifying rest stop.

Scapa

History & Heritage Tours

St Magnus Cathedral
Climb to the upper levels of Orkney's 12th-century masterpiece for a bird's-eye view over Kirkwall. The history revealed en route makes this an illuminating excursion.

Barony Mill
Listen to the wooshing waterwheel and clickety-clack machinery at work as an ancient form of barley called bere is transformed into flour. Little has changed at this mill in Birsay since the 19th century.

Scapa Flow Museum
Recently opened Scapa Flow Museum in Hoy is the perfect way to discover Orkney's wartime heritage and the history of Scapa Flow in both world wars.

Local Foodie Favourites

Beiting & Brew £
This street-food van in Kirkwall has gained a cult local following, serving up traditional Orkney ingredients with a unique twist. The menu changes regularly but the surprising combinations are constant.

Brig Larder £
Bursting with fresh local produce – this is the perfect place to pick up a local, Orkney-inspired picnic. William Shearer is another fantastic Kirkwall-based shop selling local food and drink.

Murray Arms Hotel, St Margaret's Hope ££
Regulars flock here for their seafood, landed daily from the family boat and served up in generous platters. The hand-dived scallops melt in the mouth.

Birsay Bay Tearoom £
Between April and September, this popular cafe in Birsay serves up 'Taste of Orkney' daily

TRAVELLINGFATMAN/SHUTTERSTOCK ©

Brough of Birsay

specials, best enjoyed with a cup of tea while gazing out at sea views.

Festivals & Events

Orkney Folk Festival
During May, traditional tunes, singing, conversation and laughter drift from pub doors and venues around Stromness and beyond. Festival tickets and local accommodation get booked up well in advance.

St Magnus International Festival
For a week around midsummer, the sun barely sets and the islands come alive with music, dance and theatre. Reserve some stamina for the late-night Festival Club.

North Ronaldsay Sheep Festival
Join volunteers to repair the drystone wall protecting the island's native seaweed-eating sheep. Taking place over a fortnight each summer, additional local cultural events enhance the experience.

Orkney County Show
Held each August, the County Show is the highlight of the farming calendar, providing a unique insight into island life and providing a great day out for locals and visitors alike.

SHETLAND

RAW | INSPIRING | WILD

- **Trip Builder** (p222)
- **Practicalities** (p223)
- **Exploring Fair Isle** (p224)
- **Land of the Vikings** (p226)
- **Unforgettable Unst** (p228)
- **Flora & Fauna** (p230)
- **Mousa Broch's Petrels** (p232)
- **Exploring Geology** (p234)
- **Listings** (p236)

JAMES WARWICK/GETTY IMAGES ©

SHETLAND
Trip Builder

Flanked by the North Atlantic and the North Sea, Shetland's 100-island cluster is where Scotland meets Scandinavia. Closer to the Arctic Circle than London, the dramatic landscape, shaped by fire and ice, has an ingrained Norse feel unlike anywhere else.

Hike to the most northerly part of the UK at **Hermaness** (p228)
½ day

Go beyond Ronas Hill and discover the **Lang Ayre's secluded beach** (p235)
1 day

Stand on the flank of a volcano at **Eshaness** (p235)
½ day

Hop on a boat trip to the seabird colonies of **Noss** (p235)
½ day

Take a jewellery-making workshop at **Red Houss** in Burra (p236)
1 day

Walk through 5000 years of human history at **Jarlshof Prehistoric & Norse Settlement** (p236)
2hr

Practicalities

ARRIVING

Sumburgh Airport Located 24 miles south of Lerwick, handles regular flights from Aberdeen, Edinburgh, Glasgow, Inverness and Kirkwall.

NorthLink Ferry Terminal Just 2 miles from Lerwick town centre, sails daily to and from Aberdeen.

FIND YOUR WAY

Buy an OS map for hiking or download the OS Maps app. Roads are well signposted and locals are happy to give directions.

MONEY

Carry cash – many shops, attractions, honesty boxes and ferries don't accept card payments and ATMs are restricted to Lerwick.

WHERE TO STAY

Town/Village	Pro/Con
Lerwick	Guesthouses and B&Bs are best. Close proximity to pubs and eateries.
Scalloway	Picturesque, close to town and a welcoming village feel.
North Isles	Immerse yourself in the North Isles and enjoy a quiet self-catering island retreat.

GETTING AROUND

Car The best way to reach Shetland's beauty spots. Buses are frequent, but routes are limited.

Ferry Inter-island ferries provide sea links to nine of Shetland's inhabited islands by car or as a foot passenger.

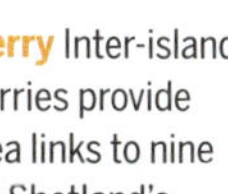

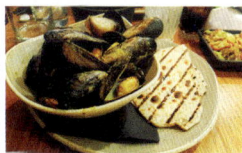

Hiking The best way to enjoy the stunning coastal scenery.

EATING & DRINKING

Locally sourced Look out for local mussels at The Dowry (p236), and the locally sourced, seasonal ingredients at No 88 (p237). Experience the unforgettable taste of Shetland lamb and Uradale Farm beef, savouring the tang of the salt-kissed flavours.

Honesty boxes and cake fridges Roadside honesty boxes and cake fridges sell everything from cakes and bannocks to eggs and jams. Remember to carry cash!

Best breakfast
Fjara Cafe Bar (p237)

Must-try drink
Shetland Reel Gin

JAN–MAR
These are often the coldest months but spring emerges slowly. Up Helly Aa is the highlight.

APR–JUN
Temperatures can remain cool. June sees 19 hours of daylight.

JUL–SEP
Average August temperatures are 15°C. This is the busiest season.

OCT–DEC
Stormy weather is common. Look out for the Northern Lights (aurora borealis).

43 Exploring FAIR ISLE

KNITTING | BIRDWATCHING | ISOLATION

Fair Isle, the UK's most geographically remote inhabited island, is a vibrant community. Home to Shetland's world-famous colourful Fair Isle knitwear and with unparalleled birding and hiking opportunities, Fair Isle offers something for everyone. If you want to remove yourself from the hustle and bustle of everyday life, immerse yourself in nature, and breathe in the salt-laden air, then Fair Isle is for you.

CHRIS MORPHET/REDFERNS ©

How to

Getting here There are two options: ferry or plane. The 12-passenger ferry departs from Grutness, close to Sumburgh Airport, and takes 2½ hours. Flights depart from Tingwall Airport, carry a maximum of six passengers and take 25 minutes. Booking in advance is essential, with only several sailings and flights a week.

When to go May to September for fair weather and seabirds.

Top tip Fair Isle involves careful planning and the necessity to be adaptable and flexible. Boat crossings can be rough.

MARIANNE TAYLOR/SHUTTERSTOCK ©

Far left Fair Isle knitwear
Bottom left Arctic skua in flight
Left Sheep on Fair Isle

A Haven for Knitters & Birders

Halfway between Shetland and Orkney, Fair Isle is home to about 60 people. Clearances and emigration led to a drastic decline in population in the 19th century. The island was bought by the National Trust in 1954 and has since bucked the trend of island depopulation.

Birding An important ornithological centre, Fair Isle's world-famous **Bird Observatory** was lost to fire. It is scheduled to reopen in 2025, providing much-needed accommodation and research facilities. Its position makes Fair Isle a handy stopping-off point for rare and common migrant birds – and a world-class destination for birders hoping to spot them during the spring and autumn migrations, or to observe the internationally important seabird colonies.

Knitwear Fair Isle knitwear, featuring bright colours and bold designs, is a style that has swept through the knitting world and is celebrated during the annual **Shetland Wool Week** festival. For an immersive experience, book a knitting holiday with Fair Isle with Marie and experience life on a real working croft.

Culture & hiking Fair Isle has some of the most beautiful walks in Shetland with highlights including the impressive **Sheep Craig** and **Malcolm's Head**. It has a rich cultural tradition of music, fishing and the famous straw-backed Fair Isle chairs, stylistically different to those from Orkney (p212). Fair Isle's cultural heritage is thoughtfully depicted in the small **George Waterston Museum**. The island is also home to notable shipwrecks including the Armada ship *El Gran Grifon*.

Shetland TV Series

Shetland has become increasingly popular as a destination in recent years. The islands' starring role in the *Shetland* series, a fictional TV crime drama based on the popular novels by author Ann Cleeves, has helped to raise its profile, planting it on the worldwide stage. The main character in the formative seasons, Detective Inspector Jimmy Perez, came from Fair Isle, and several episodes were filmed in the isle. Douglas Henshall, who plays DI Perez, has supported fundraising efforts to rebuild the island's world-famous Bird Observatory.

Land of the Vikings

ON THE TRAIL OF THE VIKINGS

Visitors are instantly struck by the 'otherness' of Shetland. The Vikings left an indelible mark on the people, place and landscape, and the lack of Scottishness is marked by the absence of the ubiquitous haggis, kilts and bagpipes. Shetland is culturally Scandinavian, with Norse place names and dialects, flaming fire festivals and a history that sits apart from Scotland.

Left A replica Viking boat, Unst
Middle Scalloway Castle
Right Participants in Up Helly Aa

Viking Shetland

Evidence of Vikings in Shetland is found from the settlement sites at Jarlshof in the south to Unst in the north. No part of the islands escaped this assimilation into Scandinavia from around 850 CE, giving rise to 600 years of Norse rule. Viking rule more or less obliterated pre-Norse culture in Shetland. There is little indication of what place names and language looked like before the Vikings arrived from western Norway and, until a few hundred years ago, the main language spoken in Shetland was a form of Old Norse, known as Norn. Shetland's unique position in the centre of the North Atlantic made it the perfect stepping-stone for Norse colonisation westward. Shetland lies equidistant to Norway and Scotland, and the cultures of both have fed the unique character and cultural heritage of the islands.

Scottish Assimilation: 1469

The 600-year period of Scandinavian rule ended in 1469 when Shetland and Orkney were pawned to Scotland as a wedding dowry. Princess Margaret of Denmark was to marry King James III of Scotland, but King Christian of Denmark couldn't afford the dowry. To secure the marriage and retain peace between nations, he pawned Orkney and Shetland, intending to repurchase them later. This never happened, and Shetland has remained part of Scotland ever since. Where Shetland had once sat proudly in the Viking world's centre, it now sits on the UK's periphery.

Shetland's transition into Scotland wasn't an easy one as land-hungry Scottish landowners moved on the isles in the hope of extending power and influence in the courts of Edinburgh with their newly gained northern estates. Scalloway Castle, built by the notorious Earl Patrick Stewart, stands as a ruin and testament to this oppressive time.

YURIY CHERTOK/SHUTTERSTOCK ©

ANDREW J SHEARER/SHUTTERSTOCK ©

Up Helly Aa

Shetland's Scandinavian heritage is celebrated in 12 annual Up Helly Aa fire festivals between January and March. The largest is held in Lerwick on the last Tuesday of January, attracting thousands of visitors annually.

The torchlit procession, led by the Guizer Jarl, weaves its way around the streets of Lerwick with over 1000 torchbearers and culminates with *guizers* (participants) tossing their burning torches into a replica Viking longship. The atmosphere is electric as street lights are extinguished: visitors throng the streets, jostling for the best view, and the smell of paraffin and smoke permeates everything. After the ceremonial burning, a night of celebration commences as a dozen halls welcome the squads of *guizers* to perform a sketch or dance, and festivities continue until the following morning.

> Shetland's transition into Scotland wasn't an easy one...

Despite what is thought, Up Helly Aa is not an ancient festival from Norse times but is rooted in Shetland's Victorian era. Until 2023, women were not allowed to participate in the procession, and in 2024, history was made with the first females joining the Jarl Squad.

A Musical Tradition

Shetland's musical culture is unlike any other, and the tradition of fiddle playing is strong. Rooted in the islands' Scandinavian past, Shetlanders are renowned for their musical abilities. This is celebrated in the annual **Shetland Folk Festival**, attracting thousands of musicians every year.

Viking Place Names

Around 870 CE, Viking explorer Flóki Vilgerðarson, known as Hrafna Flóki (Raven Flóki), visited Shetland with his family before sailing northwest to discover Iceland. Preparing to leave, Flóki went into the hills to gather young ravens. Used as navigational aids, ravens help find land. While absent, his daughter, Geirhildr, fell through the ice on Girlsta Loch and drowned. Local legend tells that her body was buried on the loch's island. Girlsta is a derivation of her name, Geirhildr, coming from Geirhildarvatn (Geirhildr's lake/water). About 95% of place names in Shetland derive from Old Norse.

44 Unforgettable UNST

WILDLIFE | HIKING | ARCHAEOLOGY

Combining outstanding wildlife experiences and a sunset hike to the UK's most northerly point, this one-day trip is an unforgettable adventure. Scout for otters in the morning with a local guide before striding out across some of Shetland's most dramatic landscapes to chase the sunset and spot puffin and gannet colonies.

How to

Getting here Unst is a two-ferry hop from Shetland's Mainland; to get there, hire a car or go with a guide, as transport links within Unst are limited. Follow the A970 from Lerwick to Toft before catching the 15-minute ferry to Yell. Drive through Yell (18 miles) to the ferry at Gutcher, which takes you on the five-minute crossing to Belmont, Unst. Booking is recommended.

Tours Otter-sighting tours can be booked with Shetland Nature.

Wildlife spotting Start by tracking the charismatic otter with local guides **Shetland Nature**. Unst is one of the best places to see otters in their natural environment. Known locally as the *draatsi*, Shetland's otters live on the saltwater shores. The best way to spot these elusive creatures is with an expert guide.

Hiking Hike to the UK's most northerly point, **Hermaness National Nature Reserve**, for an 'edge of the world' feeling, and enjoy views of **Muckle Flugga Lighthouse** and **Out Stack**. Hermaness boasts large colonies of puffins and gannets, and sometimes a passing whale. Time your visit with the setting summer sun.

Top right Eurasian otter
Right Atlantic puffins, Hermaness National Nature Reserve

JAMES WARWICK/GETTY IMAGES ©

JAMES WARWICK/GETTY IMAGES ©

Eurasian Otters in Shetland

A carnivorous four-legged and semi-aquatic mammal that feeds primarily on fish, and with a face as cute as any teddy bear, it is little wonder Eurasian otters are as popular as they are charismatic. Living their lives along our remote coast to the rhythm of Shetland's tides and feeding from our rich inshore seas, they are found here in higher density than anywhere else in the world.

Brydon Thomason, *native Shetland naturalist, otter specialist and tour operator at Shetland Nature*

Archaeology Unst is thought to be the Vikings' first landfall, and with 60 known longhouse sites, it's clear that it was an important place. Visit the reconstructed longhouse and longship at **Haroldswick**. Step back into neolithic Shetland at the **Lund** standing stone, an impressive 3.5m monolith. Visit the ruined **St Olaf's church** featuring Viking graves (9th to 11th century) and Hanseatic merchant Segebad Detken (1573). Keep your eyes peeled for seals hauled up on the nearby beach. And, following the Vikings, visit the excavated longhouse and Iron Age broch at **Underhoull**.

FLORA & FAUNA

01 Killer Whales
Killer whales can often be seen hunting seals inshore. The same animals move between Iceland, Shetland and mainland Scotland.

02 Otters (Draatsi)
Shetland has the highest density of otters in Europe. See them feeding just offshore at mid to low tide.

03 Seals – Common and Grey (Selkies)
Shetland has two species present in nationally important numbers. Common seals pup in June and grey seals in October.

04 Puffins (Tammie Nories)
Shetland's auks – puffins, razorbills and black guillemots – mate for life and return to the same nest site every spring.

05 Gannets (Solans)
With huge wingspans enabling long-distance feeding trips, and a liberal diet, populations of this large seabird have increased.

06 Red-necked Phalaropes (Peerie Deuks)
In an unusual role reversal, males raise chicks while females seek another partner. Incredibly, they winter near the Galapagos Islands!

07 Arctic Terns (Tirricks)
With the world's largest migration, terns see more daylight than any other species, but are threatened by changing sea temperatures.

08 Great Skuas (Bonxies)

Shetland hosts 40% of the world's population. Recent avian flu outbreaks have seriously reduced their numbers.

09 Fulmars (Maalies)

Shetland's most abundant seabirds have a distinctive stiff-winged flight and have only been resident since the late 19th century.

10 Rare Plants

Edmondston's chickweed is found only on the Unst serpentine. On the Keen of Hamar it grows alongside other rare Arctic alpines.

11 Orchids (Curl-dodie)

Shetland remains flower-rich – visitors are able to enjoy a proliferation of wildflowers, including several species of orchid.

12 Curlews (Whaaps)

Less intensive farming in Shetland, compared to mainland UK, means Shetland's populations of curlew, lapwing and redshank are stable.

13 Blanket Bog

Shetland's blanket bog is globally important, capturing and storing carbon, regulating water, and supporting plants and birds.

45 Mousa Broch's PETRELS

BIRDS | ARCHAEOLOGY | SIMMER DIM

The incredible culmination of one of the wonders of the natural world takes place within the walls of a 2000-year-old broch, the best preserved in the world, under the magical half-light of midsummer. The sight of the storm petrel, one of Britain's smallest seabirds, returning to its nesting grounds will leave a lasting impression.

LISA STRACHAN/SHUTTERSTOCK ©

How to

Getting here The 15-minute crossing departs from Sandsayre pier in Sandwick (unless otherwise advised); all sailings are weather dependent.

When to go The Mousa Boat operates evening tours (Monday, Wednesday and Saturday) from late May to mid-July and daily trips from April to September. Tours allow two to three hours on the island.

Cost Evening trips cost £30/10 per adult/child. Day tours, without the storm petrel experience, cost £18/8 per adult/child (mousa.co.uk).

AGAMI PHOTO AGENCY/SHUTTERSTOCK ©

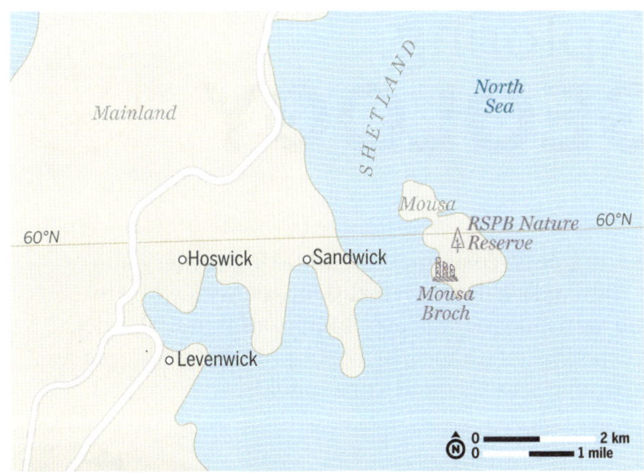

Top left Mousa Broch
Bottom left European Storm petrel

Mousa: Wildlife & Archaeology Collide

Unforgettable wildlife Nesting within the walls of a 2000-year-old broch, the tiny and enigmatic storm petrels are the star of this evening tour. The drystone walls of the magnificent Iron Age structure are brought to life as the seabirds return to their nests from the sea. With an unmistakable call, described by ornithologist Bobby Tulloch as similar to a 'fairy being sick', these night-time marvels make for a stirring sight.

60° north Mousa is metaphorically sliced in half by the 60° north latitude line that passes through the island. Visitors can take a moment to rest on a driftwood bench that marks this milestone positioning that gives 19 hours of daylight in summer and only six hours in the winter.

RSPB Nature Reserve Mousa is rich in wildlife, with a colony of noisy Arctic terns, and the ever-present great skua breeds on open moorland. Other birds to expect are shags, black guillemots, fulmars, red-throated divers and the Shetland wren, a unique subspecies, slightly larger and darker with a flatter song than its UK counterpart. Both common and grey seals are to be seen, and, if you're lucky, an otter or passing whale.

Abandoned Remnants of a thriving 19th-century community can be viewed in the stone remains of homes on the island, which once supported 11 families.

A Note on Brochs

Unique to the north and west of Scotland and built throughout the mid-Iron Age (2000 years ago), brochs are archaeological enigmas. Shetland boasts around 120 brochs, most standing in ruin. Brochs are round, stone structures constructed using two drystone walls – an inner and outer – with a staircase between to reach the top. Archaeologists debate their purpose – were they defensive or offensive? Were they storehouses or high status 'manor houses' for local chieftains? Nobody knows. Shrouded in mystery, they carry much intrigue about how past societies lived and worked.

46 Exploring GEOLOGY

DAY TRIPS | TOURING | ADVENTURE

Enjoy stunning hikes, dramatic coastlines, breathtaking scenery and uninterrupted horizons at Shetland's Unesco Global Geopark, formed by fire, ice, colliding continents and vanishing oceans over billions of years. The rich and varied geology can be experienced on foot, by boat or paddle, with each area offering a distinct set of experiences as the landscape unfolds.

ZDENKA MLYNARIKOVA/SHUTTERSTOCK ©

How to

Getting around You'll need a car and a good Ordnance Survey map to cover the whole island.

Slow down Journey to all four corners of Shetland's Mainland and the island of Unst, taking in the greatest geological treasures. Travel at your own pace and work these suggestions into your itinerary, ensuring that you don't miss any highlights.

Planning tip Treat this as a weeklong itinerary, with each area taking at least a day.

LIZ MILLER/SHUTTERSTOCK ©

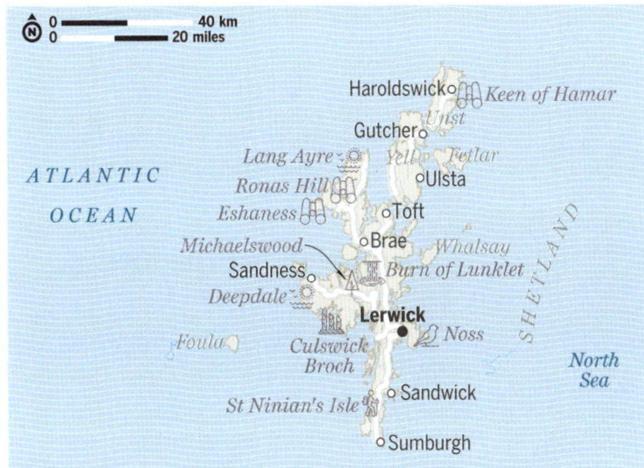

Northmavine Explore the rugged north, home to gneisses almost three billion years old – over half the Earth's age. At **Eshaness**, discover Shetland's volcanic past and stand on the UK's best cross-section through a volcano. Explore the tundra-like landscape of **Ronas Hill**, searching for rare Arctic alpines, and hike on to the **Lang Ayre**, one of Shetland's longest and most isolated beaches.

Unst Search the rocky hillside of **Keen of Hamar** for Edmondston's chickweed – endemic to this one hillside. The geological diversity of Shetland has allowed for many species of rare plants to thrive. Explore the ophiolite, discovering areas where pieces of oceanic plate have been thrust from the seabed in the island's geological past.

East coast Experience the impressive 180m-high sandstone cliffs of **Noss**, where a boat trip or island hike will take you into the heart of one of the UK's most important seabird colonies, home to thousands of nesting gannets, guillemots, puffins and more.

West Mainland Hike to **Deepdale**, a shingle beach at the foot of a deep valley formed by glacial meltwater – best done to coincide with the summer sunset over the bay. Alternatively, discover the rich-red granite of **Culswick Broch** or visit the dinosaurs at **Michaelswood** before picnicking up the **Burn of Lunklet**.

South Mainland Stroll across the sandy tombolo at **St Ninian's Isle** and walk the island circular towards the impressive 9th-century treasure hoard discovered within the remains of a 12th-century chapel in 1958.

Left Rock formation at Eshaness
Bottom left Edmondston's chickweed

Shetland's UNESCO Global Geopark

Shetland's unique landscapes, seascapes, natural history, human history and culture all grew from the underlying geology. Geologically speaking, Shetland is mainland Scotland in miniature. Within an hour's drive, you can stand on the bed of an ancient desert lake, look over the wall of an eroded volcano, or walk on the roots of a vast mountain range or across the Earth's mantle rocks beneath a vanished ocean. Shetland's landscape has been described as a 'Wow! around every corner', and an 'Open-air museum of rocks'.

By Allen Fraser, *Shetland geologist whose vision began Shetland's journey to becoming a UNESCO Global Geopark.*

Listings

BEST OF THE REST

Prehistoric Treasures

Jarlshof Prehistoric & Norse Settlement
One of Shetland's archaeological highlights lies on its southernmost point. Visitors are transported through the ages from the neolithic to the medieval.

Culswick Broch
Hike some of Shetland's best coastline to this dramatic red granite broch; enjoying commanding views, this untouched corner of Shetland is well worth exploring.

Stanydale Temple
Tucked within the heart of neolithic Shetland, this archaeological ruin is a quiet retreat.

Viking Unst
With a replica Viking longship and longhouse at Haroldswick, and excavated longhouses at Underhoull, Hamar and Belmont, Unst represents the first landfall of the Vikings in the UK.

Heritage Highlights

Shetland Museum & Archives
This museum nestled on Lerwick's historic waterfront is the best starting point for understanding Shetland's history.

Old Haa Museum
Housed within a 17th-century laird's house on the island of Yell, this museum has local history displays, a gift shop, a tearoom, an exhibition space and an impressive walled garden.

Scalloway Museum
Discover Scalloway's rich cultural history (May to October). Uncover stories about heartbreaking witch trials, fishing, whaling and the Shetland Bus – an undercover WWII operation between Shetland and Nazi-occupied Norway.

Journey Through the Arts

Craft Trail
Visit open studios throughout the islands (shetlandartsandcrafts.co.uk).

Shetland Gallery
The UK's most northerly gallery features contemporary island artists in its spacious and modern gallery in Yell.

Red Houss Shetland
Red Houss studio is a treasure trove of creativity, selling watercolours of iconic Shetland crofthouses and handcrafted silver jewellery. Hosts silversmithing and painting workshops, too.

Lerwick's Food Highlights

Dowry £
For Scandi-style and delicious local produce, including local lobster, the Dowry adds a real cosmopolitan feel to Lerwick's Commercial St.

Shetland Museum & Archives

No 88 Kitchen & Bar £

The champions of local produce, the chefs at No 88 carefully blend local ingredients with a modern twist in this vibrant streetside restaurant that bursts with personality. Booking required!

C'est la Vie £

This unassuming small cafe-restaurant is an unexpected treasure amid the bustle of Commercial St, selling delicious provincial French cuisine.

Fjara £

Sitting on the water's edge at Breiwick, this is an ideal spot to watch for passing otters and seals.

Trips & Tours

Sea Kayak Shetland

Explore Shetland's geology from the water – with caves, geos, voes and stacks, every inch of the coastline is waiting for you.

Knitting & Hiking with Shetland Wool Adventures

If knitting needles and hiking boots get your creativity flowing, this is the perfect combination of textile exploration and off-the-beaten-track hikes.

Noss Boat

Visit the heart of one of Shetland's main seabird colonies on a short boat trip from Lerwick. Two tour operators provide daily tours (April to September).

Garths Croft

Take a tour around a traditional working croft on the island of Bressay where you have the opportunity to hand feed native Shetland sheep and see other heritage breeds.

Knitwear

Shetland Textile Museum

Two miles from the town centre, knitters and spinners demonstrate local skills in a restored 18th-century fishing *böd* featuring Fair Isle, lace and tweed exhibitions.

Jamieson's of Shetland

Jamieson & Smith

Located 1 mile from Lerwick's town centre, you'll find a range of yarns, kits, books and homeware made from 100% Shetland wool.

Jamieson's of Shetland

Specialising in native Shetland wool, the shop in Lerwick (home to the world-famous yarn wall!) is worth a visit.

Anderson & Co

Anderson & Co in Lerwick is perfect for traditional hats, gloves, mittens, jumpers and cardigans with the signature Fair Isle yolks.

A Musical Journey

Mareel

Music, cinema and creative arts centre in Lerwick hosting regular live gigs from local and visiting musicians (shetlandarts.org).

The Lounge & Douglas Arms

Tucked up one of Lerwick's picturesque historic lanes, the Lounge has weekly live music and impromptu live sessions. The Douglas Arms hosts live-music nights, too – check its Facebook page for details.

Practicalities

240

242

244

245

246

248

250

Right Hiker, West Highland Way (p163)

EASY STEPS FROM THE AIRPORT TO THE CITY CENTRE

Edinburgh is the primary point of entry for most visitors to Scotland, with the country's biggest international airport here. Located 8 miles west of the city centre, the airport has one terminal and it is easily navigable. The terminal has the usual selection of pubs, restaurants, shops, ATMs and car-hire desks. You can also fly into Glasgow, Aberdeen and Inverness.

AT THE AIRPORT

SIM CARDS

Prepaid SIM cards for unlocked phones can be purchased at the airport's WHSmith branch. There are four branches of the retailer inside the terminal. Shops are open based on daily flight departure times.

CURRENCY EXCHANGE

International Currency Exchange (ICE) outlets are located in the middle of the departure lounge after security and at International Arrivals. Opening hours are timed to flight departures and arrivals. Rates are better at banks in the city.

NATALIA SVISTUNOVA/SHUTTERSTOCK ©

WI-FI

Free wi-fi (two hours only) is available for all passengers and customers at Edinburgh International Airport.

ATMS

There are a number of bank machines in the airport – bear in mind they issue the Scottish pound sterling (£).

CHARGING STATIONS

Plug-sockets-a-plenty are dotted around the terminal.

ENTRY & EXIT FORMALITIES

Entry Make sure you've got your passport and supporting documents (visas and landing cards; double-check on the UK government website at gov.uk/government/organisations/uk-visas-and-immigration). If arriving on a domestic flight from elsewhere in the UK, head straight to baggage claim.

Exit Prepare for your departure by knowing what you can and cannot take through security; see edinburghairport.com/prepare. If taking whisky home, check your home country's customs rules.

GETTING TO THE CITY CENTRE

Edinburgh Trams offers a super-smooth 35-minute ride direct from the arrivals plaza, with 15 stops between the terminal and St Andrew Sq in the city centre. Key stops en route include Haymarket, the West End and Princes St. Purchase tickets from staff or at the ticket machine.

Airlink 100 departs every 10 to 30 minutes (4.30am to 12.30am) Monday to Sunday from directly outside the Arrivals hall to St Andrew Sq, taking 25 minutes. Other services include Skylink 200 to Ocean Terminal, Skylink 300 to Surgeons' Hall and Skylink 400 to Fort Kinnaird. Pay with cash or use a contactless bank card.

By bike Edinburgh's terminal is linked to the local cycle path network by Eastfield Rd. From here, cycle paths and quiet routes can be followed almost all the way into the city centre.

HOW MUCH FOR A

TAXI

Edinburgh's black cabs are the fastest way into the city. Trips take around 20 to 30 minutes. The Uber drop-off/pick-up zone is in the car park outside the Arrivals hall.

PLAN YOUR JOURNEY

Download the Traveline Scotland app to figure out the most convenient way to get wherever you want to go in the city or further afield.

TRAVEL CARD

Purchase a Ridacard for unlimited travel across all Edinburgh Trams (all zones), Lothian city buses, NightBus services and airport buses. A one-week pass costs £22/19/11 for an adult/student/child (aged five to 15). Lothian DAYtickets, excluding Airlink, cost £4.50/2.20 for an adult/child.

OTHER POINTS OF ENTRY

Glasgow Airport is 9 miles west of the city. Taxis pick up outside the arrivals gate. Expect to pay around £30; it takes about 20 to 30 minutes. Glasgow Airport Express service 500 runs 24/7, to and from Buchanan Bus Station. Tickets cost £10.50/6 for an adult/child.

Aberdeen Airport is 6 miles northwest of Aberdeen's city centre. The journey to Union Square Bus Station takes 20 minutes. There are a number of airline services, including First Bus X27, Jet Service 72 and Service 747. Tickets cost £3.70/2.20 for an adult/child.

Inverness Airport is 9 miles northeast of Inverness city centre. The journey takes around 15 minutes. Service 11 is your direct connection between the airport and city centre. Buy tickets from the driver or online in advance. Tickets cost around £3.10.

Ferries There are a number of car and passenger ferries to Scotland. Popular routes include those from Belfast (Northern Ireland) to Cairnryan in Dumfries and Galloway with Stena Line and Larne (Northern Ireland) to the Cairnryan with P&O.

TRANSPORT TIPS TO HELP YOU GET AROUND

Scotland's cities, glens and far-flung islands are most memorably explored with your own wheels. Vehicle hire is straightforward, and exploring the network of single-track roads north of the Central Belt is all part of the adventure. Public transport can lower your carbon footprint between the main cities, but beyond urban centres services can at times be rudimentary.

CAR OR CAMPER VAN HIRE

Car hire is available countrywide, with rates slightly more expensive the further north you travel. Camper vans are ideal for exploring the Highlands and islands, though it's worth noting that road trips are now more popular than ever and locals have a love-hate relationship with RVs and motorhomes.

AUTOMOBILE ASSOCIATIONS

The AA, RAC and Green Flag offer breakdown cover and roadside assistance throughout Scotland. They are also handy resources, providing online travel tools, including route planners, traffic alerts and maps. Check for reciprocal agreements with organisations in your own country before travel.

CAR RENTAL COSTS

From £18 per day

Petrol approx £1.44/litre

Car ferry ticket from £18

GO GREEN

Scotland, with over 2600 public EV charging points, is embracing green energy and sustainable travel. ChargePlace Scotland's website lists all EV charging points, and Orkney sets the standard high with more charging stations per kilometre than anywhere else in the UK, as well as Britain's first fleet of e-campervans. The country's cycle network is also expanding, with the Great North Trail offering a route from the Borders to Cape Wrath.

ROAD CONDITIONS

Passing places (pullouts), potholes, wayward sheep: beyond Scotland's highway-connected cities and towns, there are as many hazards as highlights and the road network can at times seem pretty basic. Plan longer than the satnav suggests and check for roadworks before travel. trafficscotland.org is a great resource.

INSURANCE

For minimum stress on the road, take comprehensive or third-party insurance, covering accidental damage to other vehicles if you are at fault. Some rental companies will add a second named driver onto your policy for free.

DRIVING ESSENTIALS

Drive on the left; the steering wheel is on the right.

On single-track roads, use passing places to let oncoming drivers pass.

Speed limits, unless otherwise stated: 30mph (urban areas); 60/70mph (single/dual carriageway).

A zero tolerance policy to drink driving is in effect. Blood alcohol limit 0.05%.

Pay attention to deer warning signs, particularly at nighttime.

PLANE
A secret pleasure is flying to Scotland's islands. Swoop low over silver sands to Islay or Shetland, or land on the world's only tidal beach runway on Barra. In Orkney, you can take the world's shortest commercial flight between Westray and Papa Westray at just 90 seconds. Loganair is the main carrier.

TRAIN Reliable, if expensive, national rail provider ScotRail connects everywhere from Burns Country to Thurso and Wick in the far north. For particularly scenic routes, consider the West Highland Line from Glasgow to Mallaig or the Kyle Line from Inverness to Kyle of Lochalsh. Find timetables and tickets at scotrail.co.uk.

FERRY Caledonian MacBrayne (shortened to CalMac) offers the lion's share of routes to the Inner and Outer Hebrides, while NorthLink Ferries and Pentland Ferries are the best bets to get to Orkney and Shetland.

KNOW YOUR CARBON FOOTPRINT
A road trip from Edinburgh to Inverness would emit 43.6kg in a car and 21.8kg on a motorbike, per passenger. The same journey by train emits 13.8kg and 7.7kg by bus. There are a number of carbon calculators online that allow you to estimate the carbon emissions generated by your journey.

ROAD DISTANCE CHART (MILES)

	Edinburgh	Glasgow	Aberdeen	Dundee	Perth	St Andrews	Inverness	Dumfries	Portree	Fort William
Edinburgh	–									
Glasgow	42	–								
Aberdeen	127	146	–							
Dundee	57	81	55	–						
Perth	44	63	87	22	–					
St Andrews	52	73	80	14	34	–				
Inverness	157	169	104	137	112	147	–			
Dumfries	73	76	210	145	123	137	232	–		
Portree	236	216	215	216	192	226	114	288	–	
Fort William	146	110	154	126	102	140	67	180	108	–

SAFE TRAVEL

The biggest threat to travellers in Scotland is heading into the great outdoors unprepared. Crime rates in the cities are on a par with others across the UK, but it's still advisable to show common sense and treat people and places with the same respect you would back home.

MOUNTAINS

Scotland's mountain environments can change rapidly, bringing everything from snow, hurricane-force winds and sunburn. Leave your route details with someone, take the right kit and don't exceed your limits. If you have an accident, call 999 or 112 and ask for the Police and Mountain Rescue (scottishmountainrescue.org). Download the What3words app.

SEAS & RIVERS

Those beautiful bays, rivers and crystal-clear water look appealing, but unexpected North Atlantic swells and strong currents are all too common. Keep an eye on tide times and the weather, and check with locals before taking the plunge.

ROADS

Scotland has plenty of roadside hazards, ranging from fence-hopping deer to wayward sheep and cattle. The best advice is to drive slowly and avoid dusk and dawn, when animals like red deer are at their most active.

Theft and street attacks do sometimes occur in Scotland's largest cities. Glasgow, Edinburgh and Aberdeen city centres see the majority of problems, especially late on a Friday or Saturday night and commonly involving alcohol or drugs. Dial 999 in an emergency.

EDINBURGHCITYMOM/SHUTTERSTOCK ©

ARTVELL/SHUTTERSTOCK ©

MONEY Scotland is moving towards a cashless society and contactless bank cards are the norm in cities and towns. Remote island communities and villages lag behind – carry cash and a card so you don't get caught out.

BITES & STINGS

To avoid being bitten by midges, horseflies and ants, cover your arms and legs and stick to places where there is a breeze. Ticks, found in wet woodland, moorland and long grass, can carry Lyme disease, so they should be removed quickly.

VACCINATIONS AND HEALTHCARE

No infectious disease vaccinations are currently required to travel in Scotland. Unlike locals you are likely to have to pay for health care while you are here. Get travel insurance with medical cover.

QUICK TIPS TO HELP YOU MANAGE YOUR MONEY

CREDIT CARDS (Visa, MasterCard)
Accepted everywhere and a prerequisite for car hire, credit cards can also be used for cash advances at banks and from ATMs, but such transactions can incur hefty charges. Amex cards are not always accepted, and it's a good idea to carry some cash.

ATMS
ATMs can be found across the country, though, increasingly, high street banks are closing, with services going online. Contactless payment is available practically everywhere.

BANKNOTES
The variety of different British banknotes can be baffling. All pound sterling (£) notes printed in Scotland are valid across the United Kingdom.

CURRENCY

Pound sterling £

HOW MUCH FOR A

Coffee
£3.40

Dram of whisky
£4

Dinner for two
£55

COSTS
Factor in a £95-a-night hotel, a £20 train ticket, £40 on food and a few £10 pub rounds and you won't get much change from a daily budget of £150. If hostelling or camping, £70 to £100 is more realistic.

DRINKING WATER
Scotland has some of the freshest, cleanest water anywhere on the planet. Bring a reusable bottle and help save on plastic and your budget.

TAXES & REFUNDS
Following Brexit, Britain is no longer an EU member state and the practice of refunding VAT paid by travellers has ended.

DISCOUNTS & TIPS
Many attractions, activities and transport options offer discounts for seniors, students and families travelling with children.

Sights Historic Scotland offers the money-saving Explorer Pass, which includes free entry to more than 70 attractions.

Train Fares are cheaper when you travel at less busy, off-peak times.

Ferries Ferry operator CalMac offers 30 different island-hopping tickets that are valid for one month to help save time with bookings.

TIPPING
Although there are no fixed rules, a 10% to 15% gratuity is now expected by most waiters, particularly in cities and large towns. Often, this will be included in your bill, however, you are not obliged to pay it. For taxis, most people round the fare up to the nearest pound.

RESPONSIBLE TRAVEL

Tips to leave a lighter footprint, support local and have a positive impact on local communities.

ON THE ROAD

Shoulder season allows you to embrace the explosion of autumnal amber or the wildflowers of spring while avoiding the summer crowds. This supports tourism year-round and reduces pressures.

Observe the Scottish Outdoor Access Code (outdooraccess-scotland.scot). The act provides a guide for everyone to explore the great outdoors in a safe and responsible manner.

Go electric. It's easy to hire an electric vehicle and take advantage of charge points: Scotland is home to more than 2600 chargers country-wide (chargeplacescotland.org/live-map).

Avoid crowded places and come back when it's less busy. Stick to marked roads, tracks and paths, leaving only footprints.

Be beach safe. Scotland's seas are unpredictable, with cold temperatures and rip currents, even during the height of summer. Visit RNLI (rnli.org) for guidance.

Take part in habitat restoration, or volunteer to help save Scotland's red squirrels. For listings of volunteer programs, see Visit Scotland (visitscotland.com).

CHRISTIAN MUELLER/SHUTTERSTOCK ©

GIVE BACK

Shop local at farmers markets and farm shops to sample fresh products and support Scottish businesses throughout all four seasons.

Choose visitor attractions, sights and distilleries that are committed to sustainable practices and responsible tourism ahead of ones that aren't. A good resource is Visit Scotland (visitscotland.org).

Enjoy Scotland's two stunning national parks – the Cairngorms and Loch Lomond & the Trossachs – responsibly. You'll need a permit if you wish to wild camp, and fires are not permitted in some areas.

Plant a tree. Join charity Trees for Life in planting native woodland to restore Caledonian Forest in the Highlands (treesforlife.org.uk).

DOS & DON'TS

Do 'Fàilte' (embrace) and respect the Gaelic language.

Don't forget that tap water is safe to drink, and pure unfiltered waters run from rivers and streams.

Do eat out for a good cause at Social Bite (social-bite.co.uk). Its Edinburgh, Glasgow and Aberdeen restaurants and cafes support Scotland's homeless community.

LEAVE A SMALL FOOTPRINT

Spend more time in one area. Travel slowly to reduce the pressure on the country's most famous destinations and don't cram too much in. Save the stress, and become more richly acquainted with this beautiful country.

Use designated toilets and dispose of motorhome and camper van chemical waste and grey water responsibly. The Northwest Highlands, in particular, has only a limited number of accessible facilities.

#TakItHame. Carry a spare bag and if you see rubbish when out hiking, walking or climbing, pick it up and take it with you.

LEONARD ZHUKOVSKY/SHUTTERSTOCK ©

SUPPORT LOCAL

Eat locally. From bread to beer to fish to fresh fruit, buy from local producers around the country (foodanddrink.scot/support-local).

Source unique souvenirs like Harris Tweed and Orkney handicrafts directly from the makers. Social enterprise platforms **Buy Social Scotland** (buysocialscotland.com), **Love Local Scotland** (lovelocal.scot) and **isle20** (www.scottishislandgifts.com) list recommended artisans.

CLIMATE CHANGE & TRAVEL

Lonely Planet urges all travellers to engage with their travel carbon footprint, which will mainly come from air travel. While there often isn't an alternative, travellers can look to minimise the number of flights they take, opt for newer aircrafts and use cleaner ground transport, such as trains.

One proposed solution—purchasing carbon offsets—unfortunately does not cancel out the impact of individual flights. While most destinations will depend on air travel for the foreseeable future, for now, pursuing ground-based travel where possible is the best course of action.

The UN Carbon Offset Calculator shows how flying impacts a household's emissions:

The ICAO's carbon emissions calculator allows visitors to analyse the CO2 generated by point-to-point journeys:

RESOURCES

visitscotland.com

outdooraccess-scotland.scot

johnmuirtrust.org

keepscotlandbeautiful.org

UNIQUE AND LOCAL WAYS TO STAY

Sleep in a medieval town house surrounded by history or camp under the stars for free on a beach – Scotland offers something for every taste and budget. Often hotels and guesthouses are located inside historic buildings gone glam – from castles to coaching houses – and nothing beats them for atmosphere. For an only-in-Scotland experience, rough it at a remote bothy.

HOW MUCH FOR A

Bothy Free

Campsite from £12 per pitch

City-centre hotel £95

MARK CANNING/SHUTTERSTOCK ©

WILD CAMPING

Wild camping is permitted throughout Scotland, offering unrivalled access to the country's dramatically different landscapes and seasons. There are exceptions to this rule: in popular spots throughout the Cairngorms (pictured above) and Loch Lomond & the Trossachs, wild camping is restricted to certain permit-only pitches, and by-laws prohibiting camping and firelighting are in effect.

HOSTELS

Not-for-profit charity Hostelling Scotland (hostellingscotland.org.uk) has more than 60 properties scattered across the country. From the lochside to the trail path, highlights include those on the West Highland Way and the North Coast 500. A standout is the Loch Ossian Youth Hostel at Corrour, with no vehicle access and located on a wildly remote swathe of Rannoch Moor.

NINA ALIZADA/SHUTTERSTOCK ©

BLACKHOUSES

Once used to house both crofters and livestock, a blackhouse is a frozen-in-time, thatched dwelling synonymous with the Highlands and islands. Inside, they exude a country-chic vibe, with history hewn into the walls. Lewis, in particular, has a number to stay in or rent, including Gearrannan (pictured; gearrannan.com), a self-catering option on the windswept Atlantic coast.

DAVE A BENNETT/SHUTTERSTOCK ©

BOTHIES

Bothies are a uniquely Scottish form of rustic, shelter-style accommodation, and to stay in one is to see the country's landscape at its rawest and most unadorned. Many are off-grid, almost closely guarded secrets, requiring long walks or bike rides to reach their random locations. Others offer different sorts of challenges, sitting on unsignposted, lonely passes, with only the most basic of facilities.

Commonly, all are free to stay in as long as you embrace the bothy philosophy. You'll have to embrace the slow pace, carry in all your supplies (food, sleeping bag and candles), fetch water from a nearby stream and share the cottage with whoever else turns up for the night. Due to their popularity, some have stoves and sleeping platforms, but most are no-frill, two-roomed shepherd's cottages with a dusty fireplace. It's also worth noting that there is no booking system and reserving a bed at one isn't possible. And yet, what an adventure. A night overlooking an empty beach or picturesque glen? It's what backpacking dreams are made of.

The Mountain Bothies Association (mountainbothies.org.uk) is an excellent resource.

Price: Free

BOOKING

Book well in advance in peak tourist season, from June to August. Edinburgh is at its busiest throughout the Fringe Festival in August and during Hogmanay in December. It's worth booking accommodation up to a year in advance of travel. Note that Visit Scotland's iCentres are all set to close as Visit Scotland goes fully digital.

Lonely Planet (lonelyplanet.com/hotels) Find independent reviews, as well as recommendations on the best places to stay, and then book them online.

The Camping and Caravanning Club (campingandcaravanningclub.co.uk) Membership association with a great selection of top-rated sites.

Hidden Scotland (hiddenscotland.co/accommodation) Holiday bookings with everything from lodges and log cabins, to dog-friendly options and hot-tub havens.

Scotland's Best B&Bs (scotlandsbestbandbs.co.uk) The only 4- and 5-star B&B association in the country, offering a great selection of reliable guesthouses.

isleHoliday (isleholiday.com) The ethical alternative to big booking sites for the Scottish islands. Enjoy sustainable island holidays!

VisitScotland (visitscotland.com/accommodation) Online accommodation bookings, especially good for quirky options, glamping and guesthouses.

WHAT3WORDS

Download the What3Words app if you are heading out into the hills. This geo-code system is designed to identify any location on the surface of Earth with a resolution of about 3m. Every $3m^2$ of the world has been given a unique combination of three words. It can be used by emergency services if you are in need of assistance.

ESSENTIAL NUTS-AND-BOLTS

ALCOHOL

It's the lifeblood of Scotland and 'taking a drink' is deeply rooted in the country's national psyche, whether for better or worse. And it's spelt whisky, without the 'e'.

TIPPING

There isn't a big tipping culture in Scotland, though it is common in restaurants and for taxi journeys.

SMOKING & VAPING

It's illegal to smoke or vape in any pub, restaurant, nightclub or hotel, except within designated outdoor areas.

FAST FACTS

Time Zone
GMT

Country Code
+44

Electricity
230V/50Hz

GOOD TO KNOW

Citizens from 139 countries are automatically issued a temporary visa on arrival, typically valid for 90 days.

Scottish banknotes are different from those in England.

Driving etiquette: move into lay-bys to let oncoming traffic pass.

The legal drinking age in Scotland is 18.

Mobile phone signal can be hit or miss across the country – even close to a major city.

ACCESSIBLE TRAVEL

Larger hotels have wheelchair-friendly rooms (book in advance). Euan's Guide reviews hotels with all write-ups done by disabled travellers (euansguide.com).

Accessible dining varies dramatically. It's always best to call the restaurant, cafe or pub in advance to make sure of access.

City transport stations have elevators or ramp access at street level. Station staff will help you on and off the train with a temporary slope. Ask at the ticket counter.

Museums and attractions often have different entrances, but varying is considered 'accessibility'. Accessible Travel Hub (accessibletravel.scot) is a great resource for planning journeys.

Wheelchairs and other equipment can be booked for short-term use from the British Red Cross (redcross.org.uk).

WINTER

Many attractions, museums, guesthouses and hotels close in winter (usually from November to March).

BREXIT

Since 1 October 2021, you need a valid passport to enter the UK from the EU; EU identity cards can no longer be used.

FOOTBALL

The national sport can be a divisive subject and unsavoury. Especially in Glasgow, which splits into either Rangers or Celtic.

FAMILY TRAVEL

Licensing laws mean children under 14 often can't be in pubs that sell meals after a certain time.

Admission to castles, museums, art galleries and more is often wonderfully free for all ages.

Restaurants commonly have high chairs and children's menus.

Train travel is £1 return each for up to four kids for every paying adult at the weekend. See scotrail.co.uk.

Breastfeeding in public is widely accepted and actively encouraged by government campaigns.

Child seats are not available in taxis.

PUBS These are hubs of community life and not just for drinking world-class beers, ales and whiskies in. They act as social centres for live music, quizzes, events and getting the lowdown on what's going on. You'll also pay a fraction of the price for meals compared to a restaurant, and breakfast, lunch and dinner are often on the menu.

KILTS

Non-Scots are actively encouraged to wear and buy kilts – this is taken as a heartfelt tribute, not an act of cultural appropriation.

There are few do's or don'ts: go casual or formal, with a jacket or without. It's all about the freedom.

Underwear is optional, but the proper way to wear a kilt is without.

LGBTIQ+ TRAVELLERS

Outright discrimination is unusual and the Scottish government actively campaigns for inclusivity regardless of sex or gender; however, travellers have reported isolated incidents of being turned away when checking into hotels in rural areas.

The Rainbow Index presents information on Europe's LGBTI Rights Rankings annually in an intuitive and interactive way.

Glasgow and Edinburgh have large, vibrant gay and lesbian communities, with annual Pride events and parades celebrating Scotland's LGBTQI+ heritage and future.

Follow Pink Saltire (@PinkSaltire) to keep up with issues and learn about events and meet-ups.

Index

A

Aberdeenshire Coastal Trail 116-19
accessible travel 250
accommodation 248-9
activities 16-23 *see also individual activities*
Ailsa Craig 88
airports 241
alcohol 250
Alloway 89
animals 48, 162, 230-1, *see also individual animals*
Anstruther 97
archaeological sites 142-3, 210-11
 Calanais Standing Stones 200
 Dunadd Fort 143
 Jarlshof Prehistoric & Norse Settlement 236
 Kilmartin Glen 144-5
 Knap of Howar 208
 Nether Largie Standing Stones 143
 Temple Wood Stone Circle 143
 Unst 229
 Viking Unst 236
Argyll 139
art 16, 66-7
art galleries, *see* museums & galleries
Arthur's Seat 56
ATMs 240

B

Ballater 161
Barony Mill 219
Barra 198-9
Barrhill 87
Battle of Bannockburn Visitor Centre 109

000 Map pages

Bealach na Bà 170
beavers 109
Beinn Eighe 170
Beltane Fire Festival 24
Ben More 133
Ben Nevis 158-9
Berneray 198
bicycle travel, *see* cycling
birdwatching
 Cape Wrath 173
 Fair Isle 225
 Loch of the Lowes 101
 Mousa Broch 232-3
 Mull 146
 Mull of Galloway 88
 Noss 235
 Staffa 133
blackhouses 200, 248
blanket bog 231
boat tours
 Central Highlands 163
 Inner Hebrides 132-3, **133**
 Loch Ness 155
 Northern Highlands 177, 181
 Outer Hebrides 198-9, **199**
 Shetland 237
Bonnie Prince Charlie 176
Bonnie Prince Charlie Trail 193
booking services 249
books 36
bothies 249
Braemar Gathering 20
Braid Hills 53
Braveheart 156
breweries
 Campervan Brewery 55
 Orkney Brewery 218
 Swannay Brewery 218
Brexit 251
Brough of Birsay 218
Burns Night 22
Burns, Robert 27, 89

C

Caledonian Canal 155
Calum's Road 194-5
camping 248
Canna 162
canoeing & kayaking 109, 133, 163, 199, 237
Cape Wrath 172-3
car travel 242, 244, *see also* driving tours
Castlebay 199
castles 10, 102-5, 106-7
 Aldourie Castle 154
 Armadale Castle Garden 202
 Balmoral Castle 161
 Blackness Castle 47
 Blair Atholl Castle 161
 Bothwell Castle 74
 Carnasserie Castle 143
 Castle Campbell 105
 Castle Kennedy Gardens 87
 Castle Stalker 146
 Craigmillar Castle 47
 Culzean Castle 83
 Doune Castle 105
 Drumlanrig Castle 83
 Dumbarton Castle 72-3
 Dunnottar 118
 Dunrobin Castle 175
 Dunure Castle 85
 Dunvegan Castle 203
 Edinburgh Castle 47
 Floors Castle 83
 Glamis Castle 125
 Gordon Castle Walled Garden 125
 Hermitage Castle 85
 Inveraray Castle 146
 Inverness Castle 177
 Kisimul Castle 199
 Lauriston Castle 47
 Lochleven Castle 104

New Slains Castle 119
Old Castle Lachlan 141
Rothesay Castle 147
St Andrews Castle 108
Stirling Castle 104-5
Thirlestane Castle 88
Threave Castle 85
Urquhart Castle 155
cathedrals, *see* churches & cathedrals
Ceannabeine 175
Central Highlands 148-63, **150-1**
accommodation 153
drinking 153, 163
festivals & events 153
food 153
money 153
navigation 153
planning 150-1
travel seasons 152
travel to/from 152
travel within 152
Central Scotland & the East itineraries 30-1, **30-1**
children, travel with 251
churches & cathedrals
Elgin Cathedral 125
Glasgow Cathedral 69
Kilmorie Chapel 141
St Magnus Cathedral 217, 219
St Magnus Church 217
St Magnus Kirk 217
climate 18-25
climate change 247
convents & monasteries
Arbroath Abbey 124
Dundrennan Abbey 88
Inchcolm Abbey 57
Melrose Abbey 85
Paisley Abbey 74
Pluscarden Abbey 124-5
Corstorphine Hill 53
Cowal Way 141
crafts 124, 147
Fair Isle 225
Northern Highlands 181
Orkney 212-13, 214-15, **213**
Outer Hebrides 203
Shetland 236-7
Skye 203
Crail 97
Crannog Centre 108
credit cards 245
Crinan Canal 142
Culloden Battlefield 177
Culswick Broch 235
curlews 231
currency 245
cycling 12-13, **12-13**
Cape Wrath 173
Crinan Canal 142
Great Cumbrae 88
Highlands 176-7, **177**
Loch Ness 154-5
Outer Hebrides 198-9, **199**
Southern Scotland 86-7, **87**

D

Dalkeith Country Park 57
Dean Village 49
design 122-3
disabilities, travellers with 250
distilleries 115
Ardbeg 135
Ardnahoe 135, 137
Balblair Distillery 180
Bowmore Distillery 136
Bruichladdich Distillery 135
Bunnahabhain 135
Caol Ila Distillery 135
City of Aberdeen Distillery 125
Clydeside Distillery 75
Dalwhinnie Distillery 162
Deerness Distillery 218
Dewar's Aberfeldy Distillery 162
Edinburgh Gin Distillery 57
Glenegedale 135
Glenlivet, the 162
Glenmorangie Distillery 180
Glenrinnes Distillery 125
Highland Park 218
Isle of Raasay Distillery 194
Kilchoman 135
Kingsbarns Distillery 97, 109
Lagavulin Distillery 135
Laphroaig 135
Orkney Distillery, the 218
Royal Lochnagar Distillery 161
Scapa 218
driving tours 14-15, *see also* car travel
Central Highlands 160-1, **161**
Clearances Trail 174-5, **175**
Destitution Road 169
Golden Road 201
Harris 200-1, **200**
Lewis 200-1, **200**
North Coast 500 181
Secret Coast 140-1, **140**
Snow Roads Scenic Route 162
Uist 192-3, **193**
Wester Ross 168-71, **171**
Drumnadrochit 155
Dundee 122-3
Dunfermline 103

E

Edinburgh 38-57, **40-1**
accommodation 43
drinking 43, 56-7
food 43, 56, 57
hills 52-3
money 43
navigation 43
planning 40-1
travel seasons 42
travel to Edinburgh 42
travel within 42
Edinburgh Festival Fringe 19, 44-5
Eigg 162
Eildon Hills 81
Eriskay 193
etiquette 247, 251
Eurasian otters 228, 229, 230
events, *see* festivals & events

F

Fair Isle 224-5
Fairy Glen 190
Fairy Pools 202

family travel 251
Far North Line 180
ferries 243
festivals & events 16, 18-25, 43, *see also individual events*
Borders & Wigtown 89
Braemar Gathering 160
Ceòlas week 193
Common Ridings, the 89
Edinburgh International Book Festival 45
Edinburgh International Film Festival 45
Edinburgh's Hogmanay 45
Highland Games 121
North Ronaldsay Sheep Festival 219
Orkney County Show 219
Orkney Folk Festival 219
Scottish Traditional Boat Festival 117
Shetland Folk Festival 227
Shetland Wool Week 225
Spirit of Speyside Festival 121
St Magnus International Festival 219
Up Helly Aa 227
Fife, *see* Stirling, Fife & Perthshire
Fife Coastal Path 96-7
film locations 156-7
films 37
food 11, *see also individual locations*
football 251

G

Gaelic language 192
gannets 230
gay travellers 251
geography 34
geology 234-5
Glasgow 58-75, **60-1**
accommodation 63
drinking 63, 64-5, 75
entertainment 65, 71, 74-5
food 63, 64-5, 75
history 68-9, 70-1
money 63
navigation 63
planning 60-1
shopping 63
tours 74
travel seasons 62
travel to/from 62
travel within 62
Glen Clova 162
Glenan Wood 141
golf 53

H

Halloween 20
Harray 213
Harris 8, 200-1
Highland Clearances 174-5
Highland Games 178-9
Highlands & Islands itineraries 28-9, **28-9**
hiking 10, 12-13, **12-13**
Aonach Eagach 159
Ben Nevis 158-9
Braeriach 159
Buachaille Etive Mòr 159
Crinan Canal 142
Culswick Broch 236
Dalriada Heritage Trail 142-3, **143**
Deepdale 235
Dùn Caan 195
Fife Coastal Path 96-7, **97**
Fair Isle 225
Great Cumbrae 88
Hermaness National Nature Reserve 228-9
Loch Leven Heritage Trail 104
Loch Ness 154
Lowlands 80-1, **81**
North Hill Nature Reserve 208-9
Old Man of Hoy 218
Schiehallion 99, 159
St Abbs Head Nature Reserve 81
St Magnus Way 216-17, **217**
Trotternish 188-91
Yesnaby 218
Hirta 197
history & historic sites 10, 95
Battle of Bannockburn Visitor Centre 109
Culloden Battlefield 177
Grave of Flora MacDonald 190
Moot Hill 103
St Magnus 216
Stirling Old Bridge 105
Holm of Papay 209

I

immigration 240, 251
Inner Hebrides 132-3
internet access 240
internet resources 247
Iona 133
Island of Rousay 211
islands 8-9, **8-9**
Islay 134-5
Isle of Raasay 194-5
itineraries 26-33, **26-7**, **28-9**, **30-1**, **32-3**, *see also individual regions*

K

kayaking, *see* canoeing & kayaking
killer whales 230
Kilmartin Glen 144-5
kilts 251
Kirkwall 213
Knoydart 163

L

language 35, 118
Largs Viking Festival 21
Leith 54-5
Lewis 200-1
Lewis Chess Pieces 201
LGBTIQ+ travellers 251
Library of Innerpeffray 109
lighthouses
Ardnamurchan Lighthouse 162
Cape Wrath Lighthouse 173

000 Map pages

Muckle Flugga Lighthouse 228
Mull of Galloway lighthouse 88
Lismore 146
literature 36, 50-1
Loch Morlich 163
Loch Ness 154-5
Lochinver 180
Lunga 133

M

Mackintosh, Charles Rennie 67, 69
Mackintosh House 69
Malt Whisky Trail 7, 121
Meall Fuar-mhonaidh 154
midges 35
Mingulay 198
mobile phones 34, 240
monasteries, *see* convents & monasteries
money 240, 245
monuments & memorials
Emigrants Statue 175
National Wallace Monument 105
Our Lady of the Isles 202
Scott Monument 51
William Wallace Statue 88
Mousa Broch 232-3
Mull 8, 133
murals 66-7
Murrayfield Stadium 49
museums & galleries 57
Burrell Collection 69
Dandelion Designs 203
Devil's Porridge Museum 89
Dundee Contemporary Arts 123
Dunvegan Castle 203
Gairloch Museum 171
Gallery of Modern Art 74
George Waterston Museum 225
Holland Farm 208
House for an Art Lover 74
Hoxa Tapestry Gallery 213
Island Darkroom 203
Jim Clark Motorsport Museum 89
Jupiter Artland 57
Kelvingrove Art Gallery & Museum 69
Kildonan Museum 193
Kilmartin Museum 143
McManus Art Gallery & Museum, 123
Museum nan Eilean 202
Museum of Lead Mining 89
National Museum of Scotland 57
Old Haa Museum 236
People's Palace 69
Perth Museum & Art Gallery 108
Raasay Gallery 203
Red Houss Shetland 236
Riverside Museum 69
RRS *Discovery* 123
Scalloway Museum 236
Scapa Flow Museum 219
Scottish Fisheries Museum 108
Scottish National Gallery of Modern Art 49
Seallam 202-3
Shetland Gallery, the 236
Shetland Museum & Archives 236
Skoon Art Gallery 203
Skye Museum of Island Life 190
Staffin Dinosaur Museum 202
Taigh Chearsabhagh Museum and Arts Centre 193
Ullapool Museum 171
V&A Dundee 16, 123
Writers' Museum, the 51
music 15, 36, 65, 74-5, 237
Belladrum Tartan Heart Festival 18
Celtic Connections 23

N

national parks & reserves
Balranald Nature Reserve 202
Black Wood of Rannoch 99
Falls of Clyde 81
Fowlsheugh Nature Reserve 118
Galloway Forest Park 80, 81
Hermaness National Nature Reserve 228-9
North Hill Nature Reserve 208-9
RSPB Nature Reserve 233
St Abbs Head Nature Reserve 81
UNESCO Global Geopark 234-5
neolithic sites 210-11
Barnhouse 211
Calanais Standing Stones 200
Cuween Hill Chambered Cairn 211
Island of Eday 211
Island of Rousay 211
Jarlshof Prehistoric & Norse Settlement 236
Lund standing stone 229
Maeshowe 211
Nether Largie Standing Stones 143
Ring of Brodgar 211
Skara Brae 211
Standing Stones of Stenness 211
Stanydale Temple 236
Temple Wood Stone Circle 143
Unstan Chambered Cairn 211
New Luce 87
Northeast Scotland 110-25, **112-13**
accommodation 115
drinking 115
food 115, 124
money 115
navigation 115
planning 112-13
travel seasons 114
travel to/from 114
travel within 114
Northern Highlands 164-81, **166**
accommodation 167
drinking 167
food 167
money 167
planning 166
travel seasons 167
travel to/from 167
travel within 167

Northern Scotland itineraries 30-1, **30-1**
Noss 235

O

Oban 138
Old Man of Storr 191
orchids 231
Orkney 9, 204-19, **206**
  accommodation 207
  drinking 207
  food 207, 219
  money 207
  planning 206
  travel seasons 207
  travel within 207
Outer Hebrides, *see* Skye & the Outer Hebrides
oysters 138-9

P

Pabbay 198
palaces & stately homes 82-3
  Abbotsford 83
  Falkland Palace 104
  Mellerstain House 88
  Palace of Holyroodhouse 47
  Scone Palace 108, 161
  Traquair 83
Papa Westray 208
parks & gardens
  Armadale Castle Garden 202
  Attadale Gardens 181
  Castle Kennedy Gardens 87
  Glamis Castle 125
  Gordon Castle Walled Garden 125
  Inverewe Garden 170
  Johnston Gardens 125
  Jupiter Artland 57
  Langley Park Gardens 125
  Logan Botanic Gardens 88
  Mellerstain House 88
  Pitmedden Garden 125
  Royal Botanic Garden 49
passports 240, 251
Pentland Hills 53
Perthshire, *see* Stirling, Fife & Perthshire
Peterhead Prison 119
petrels 232-3
Pittenweem 97
plants 231
politics 34
ponies 193
Port Ban 133
Portpatrick 87
Potter, Harry 51, 156
Princes Street Gardens 56
pubs 251
Puck's Glen 140
puffins 133, 197, 230

Q

Quiraing 189

R

Rannoch 98-9
Rannoch Moor 99
responsible travel 246-7
River Tay 100-1
River Tummel 99
road trips, *see* driving tours
round towers 200
Rowling, JK 50, 51
Royal Deeside Steam Railway 161
Royal Highland Show 19
Royal Mile 47
Royal Observatory 56
RRS *Discovery* 123
ruins
  Dun Carloway Broch 200
  Dunadd Fort 143
  Glenluce Abbey 87
  New Slains Castle 119
  Old Castle Lachlan 141
  St Olaf's church 229
  Urquhart Castle 155
Rum 162

S

safe travel 244
salmon 101
Scottish culture 16
sea eagles 132, 146
seafood 96-7, 108, 138-9
seals 117, 230
sharks 146
Shetland 220-37, **222**
  accommodation 223
  drinking 223
  food 223, 236
  history 226-7
  money 223
  navigation 223
  planning 222
  travel seasons 223
  travel to/from 223
  travel within 223
Shetland Wool Week 21
skiing 22, 163
Skye & the Outer Hebrides 8, 182-203, **184-5**
  accommodation 187
  drinking 187
  food 187
  money 187
  planning 184-5
  travel seasons 186
  travel to/from 186
  travel within 186
smoking 250
Smoo Cave 180
Soay sheep 197
Southern Highlands & Islands 126-47, **128-9**
  accommodation 131
  drinking 131
  food 131
  money 131
  navigation 131
  planning 128-9
  travel seasons 130
  travel to/from 130
  travel within 130

000 Map pages

Southern Scotland 76-89, **78**
accommodation 79
drinking 79, 89
food 79, 89
itineraries 26-7, **26-7**
mobile phones 79
money 79
planning 78
travel seasons 79
travel to/from 79
travel within 79
Southern Scotland itineraries 26-7, **26-7**
Speyside 120-1
sporting events
Braemar Gathering 20
Halkirk Highland Games 181
Highland Games 121, 178-9
Mountain Bike World Cup 163
Mountain Biking World Cup 25
Six Nations 24
St Andrews 97
St Andrews Day 21
St Kilda 196-7
St Magnus Way 216-17, **216**
St Monans 97
St Ninian's Isle 235
Stac an Armin 197
Stac Lee 197
Stac Pollaidh 180
Staffa 133
stargazing
Cairngorms Dark Sky Park 162
Coll Bunkhouse 133
Galloway Forest Park 80
Royal Observatory 56
Stirling, Fife & Perthshire 90-109, **92-3**
accommodation 95
drinking 95
food 95, 108, 109
money 95
planning 92-3
travels seasons 94
travel to/from 94
travel within 94
Stockbridge 49
Stone of Destiny 103
storm petrels 232-3
Strathnaver 175
street art 66-7
Stromness 213
surfing 117, 181
swimming 53, 119

T

Tankerness 213
taxis 241
terns 230-1
tipping 245, 250
Tiree 133
tours, *see also* boat tours, cycling, driving tours, walking tours
Glasgow 74
Inner Hebrides 146
Jura Island 146
Orkney 219
Shetland 228, 232, 237
Traigh Mhòr 199
train travel 243
travel seasons 18-25, 251
travel to/from Scotland 240-1
travel within Scotland 242-3
Trotternish 188-91

U

Uist 192-3, **193**
Ullapool 169
UNESCO Global Geopark 234-5
Unst 9, 228-9
Up Helly Aa 23

V

Vat of Kirbister 218
Verdant Works 123
viewpoints 56
Bullers of Buchan 118
Dumbarton Rock 73
Kilt Rock 189
Kyles of Bute 140
Mull of Galloway 88
Vat of Kirbister 218
Vikings 215, 226-7, 229, 236
Village Bay 197

W

Wallace, William 73, 88, 105
walking tours
Dundee 122-3, **123**
Edinburgh 48-9, 50-1, 54-5, **49**, **51**, **55**
Glasgow 64-5, 66-7, **65**, **67**
Water of Leith 48-9, **48-9**
waterfalls
Allt Robuic 140
Falls of Measach 169
Grey Mare's Tail 81
Mealt Falls 189
Victoria Falls 169
weather 18-25
websites 37
West Highland Way 163
West Island Way 146
Wester Ross 168-71
Westray 208
whale-watching 19, 146
whisky 6-7, 136-7
Edinburgh 56-7
Glasgow 75
Islay 134-5
Northern Highlands 180
Speyside 115, 120-1
white-water rafting 99, 109
wi-fi 34, 240
wildlife-watching, *see also* animals
Black Wood of Rannoch 99
Cape Wrath 173
Central Highlands 162
Islay 135
Perthshire 109
River Tay 101
Southern Highlands & Islands 146
Unst 228-9
Water of Leith 48
winter sports 22

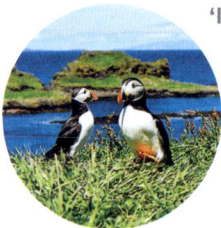

LINDSAY R BELL/SHUTTERSTOCK ©

'I love taking a boat trip to the turquoise-fringed shores of Lunga (p133) to see thousands of puffins up close: a sight you never forget.'

KAY GILLESPIE

'Weather and tide finally cooperated, allowing the Solan IV to sail through the Giant's Leg natural arch on our way to Noup of Noss (p235) in Shetland.'

NEIL WILSON

'My favourite experience is the Far North Line (p180). I love the changing landscape and hopping off at rural stations to explore on my bike.'

COLIN BAIRD

'My favourite experience is witnessing the return of the storm petrels to the 2000-year-old Mousa Broch (p232) at midsummer. The culmination of nature and archaeology is breathtaking.'

LAURIE GOODLAD

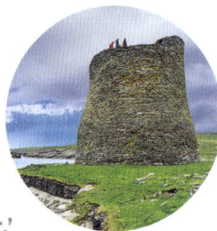

'My first experience of the Edinburgh Fringe (p44) was as a playwright. Trust me: it's much more fun as a punter.'

JOSEPH REANEY

ARTERRA/UNIVERSAL IMAGES GROUP VIA GETTY IMAGES ©

THIS BOOK

Destination editor
Amy Lynch

Product editor
Katie Connolly

Cartographer
Alison Lyall

Book designer
Clara Monito

Assisting editors
Helen Koehne, Tasmin Waby

Cover researcher
Kat Marsh

Thanks Hannah Cartmel, Melanie Dankel, Claire Rourke